RACING THROUGH THE DARK

RACING THROUGH THE DARK

THE RISE AND FALL OF DAVID MILLAR

DAVID MILLAR

IN COLLABORATION WITH JEREMY WHITTLE

Copyright © David Millar 2011

The right of David Millar to be identified as the author
of this work has been asserted by him in accordance with the
Copyright, Designs and Patents Act 1988.

This edition first published in Great Britain in 2011 by
Orion Books
an imprint of the Orion Publishing Group Ltd
Orion House, 5 Upper St Martin's Lane,
London WC2H 9EA
An Hachette UK Company

1 3 5 7 9 10 8 6 4 2

A CIP catalogue record for this book
is available from the British Library.

ISBN: 978 1 4091 1494 9 Hardback
ISBN: 978 1 4091 3441 1 ETPB

Typeset by Input Data Services Ltd,
Bridgwater, Somerset

Printed and bound in the UK by CPI Mackays,
Chatham, Kent

The Orion Publishing Group's policy is to use papers that
are natural, renewable and recyclable and made
from wood grown in sustainable forests. The logging
and manufacturing processes are expected to conform to
the environmental regulations of the country of origin.

Every effort has been made to fulfil requirements with regard
to reproducing copyright material. The author and publisher will
be glad to rectify any omissions
at the earliest opportunity.

www.orionbooks.co.uk

To the love of three women, my mother Avril, my sister Frances, and my wife Nicole. Thank you for being so kind.

And the peloton, I treasure the small amount of time I have left with you, even though you can be so cruel.

'It is very difficult to know people ... For men and women are not only themselves; they are also the region in which they are born, the city apartment or the farm in which they learnt to walk, the games they played as children, the old wives' tales they overheard, the food they ate, the schools they attended, the sports they followed, the poets they read, and the God they believed in. It is all these things that have made them what they are, and these are the things that you can't come to know by hearsay, you can only know them if you have lived them.'

W. Somerset Maugham, *The Razor's Edge*, 1943

'The man is greater than his victories and defeats. The man is worth more than the cyclist. In the champion, beats the heart of a boy, a heart that needs normality and that cannot be sacrificed at the altar of exploitation.'

Bishop Antonio Lanfranchi's eulogy at the funeral of Marco Pantani

CONTENTS

ACKNOWLEDGEMENTS

JEREMY 'JUDGE' WHITTLE and DAVID 'KAISER' LUXTON, without whom there would be no book, you always believed in it; thank you for teaching me how to do it and doing it when I didn't learn. IAN 'PRIEST' PREECE who has been a wonderfully patient and skillful editor, thanks for putting up with my 'naivety' and allowing me to create the book I wanted.

The photographers: GRAHAM WATSON, to whom I will always be 'The Junior'; you've seen more of me race than anyone else, and have seen my ups and downs far closer than anybody else, thanks for giving me the memories. TIM DE WAELE, for his generosity and gift of being in the right place at the right time, which has created some of my favourite photographs. BRUNO BADE, from the 1997 Tour de L'Avenir prologue to the 2010 Chrono des Nations, thank you for scouring your archives. TIMM KÖLLN, the Catalan German, kudos for creating the peloton book and thank you for the photographic epilogue to this book. CHRIS MacPHERSON, our man in LA, thanks for capturing that Californian moment and for that drink in that random bar. CAMILLE 'THE CHRONICLER' McMILLAN, legend.

Cycling allows me to meet some interesting people. KADIR GUIREY is one of them, and through him I met NADAV KANDER. Nadav, thank you for creating the cover portrait. I thought I had it in my head. Evidently I didn't, you did. Look forward to cycling together in the future, with the occasional stop for chicken soup and heartfelt chat.

To the esteemed members of Velo Club Rocacorba, thank you for putting up with your president's folly, and offering your help and advice when it came to the book. There is no opinion I value higher than your 51.

My cycling team, SLIPSTREAM, more commonly now known as TEAM GARMIN. In particular DOUG ELLIS, who believed in us and made it possible for us to achieve what nobody else thought possible.

My wife, NICOLE MILLAR, who watched me turn into a Howard Hughes-like figure while writing this book. I may have spent the off-season at home, but I wasn't really there; thank you for taking me out and 'airing' me on occasions. And for not getting annoyed when I couldn't remove my head from my hands at the end of the kitchen table, oblivious to anything beyond the screen in front of me. You are an angel.

FOREWORD

Life is about making decisions and my relationship with David Millar has informed some of the toughest and most critical decisions in my career. Looking back, his experience has also been pivotal in fuelling my passionate belief in clean sport.

I first crossed paths with David in 2002 at the World Road Championships in Belgium. I was working as Performance Director to Team GB and he was riding for the British team. It was clear from the outset that he was different to any other bike rider I'd met before. Hugely talented, ambitious and extrovert, Dave was a thoroughbred.

He was intelligent and strong-willed, yet also very vulnerable. It is rare for me to mix personal with professional, but we got on immediately and he is one of the few riders that I have also become close friends with.

Dave was already clearly frustrated with the 'old school' thinking of the European scene. We talked about working together, developing new ways of thinking about racing and equipment, and about taking those ideas into Europe. I knew that with the right environment he could go on to great things.

Yet in hindsight, I can look back and see that there were nagging worries. Dave was something of a wild child, living life to the full, lacking the kind of mentoring that he needed at the time. I knew he had doubts about the team that he was in, that he was under a lot of pressure, that some aspects of his lifestyle were extreme, but I didn't know how far that extreme lifestyle had gone, or that there was another side to his life that he couldn't share.

I had just come back to Biarritz with him, after watching him race in the build-up to the Athens Olympics, when it all came tumbling down. I looked on in horror and disbelief as the French police arrested him, just as we settled down to dinner in one of his favourite restaurants in Biarritz. It was a shocking moment, something I never want to experience again. Only then, did I begin to understand his secret life and how deeply ashamed he was of betraying his ideals and his family and friends.

Dave's arrest put me in a difficult situation. I was advised, in no uncertain terms, to leave as quickly as possible, to ensure that British Cycling was not tarnished by scandal. Ultimately though, I had nothing to hide and had done nothing wrong. I was warned that it could be damaging to my reputation but I felt that I had a duty of care to Dave. I decided that the right thing to do was to stay.

He was in custody for seventy-two hours. The French police were brutal and very aggressive. I was interrogated for almost five hours, but they finally completely acknowledged that I had no involvement at all. I waited until Dave was released, exiting through the back door of the police station to avoid the media. Then I told him to tell me everything.

Over the next few days, as we talked openly about what he had done and what he had been through, the murky world of doping – something I had never encountered – became real. It opened my eyes as I learned how the culture of doping had poisoned his life. It was a steep learning curve for me, but his experience has given me valuable insight and helped me to further develop the strong ethical values that are now the foundation for Team GB and Team SKY. I have seen first hand how doping can almost wreck an athlete's life – I am determined it will not happen to any athlete in my charge.

Dave and I came close to working together a couple of years ago, when Team SKY was being developed. The team would have benefited from his racing knowledge, from his performances and from his experience as a captain on the road. In the end, however, the premise of Team SKY, emphatically founded on creating a team that exemplifies clean sport and that has a zero tolerance on employing anybody with any doping history, made it impossible for him to come to the team.

I am convinced Dave has learned his lesson. Since his comeback, he's become a reformed character, a voluble contributor to the anti-doping debate through his work with Garmin-Slipstream, UK Sport and WADA. More remarkably, his passion for cycling is undimmed, despite everything he went through. It's very clear to anybody who knows him that he will always love riding his bike. That alone probably tells you more about who he really is, than any number of speeches.

Most importantly, Dave's story reveals what I have long believed – that, in the wrong environment, under the wrong influences, even people with the greatest integrity can make the wrong decisions. Although the culture of doping in sport is often depicted as black and white, it can be insidious and subtle; on the one hand, it exploits the vulnerable and pressurised athlete, on the other, it enables the cynical to clinically cheat. That's why the David Millar story is so valuable and so instructive to all those who care about ethics in sport.

David Brailsford, CBE
Performance Director, British Cycling and Principal, Team SKY
Manchester, May 2011

22 JUNE 2004, BIARRITZ

It is early morning.

I have been dozing. I open my eyes.

For a moment, I don't know where I am.

Then I remember the night before, the hands on my shoulders, pushing me, shoving me, the rage and the abuse, my heart racing, my palms sweating.

And then, my guts in sudden freefall, I recognise where I am, the bare walls, the rough blanket, the hanging light bulb.

I am in a French police cell, below Biarritz town hall, in an empty basement. A smell of piss and disinfectant hangs in the air. A drunken man shouts relentlessly in a cell somewhere down the corridor.

It is six in the morning. The morning of a new life. Only I don't know what kind of life it will be. What do I feel? Relief, shame, terror, emptiness, loneliness.

And tired, I am so tired.

Outside, the sun is already up, warming the rooftops. The dawn surfers will be heading down to the beach, the patisserie near my flat opening for business, the nightclubs emptying. This place has been my home. They liked me here. Not any more. Now they will look the other way. Now I don't belong.

I don't belong here, in France, where they have arrested me and where they will shame me and break me, nor in Britain where they will disown me for who I have become. Now I don't belong anywhere. Now I float, cast adrift, out to sea, a speck in the distance.

Now I know it is finished.

There are no good reasons, no easy excuses. There is no redemption.

1

Instead I am blinded now, dirty, unshaven, red-eyed – they took my phone, my belt, my shoelaces – just in case, they said.

Just in case.

I bury my head in the hood of my sweatshirt, understanding that I've lost everything I had once dreamed of, but feeling nothing but acceptance. There is no sadness – simply the recognition that I have been unhappy for a long time.

I close my eyes, pull the hood over my head and turn towards the wall. I want darkness, but here the lights never go out. The opposite wall, the one with the locked door, is made of perspex. Privacy is a thing of the past.

I can't sleep.

I can't sleep because I am guilty and I am all the more awake because of it. All I can do is think of ways to explain myself, to justify myself, but I know I can't. It doesn't stop me trying for hours and hours on end.

I lie there on the wooden bench, motionless, wondering when it's all going to start again, when will they come for me with more questions. Fourteen hours in this cell, no food, no company.

There is a bang on the door. Finally. A bolt turns and the one with the gun, the one who laughed at me, comes in.

'*Bon. On y va.*'

The walk upstairs to the interview room is humiliating. I know some of the policemen who work here. They treated me as somebody special, asked for my autograph. I'm being looked at differently now. They are embarrassed for me. I can sense pity.

For 24 hours the questions continue, in and out of the interview room. The good cop, the man in charge, seems reasonable. He plays his role.

'David, I understand the stresses you're under,' he says. 'This is all the fault of Cofidis and François Migraine. Not you. You know that? They're the ones responsible for us being here – you must remember that.'

After a while he leaves. I am on my own with the one with the sneer and the gun. And, in turn, he plays his role. He knows how to hurt me.

'I know the type of person you are, David. It's disgusting that you trick people who admire and respect you.' He moves across the room, leans in closer. 'All you are is a cheat and liar.'

By the end of the second day, I've barely slept for 48 hours.

I know I'm going to lose everything, my career and my sport, the house, the car, the prestige, the money, the lifestyle.

I do not care if I lose everything, even though I thought that it was all that mattered. It is a relief. I am going to be free. It is an epiphany.

They take me back to the interview room. I ask if I can talk to the other policeman, the third guy, the one who has never spoken to me.

He has remained in the background, seemingly the lowest ranked of this elite drugs squad. He enters the room.

'You must be tired,' he says, pouring me a glass of water.

'Yes,' I say. 'I am.'

I look down for a moment, studying my hands, tanned and wiry from the hours spent gripping the handlebars, training and racing with my Cofidis teammates, for thousands upon thousands of kilometres.

I lift my head and look at him. He is watching me.

'You know, David, this is not going to go away,' he tells me. 'We're not going to stop.'

'I know,' I say.

Now, at last, I am ready.

'I want to tell you first. I don't want to give *them* – the others – the satisfaction.'

And so I begin.

Let me tell you who I am.

My name is David Millar.

I am a professional cyclist, an Olympic athlete, a Tour de France star, a world champion – and a drugs cheat.

And I want to start again.

9 JULY 2009, BARCELONA

You might think, after everything that happened, after the bitterest humili-ation, that I would have wanted to quit professional cycling. In fact, the opposite was true. I grew to love it more than ever. I realised how lucky I was that I had a second chance. I wanted to make up for wasted time. I owed it to myself and to the idealistic, romantic kid I'd once been.

That was why, racing alone through the pouring rain, 30 kilometres from a Tour de France stage finish line in Montjuic, I still believed.

The Tour peloton was chasing me, but I was still riding faster, clinging on to my lead. Time checks, encouragement and expletives came through my radio earpiece from Matt White, my Australian *directeur sportif*, at the wheel of the team car following in my wake.

Television helicopters hovered above, flying low enough to send

litter scurrying across the road, the rotors deafening me as they swept overhead. Screaming Catalan cycling fans were crammed onto the hillside. Press cars, race *commissaires* and media motorbikes weaved around and about me. The pain in my legs and my lungs gripped me, my face tightening with the strain, as I neared the top of the final climb.

It was intense, it was excruciating.

It was wonderful.

I have lived in Girona in Catalunya for a few years now. In the past, many other professionals – Lance Armstrong, Bradley Wiggins, Floyd Landis – have also based themselves there. Even so, I never expected a Tour de France stage to start there. Stage five of the 2009 Tour, however, did, tracing a 182-kilometre route south to Montjuic in Barcelona, using roads that I trained on day after day. The Tour was in my backyard.

During the winter, prior to off-season training rides, the handful of us living in Girona often met in a café on the peaceful Placa de Independencia. This was only a couple of hundred metres from where the Tour's team buses were now lined up and where, overnight, the Tour's sprawling start village had sprung up, taking over the city centre. Those grey, cold winter days seemed a lifetime ago.

It was a hot morning and there were thousands of people milling around. I couldn't distinguish between the pavements, roads or car parks. The juggernaut of the Tour owned them all now. The biggest circus in cycling had come to town, and I was one of the performers.

Nicole and I sat in the start village with Brad and his wife Cath, their kids running circles around us. The energy levels of Brad and Cath's son Ben, a Garmin racing cap perched on his little head, reminded us of our one-year-old terrier Zorro.

At the same time, the 'performer' bit, fuelled by Nicole's prompting, was playing on my mind. The following day we would ride to Andorra and climb to the ski station at Arcalis, the first of three Pyrenean mountain stages. The previous week of racing had been very demanding; in the team time trial we had ridden out of our skin to finish second. I'd gone particularly deep that day, making myself physically sick and being unable to eat for almost 7 hours after we crossed the finish line. It had already been torrid, and horrifically hard – and there were still eighteen days of the Tour remaining.

Nicole didn't care about that. 'Should we dedicate our afternoon to Tour viewing?' she asked. 'You have to promise me you'll try and win. It's your home stage – you have to try!'

'Of course I will,' I said, indulgently. 'Just for you.'

Then I set her straight. 'Of course I'm not. In fact, if everything goes to plan you won't see me once. A sprinter will win and we'll all have a relaxed day.'

Ben tugged at his mum's sleeve. 'Mum! I need to pee,' he said. Brad put down his coffee cup and got to his feet.

'I'll take him,' he said. 'Come on, Ben, let's go find the toilets.' He climbed onto his bike and set off, Ben sprinting through the journalists, VIPs and hangers-on in his wake.

An hour and a half later, I was back in that world of pain, teetering close to my limits. The peloton was racing hard, lined out on the climb exiting Sant Feliu, at the start of a corniche road familiar from those winter training rides, that twisted relentlessly for the next 25 kilometres.

In the off-season, I would struggle up the climbs and gingerly tackle the damp descents. Now, with riders cursing and spitting all around me, after just 2 of those 25 kilometres, I was already close to my absolute maximum. We were going much faster than I thought was possible on roads I knew so well. With a speeding peloton attacking each twist and turn and change in gradient, they took on a new, far more menacing dimension.

Matt and the team car were far behind us, as the peloton snaked around the jagged coastline. Instead of tactical advice or information crackling over the radio, for the time being there was only silence.

As an athlete, it's amazing how focused it's possible to become when you're managing your body close to its limits. As I balanced between maximum effort and total collapse, every corner, every change in gradient, engraved in my memory from training, suddenly became more detailed than I would ever have thought possible.

Yet in the ebb and flow of the race, it was difficult to tell whether I was moving up through the peloton or whether the peloton was sliding backwards around me. At times like these – when you're 'on the rivet' –

the riders become desperate, clinging on to the pace by their fingernails, fighting, scrapping even, to claw themselves back into contention.

Soon, the cream rose to the top. Alberto Contador, the Schleck brothers – Frank and Andy – and Lance Armstrong started appearing in these moves, a clear sign that the peloton was now close to breaking point. Such riders only show their cards if they sense the race entering a critical phase.

I knew that the only way to escape the grasp of the peloton now would be through strength and will. Buoyed by the excitement of home advantage, any ideas I'd nurtured of taking it easy were now a distant memory. I just hoped Nicole was watching.

I couldn't suppress the romantic kid, the teenage boy who'd raced around the country parks of Hong Kong pretending to lead the Tour de France, only these days I was a born-again cycling geek racing in the world's biggest bike race. The 32-year-old battle-hardened pro sighed in resignation. He had no choice but to take a back seat as the big kid came out to play.

Another move slipped clear and the remaining strong riders at the front of the peloton surged forward again in one last effort to chase and reel it in. We hammered on the pedals again in desperation. But it was plain to see – everybody was fucked.

Perversely, now – with everybody beyond their limit – was the moment. I had lactate building up through my body – legs, arms, shoulders – and my heart rate had been over its controllable threshold for over 20 minutes. Yet there was a good chance that if a strong move went clear of the peloton it might just make it to the finish line in Montjuic.

The fittest men in the world had cooked themselves and I knew it was now or never. It was time to go.

When you take on a lone attack in professional racing, you have to commit and show utter conviction. There are no half-measures. So I changed up through the gears, used the power of my bodyweight to crush the pedals and attacked with everything I had. My body, screaming at me to stop, was overruled.

After about 30 seconds of effort, I looked under my arm and saw that nobody was following me. I switched into time trial mode, controlling my power so that I could continue for the next quarter of an hour, until a decent gap formed and hopefully an elite group of riders, capable of sharing the pace, were bridging up to me.

The reality was that my attack backfired. Everybody was so wrecked and so happy to see me go that they relaxed. Only two other riders, two of the strongest French pros, Sylvain Chavanel and Stéphane Augé, broke free. But I knew that however hard we rode, three of us were not going to get to Barcelona ahead of a pursuing peloton.

Behind us, the peloton regrouped. One by one, the riders dropped during those crazy 30 minutes on the corniche reattached themselves to the back of an ever-growing bunch. They would take a breather, snack on something, have a drink, talk tactics. Once rested, tactical decisions would be made based on the race situation.

All our efforts would probably be for nothing, yet at the same time we were live on television, our sponsors and the world were watching, and we were now under obligation to race. So we had to plough on. But we were in a kamikaze attack with close to zero chances of success. I was furious with my impetuosity, pissed off for allowing my emotions to lead me into such a hopeless situation.

The gap came down to 2 minutes and it began to rain. Now my confidence ebbed away. I started to drop behind on the descents and in the corners. For some reason, my ability to handle my bike on the slippery Catalan coastal roads had deserted me. I prayed the peloton would reel us in and put us out of our misery rather than prolonging the agony.

But cycling plays with the mind. One moment you can be in a pit of despair, the next, spirits lifted by some barely perceptible positive sensation, buoyed by optimism. Thirty kilometres from Barca, the rain started to fall more heavily than it had all day, and as the downpour intensified, I began to feel replenished.

We still had a minute's lead. There was one more climb, followed by a descent into the suburbs of Barcelona and then just 15 kilometres through the centre of the city. As we tackled the last hill, I drifted behind my long-time companions and, instinctively, launched a massive attack.

The TV motorbikes drew alongside and the helicopters buzzed overhead. The sky grew darker and the rain came down, yet I was in my element. I knew that if I stayed clear over the top of the last climb, then, as a lone rider using the full width of the road, I would be able to take time back on the descent.

After that, I'd just have to ride on a wing and a prayer.

It was eerie, deserted and dark coming off that final hill. I felt serene as my pain subsided and I rediscovered the bike-handling skills that earlier had deserted me. Ahead of me, as I sped into a corner, one of the race motorbikes wobbled and then slid into the gutter. All it would take was one little patch of oil or dirt washed across the road and I'd be on the ground too.

Now the radio came to life, and Matt White's excited voice crackled in my earpiece. '*Dave* ,' he told me, ' *you've taken time on the climb, you've got over a minute. Astana are controlling, they'll play it safe on the descent. You know what to do.*'

Now I was committed again, racing into each corner with a caution that only just outweighed risk. Once I'd made it through upright, I would sprint, stamping furiously on the pedals, until I was back up to speed.

As I headed on alone, into central Barcelona, I became more and more aware of the sheer number of people everywhere. The noise was loud, very loud, and I felt the whole of the city willing me on.

Matt (a.k.a. Whitey) was yelling now. '*Dave, mate – you're on a stormer, they can't bring you back. You're holding them at over a minute. It's chaos back here.*'

Ten kilometres remained. Ten kilometres of long, broad, boulevards, stretching ahead of me, glistened in the gloom. Now I felt Catalan, as the crowds willed me on, helping me through every corner, shouting me back up to speed in every sprint and urging me to not slow down.

My earpiece crackled again. '*Fuck me, Dave – you can do this! There are crashes everywhere behind, the teams are at their limit to bring you back. DON'T FUCKING SLOW DOWN!*'

Five kilometres to the line and still, there I was, 45 seconds ahead of the Tour de France. Now it became a straight pursuit: David Millar versus the peloton, in the biggest moment of my career since my comeback, with the world watching, my mum biting her nails at home in London, Nicole, my fiancé, barely able to watch in a bar in Girona, both of them surrounded by friends, the anxious texts flying back and forth.

But inevitably, I was tiring. I had fought to keep my speed at 50 kilometres an hour on those never-ending boulevards, but my body had stopped listening. My cadence ebbed, as the strength seeped out of me. The seconds tumbled like dominoes.

Matt wasn't throwing in the towel though. '*Thirty seconds, Dave, thirty seconds – fucking amazing, mate. You're so close! DO NOT GIVE UP!*' he bellowed. '*Anything can still happen behind, you would not believe the carnage back here.*'

But no matter how much I wanted to win, no matter how much power I wanted to generate, I couldn't do it. Even the thousands of Catalans that lined the streets, imploring me to fight on, couldn't help me. I wasn't in control any more; now it was just a matter of time until the soaked and swearing bunch swept past.

I rode into Placa d'Espanya and was faced with the magnificent spectacle that is Montjuic. Momentarily, I was taken aback, but the sight gave me a final snap of energy, as I rode alone up the steadily biting gradient, the peloton now eyeing my back wheel.

I swung right as the road climbed to the line and battled to lift my speed, but I could hear them all now, emptying themselves in their effort to get past me, to surge ahead to the line, just a kilometre further ahead.

Then, they were past me, swamping me and spitting me out.

But they were red-eyed, vacant, broken men, who looked as if they had fought their own battle, just to catch me. It made me smile: there were only forty of them left in the front group and I knew they'd been pushed to the limit.

As I exited the back of the front group, my body and mind shut down. I can remember one or two pats on the back, a couple of compliments on my ride. Maybe the day hadn't been wasted. I was getting respect from the guys whose lives I'd just made hell.

I was awarded 'Most Aggressive Rider of the Day', generally given to the most spectacular loser of the day and, rather wonderfully, sponsored by 'Coeur de Lion' (Lion Heart), a French cheese. There was a trip to the podium, a little trophy and a lot of handshakes.

People rarely remember lone breakaways – only when they succeed perhaps. It was a mad move on my part. But cycling is mad, beautifully so. The beauty, suffering, grandeur and panache are what make it special.

But that day taught me something else too: the manner in which one loses the battle can sometimes outshine the victory.

I

MY EARLY YEARS

Even though I was born in Malta – for those who need to know, on 4 January 1977– I have always thought of myself as a Scot.

My parents, Gordon and Avril, left the island when I was 11 months old and returned to Scotland. This was a homecoming, a return from abroad to our brethren. Yet because my father was in the Royal Air Force and subject to their postings, it wasn't really his choice where we ended up.

We lived in Forres. My earliest memories are of a housing estate, a school bus – with a metal bar across the top of the seat in front of me that I'd try to bite but couldn't, because of the bus bumping around – and of my grandma giving me chocolate eclairs.

The RAF housing estate was my playground. I could usually be found playing with my *Star Wars* figurines and space ships – a quiet little boy by all accounts, living in his own little world.

I've been told a story, by both Mum and Dad, about a birthday party they held for me at home. I disappeared early on, and was found playing alone in my room, asking when everybody was going home. I remember being like that when I was young.

I liked drawing. In fact, I drew a lot. There was another toddler who I was best friends with, but I can't remember his name now. My sister Frances – sometimes 'Fran', sometimes 'France'; 'Fran' to others, 'France' to me – arrived a little less than a year after our return to Scotland and she quickly became my new play partner.

Fran was a quick developer and walked and talked at a freakishly young age. When people learned that I, not Fran, was the older sibling, this confused them. I've never had a problem with it – Fran's propensity for talking, that is. I simply point out that I'm older than her anyway and claim seniority that way.

Dad was stationed at Kinloss, the RAF base not far from Forres. On occasions when he wasn't flying, he'd take me to the base and I'd play on the grass-covered aircraft hangers and run around after him amongst the aircraft. Even now, it's a vivid memory. Sometimes I'll pass a garage that will have that same smell of warm metal and diesel and I'll be back there, running among those big war machines, with my dad, in the grass-covered hangers. I wish more garages had that smell.

I was too young to understand his job, but I remember him leaving for the Falkland Islands. He just disappeared one day and we didn't see him again for what seemed like for ever. It's the only time I can remember my mum telling my sister and me to pray at night. There was never any news and it must have been very hard for her.

My godfather, Major Mike Norman, was involved in the Falklands War too. He and his wife, Thelma, were friends with my parents in Malta. Mike had given my mum a Royal Marine insignia to be flown above the house when she went into labour. She still has the flag.

Mike was something of a war hero and, years later, while I was living in Hong Kong, I learned what a significant part he had played in the conflict when I saw a BBC film called *An Ungentlemanly*

Act. Mike had been the commanding officer of the Royal Marines unit on the Falklands when the Argentinians invaded.

When it became clear that the Argentines were mounting a full invasion, he was charged with defending the island by Rex Hunt, the island's Governor. Although outnumbered, Mike led his men with courage and skill, but after hours of defending Governor's House he was ordered to surrender.

Two months later, when the Argentine army capitulated, he raised the British flag once again. Nonetheless, the war left its mark on him. Many years later, after Mike had retired, my mother spoke to Thelma on the phone and asked how he was.

'Oh, he's fine,' she said. 'He's out gardening. But you know, Avril, his knees never really recovered from that bloody yomp.'

In many ways, growing up as a forces child made us different from other kids. Our dads, whether in the RAF, army or navy, couldn't just switch off their value systems on coming home and taking off their uniforms. They worked in an environment with hundreds of years of history and standards. It made for a disciplined and regimented childhood.

My sister and I could be taken to any restaurant in the world and there would be no risk of us behaving badly. Without being too hard on us, my father was a disciplinarian. But he was also incredibly funny and loving when he was relaxed and happy, which was all the funnier because it was impossible to imagine him ever being the same when he was in his uniform.

I remember one flyer friend never stopped calling him 'Sir', even when they were both in civilian clothes.

'Why don't you just call him Gordon?' I asked him once.

'I can't, David,' he replied, deadpan. 'He's my commanding officer.'

Years later, after my dad had left the forces and joined Cathay Pacific, I appreciated what a change it must have been for him going from being a young wing commander in the Royal Air Force to a middle-aged co-pilot in a commercial airline. It couldn't have been easy for him.

My dad was reckless at times. I remember seeing him, around

the time that he was a squadron leader, standing in the dining room looking out of the window, staring at his white Lotus Elite. There was something broken about his expression – he told me that he'd crashed his car and that he felt sad.

I first learned to ride a bike in Scotland. But it was hardly the most auspicious start to my cycling career, as I rode into the back of a parked car on one of those first rides.

In fact, I was a little accident-prone. Playing tag at school, I managed to break my collarbone for the first time. It took my mum, bless her, three days to believe that I'd broken it. I'm not sure if that says more about me, or my mum.

My mum is one of the most intelligent people I know, able to maintain a challenging conversation on almost any subject. She studied engineering at Glasgow university based on her admiration for her adopted father yet, forty years on, is now on her fourth different career. She came from a loving yet unorthodox family, adopted as a baby by a couple already in their mid-forties. Today the only family she has is my sister and me, and her fabulous piano playing neighbour Terry. Her background probably explains her absolute love for France and me, yet this collarbone incident also showed she was no pushover.

Just before we left Scotland, I did it again. One of my best friends had a hill in his back garden that in winter hardened to a stony mix of frost, ice and snow. Naturally, we considered it our duty to ride down this. I must have taken it more seriously than him, because I was the one who ended up crumpled at the bottom of the hill, nursing a second broken collarbone.

There's a final memory of our time in Scotland – of leaving in 1984, and Fran and I, cocooned in the bucket seats of my dad's Lotus, singing along to Yazoo. Dad had a new posting. We were moving on again, heading south to our new house in Stone, Buckinghamshire.

It's hard to imagine Frances and I arriving in England as wee Scots, the two of us arguing away with our strong sing-song accents. The years since, travelling and living in many different places, have left me with the most neutral of accents.

If anything, what I have now is an expat Brit accent that morphs itself spontaneously to mimic those around me. It's not something I'm proud of; I would much prefer to have held on to the Scottish accent that I had as a child, because I remain very proud of being a Scot.

At times, I have to admit that, listening to my English accent while calling myself Scottish, I've felt like a fraud. But then I suppose our nomadic lifestyle made it important that we were good at 'fitting in'.

When I started school in Buckinghamshire, I would always play lunchtime football in Scottish national team kit. Looking back, I think losing my accent was a pivotal moment. Even so, I feel most at home when surrounded by Scots, and it was among Scots that I spent most of my time during my doping ban.

I didn't enjoy school that much, but out of the classroom, I had a blast, particularly after I discovered BMX and became the proud owner of a Raleigh Super Tuff Burner. Dad would take me along to the BMX race leagues in High Wycombe every other weekend.

I was 8 years old and it was the perfect introduction to racing.

The BMX boom was at its height and movies such as *ET* and *BMX Bandits* were big box office. I still haven't seen *ET*, even though, a few years later while on a family holiday in California, I was chosen out of a throng of children to ride the *ET* BMX against a blue screen at Universal Studios. I couldn't bring myself to tell them I hadn't actually seen the film.

I loved the rush of BMX racing. The start gate would come crashing down and the ten riders in the field would hurtle with childish abandon towards the first ramps and left-hand banked turn, or 'burn'. There was very little skill involved. It was more dependent on a lot of youthful courage and blind luck.

I was still on my trusty Raleigh, competing against kids on special racing BMXs. This had never bothered me, until one day, when, after finishing in the top three and while pushing my Raleigh back up the hill for the next race, I heard the commentator remark on my less than special bike. I was upset to say the least.

Despite that, in my first season I finished fourth in the county for my age group. This entitled me to a number 4 handlebar plate for the next season, but I clearly remember thinking that fourth in the county wasn't really that good.

I don't know why I would have such high expectations or put such pressure on myself at such a young age. I was competing against boys who were clearly taking it much more seriously than I was. For my dad and I, it was simply a Sunday out together. He didn't allow himself to get mixed up in 'over-competitive dad' syndrome. Any pressure or desire I had to perform came from me and me alone.

But that number 4 plate was never used because my beloved Super Tuff Burner was stolen that winter, effectively ending my BMX career. I spent years looking in ditches and scouring bike racks searching for that bike, and it took me a very long time to accept that it was never coming back.

As well as BMX, I'd taken to roller-skating much of the time, usually at roller discos. I can't remember how often the roller discos were, but they were never regular enough for me. I was a roller

disco king – Thame Leisure Centre was my kingdom.

France, in true younger sibling fashion, had taken to copying everything I did, be it BMX or roller-skating. It was never long before France was, like me, fully equipped, tagging along. Most irritatingly, everybody still thought she was my older sister, which was not cool for an already quiet, shy, introspective boy. I'm ashamed to say that I did my best to make sure that skating was the last hobby of mine that Frances copied. At the time, I didn't see the love, only the burden of a little sister.

France was so confident, so able to talk to people. She would talk to anybody at any time on any subject. We – my parents and I – would hang back and send her forward to ask all sorts of things of all sorts of people. We didn't need local knowledge or a tour guide when we were on holiday, because we had our own little search engine on legs. Frances was our Google.

My mum and dad made a significant effort to improve us both. We were both given extra tuition outside of school and I was learning to play the trombone and the piano. I was trombonist in the school jazz band and now it amazes me that I pretended to enjoy it and persevered for so long.

But there were problems at home. It became impossible to ignore the troubles between my parents. At first, it had been subtle, but now there were things that I couldn't ignore. It became harder to pretend that the fights weren't happening. I suppose it had been going on for a long while, but children choose not to see such things.

Eventually, things reached crisis point. I was woken up in the middle of the night, my tearful mum and dad sitting on my bed, telling me that they were splitting up, that it wasn't my fault and that I should look after my sister.

I don't think I cried. I certainly don't remember being tearful, but I remember being incredibly fucking angry. My childhood had come to an abrupt end. I was 11.

The next morning, I walked to school as usual, through grass covered in morning dew, my feet leaving a trail behind me.

2

THE MESS

Things changed fundamentally over the next couple of years.

Not long after Dad moved out, Terry, my mum's new partner, moved in. With Terry came his children, Simon and Sarah. Simon was a bit older than me and Sarah was the same age. It was weird at first. At that time my dad didn't have a home and was living in the officers' mess at Northwood, while we were all under one roof in a little village 15 miles from Stone.

Terry was nice enough though, and he soon won us over. He had met Mum through work, so we'd already met him before everything – my parents' relationship – had fallen apart, but it was still a new family to me.

Now, I can see that I wasn't happy. I didn't like our new home, school made me miserable and, to make matters worse, we had no money. Dad wasn't around much, although he and I would get together on Thursdays, as he lived in Aylesbury and I'd stop by his house on the journey to and from school.

Fran and I spent a few weekends at the mess in Northwood. This was not just any officers' mess, but home of the combined commander and chief officer's ward room, where we would be dining on special dispensation of the president of the mess committee.

It was more like a gentleman's smoking room, full of high-ranking older officers who'd be sitting, quietly dining with full silver service, while reading or simply enjoying the rarefied peace and quiet. France and I would be on our very best behaviour, knowing that we had no margin of error in such an environment. It was the last time such behaviour would be required of us.

But France and I had started to argue more than laugh, perhaps as much due to our adolescence as to the tumultuous times that we were living through. And I was changing, rebelling.

The upheaval caused profound changes in me over a very brief period of time. I began to doubt the wisdom of adults, and began to understand that my life was mine to control. But I was still a kid – I wasn't ready for such big changes.

School held little escape. Aylesbury Grammar's intake was largely smart state-school boys being groomed towards public-school values. Football – which most of us loved and cherished – was not on the school games list, and rugby took its place. This did not go down well. To rub salt into the wound, the one subject I liked most, art, was held in little or no esteem.

Mixing such a diverse bunch of boys together did not make for the most harmonious of classrooms. We made our French teacher cry more than once and our second-year tutor had a nervous breakdown. We were smart and rebellious, a terrible combination for a teacher.

I was still keen on cycling – I just didn't have a bike. My short-lived BMX career was already over, but I started to take an interest in mountain biking. I took on some odd jobs and dad said he would match whatever I earned so that I could buy a new bike. So on top of a paper round was added car-cleaning and lawn-mowing. My financial planning, targeting a new mountain bike, was ridiculously organised.

I had a big wall chart taped to the ceiling where I would monitor progress, relative to weekly and monthly targets, while lying in bed. I would empty my moneybox and count it all out, like a wee Ebenezer Scrooge. (This was about the most sophisticated I would ever become in planning my finances, although in fairness, I should point out that things have got better recently.) At the end of the rainbow was a Marin Bear Valley '89, black and gold and very handsome. I bought it in a shop in High Wycombe and my life in cycling began.

Soon after that, Dad told us that he was leaving for Hong Kong. I knew he was leaving the RAF and training to be a commercial pilot but Hong Kong hadn't been mentioned. We presumed he would be near us whatever happened. He immediately said that we could move out there with him, but we didn't even know where Hong Kong was, let alone what it was like. It didn't seem real, and although it wasn't to have an effect on us for a while, affect us it did.

Before he left, Dad and I went to Scotland together to look at boarding schools. I hadn't been happy at Aylesbury since the beginning. The whole experience felt so miserable, from the cold, dark, silent wait at the bus stop, through the long journey on a double-decker bus, to the death march from the bus station to the school. And then there was the school itself.

It was almost five hundred years old and had the foundations of a great institution, but it was dilapidated and frayed at the edges. Some of the teachers were wonderful, but there were also terrible teachers, young, inexperienced and badly trained.

At the beginning of my second year at the Grammar our form groups were changed around. To my horror I found myself in a class of boys I neither knew or liked, and I wrote a letter to the headmaster expressing my unhappiness at being separated from my friends. A couple of days later, the deputy head asked to see me.

He explained that the headmaster had read my letter and asked him to speak to me.

'So, David,' he began, 'I understand you are not happy with your new form group?'

I stood by my letter. 'No, sir.'

'Well, you understand that these form groups were created to help you? We are not in the habit of allowing boys to simply pick their form group. Why should we treat you differently?'

I explained that I understood the reasoning behind the form groups, and agreed it was the best way to educate us. Then I said: 'I think my situation is a little different from the other students.

'My parents recently divorced and we have moved away from all my old friends. This has all happened in the last two years and I seem to be living in constant change. I don't feel like more change, sir.'

I hadn't intended to mention my parents divorce, but as I spoke,

I realised that it was a key element in my motives for sticking with my friends and being moved to a less academic class. He got up from his chair and moved back behind his desk.

'Well, I will speak to the headmaster and give him my opinion. If we choose to make an exception and allow you to go to the form you want, you can be sure we'll be keeping an eye on you, so make sure you don't let us down.'

'Thank you, sir.'

There was a pause. 'One last thing,' he said. 'I asked around about you before this meeting. Did you know you are thought of as, er, a bit of a "*wide boy*"?'

I had no idea what a wide boy was, but I liked the sound of it. Hesitantly I replied. 'No, sir, I didn't. Should I say thank you ...?'

He smiled at that. Thanks to him my last few months at Aylesbury Grammar School were not nearly as miserable as they might have been.

Dad's new life took shape. France and I went to Hong Kong to visit him at half-term, enduring the YPTA (Young Person Travelling Alone) system of flying around the world. Even now, Frances and I feel a pang of empathy for these kids when we see them in airports with their little travel packs around their necks.

You've probably seen them too, pre-teens chaperoned on and off flights by cabin crew. They label you, putting a packet around your neck containing ticket and passport. Then you board a flight, seated alone, often surrounded by other kids with their mums and dads, heading off on holiday – together. It's a crushing experience. From the moment of leaving one parent and then meeting the other at the final destination, you are in limbo, between families.

Yet it was worth that humiliation to get to Hong Kong, because from the moment the plane landed, I fell in love with the place. I'd stepped from a black and white world into life in technicolour and I knew that was what I really wanted.

Frances and I were there for less than a week but it was enough time for me to decide that I wanted to move there. Dad had made it clear that it was an option for both of us, if we were interested.

Hong Kong offered an escape and I didn't hesitate, even though I knew that when I got back home I'd have to tell my mum.

I can't remember exactly how I told Mum, but I can remember the distress it caused. She cried every night for weeks. France was the collateral damage in it all. She didn't want to leave Mum after seeing how upset she was, and this would be what always kept her from Hong Kong. My leaving her behind was to weigh on our relationship for a decade.

Leaving Mum was hard, but I guess that part of me held her responsible for Dad moving out and for us moving houses. This wasn't – isn't – necessarily true, but believing it made it possible for me to even consider leaving.

Now, from a distance, I look back and see that it was a life-changing decision. I was a selfish, damaged 13-year-old determined to take his life into his own hands. It changed me, hardened me, and laid the foundation for the person I was to become.

Hong Kong was my escape, I was going to the Far East for the same reason as so many before me – to start afresh in a faraway place. The dreariness of Aylesbury was made all the more profound by the knowledge I was leaving for a new life. I felt sorry for everybody who had to carry on.

I didn't return to live permanently in Britain for fifteen years.

3

FLYING BALL BICYCLES

Hong Kong – 'HK' – is a strange and magical place, one of the wonders of the world. It was especially so during the years I lived there. The British lease on the territory was nearly over and the 1997 handover back to China was rapidly approaching.

HK's residents lived with the ever-present ticking of the count-down to Chinese rule as the backdrop to their everyday lives. It made for vibrant times. At first, I didn't understand this – I just loved the atmosphere and thrived in the city's electrified air. Everybody and everything seemed so much more alive than what I'd left behind in England.

The people that I met were generally positive, dynamic people, and the two cities, Hong Kong on the island and Kowloon on the mainland, were ever-changing beasts in their own right.

I never grew weary of sitting on the Kowloon waterfront, gazing across the harbour at that most famous of skylines, admiring the sheer scale of it all. I'd go to the far end of the Ocean Terminal car park, perch on a wall and look out over the water. It was an oasis of peace amongst all the chaos and noise. At night, HK was other-worldly, particularly if the clouds were low. The city's neon lights would reflect off them and illuminate an upside-down, snowy mountain range shrouding the tops of the tallest buildings. It was, and I'm sure still is, sublime.

Kowloon's growth had been stunted because of the presence of Kai Tak airport. Development could not shoot skywards because of the planning limitations imposed by the flight paths. But what it lost in height, it made up for in intensity. The most densely populated place in the world, Mongkok, was only a 5-minute walk from where

I went to school. Ten minutes in the opposite direction took me to the Walled City, a self-governed, mythical enclave that over a century had grown into what, to me, looked like the most ambitious post-apocalyptic film set ever created. It was governed by the triads and was a total no-go area for a *gweilo* like myself.

I lived with Dad and his new wife Ally in the New Territories, near Sai Kung, in a marina development built into the sea on reclaimed land and comprising scores, maybe hundreds, of big terraced town houses. The development was brand new and had attracted many expat families. There was a big group of us who would hang out and have fun. My first few years there were some of the happiest I've had – K61 Marina Cove, the home and resting place of my adolescence. I'm sure if I were to return there now I would see the ghosts of my youth.

School – the King George V, or 'KG5' – was a Hong Kong institution, built in the 1930s amongst paddy fields and farmland. KG5 sat under the flight path of one of the busiest airports in the world, sandwiched between two of the most densely populated places on the planet. We studied an English curriculum and were taught by mainly English teachers. We also wore English-style uniforms, and were the only school kids in HK to do so.

The school itself was the antithesis of what I knew. I had come from a single-sex school and was essentially a well-mannered, chivalrous boy. I was something of a novelty to my fellow students, especially as I had started halfway through the year. I'd never had much attention before and I was surprised to find that I liked it. In fact, I loved it. Initially, the curriculum itself wasn't challenging as I was about a year ahead of what was being taught, so I just sat back and luxuriated in my new life.

Unfortunately, I continued to luxuriate for the next five years.

It didn't take long for my report cards to begin their slippery downward slope. First to tumble were the effort marks, followed, before too long, by my grades. But I was having too much fun to care or even bother to try to make a difference.

I have to say that I wasn't always well advised. One of my

dad's most memorable pieces of good counsel revolved around my decision to continue studying French.

'Come on, David,' he said. 'It's not something that's going to be of any use to you in the future, is it?'

I reminded him of that particular nugget of wisdom a few years later while eking out a lonely existence as a wannabe pro cyclist in a quiet French village, cut off from local society, barely capable of ordering a *café au lait* or buying a baguette.

As having fun increasingly took precedence over learning useful things, Dad did a good job of kicking my arse into gear. After a while though, even he was having too much fun to be bothered by such trivial things as his son's performance at school.

Brit expat culture was a remnant of a colonial history in which good manners, smart uniforms and hard drinking were the only way to survive a Far East posting. It didn't take either of us long to get used to the privileges offered to us on a daily basis, and in fact we slipped into that lifestyle with ease.

The British community was small, but the majority of the locals regarded us as a ruling minority. Even the kids were treated deferentially, strolling around Kowloon in our colonial school uniforms. Perhaps it empowered us a little too much, but it also gave me confidence and any shyness I may have had dissipated rapidly.

We used this social situation to our advantage and would act as if we could do what we wanted. Our parents' underlying guilt for making us live in such a faraway place meant that, most of the time, we got off lightly. So we would push a bit further each time, seeing what we could get away with. In fact, we were all spoilt and indulged, adults and children alike, some more so than others.

There were positives to growing up there. We became multinational and multicultural, so it was a very healthy environment in that sense. Yet the 'special' status we enjoyed in HK meant that many of my friends would never quite fit in anywhere else.

But that was Hong Kong before the handover, a land of self-indulgence. We did what we wanted, when we wanted, without any thought of the future or past. It was the expat lifestyle at its purest.

*

I had other interests though, beyond the expat circuit. I'd taken my new passion for mountain biking with me to HK, and surprisingly it turned out to be a great place for riding. Hong Kong and the New Territories are very hilly, almost mountainous, and beyond Sai Kung and Sha Tin were the country parks, where we were given free rein.

Every Sunday in HK was like a scene from *End of Days*, as all the Chinese would board buses and leave the city to spend a day in the country. The KMB super big double-decker buses, always a hazard, were particularly likely to knock you off your bike on those days. They were equipped with a big red emergency 'Engine Stop' button on the back.

Sometimes, adrenalin pumping after being brushed by one of them as it overtook me, I'd give chase, catch up, lean across and push the button. I'd ride on, looking back as the bus ground to a halt, the perplexed driver standing alongside his stalled juggernaut, trying to figure out what had happened. These were my first sessions of interval training.

As I got more into riding, I was becoming a geek, a bike perv. I would hang out on a regular basis at the Flying Ball Bicycle Shop. It was a crazy shop, deep in the heart of Mongkok and the very definition of organised chaos. Tiny and with perhaps one of the most valuable equipment stocks in the world, the shop had bikes that I'd only read about or seen in magazines, kit that a bike shop in England would never dream of stocking.

Mr Lee, the owner, kept long hours. He was there seven days a week, from nine in the morning, sometimes until ten at night. He lived in a flat above the shop with his family and must have had the patience of a saint, because I surely annoyed the hell out of him, hanging around the shop, getting in the way and not buying anything. It was here that I saw a notice for some races in one of the country parks. I told the boys about them and we all set about training for them.

Back then, my idea of quality training was to come home from school, eat a bowl of cereal and then set out on my mountain bike up Hiram's Highway, a 4- or 5-kilometre climb, starting not far from the main entrance of Marina Cove. I would shoot out of the blocks as fast as I could and be tasting blood by about halfway up the climb. This was a sure sign I was 'in the zone'.

At the top of the hill, I'd turn around and head back down, taking as many risks as possible to get back home as fast as I could. There was one corner where I considered myself a chicken if I couldn't get around it at 30 mph. It served me well though, because in the races, I was usually able to finish in the top five. I was a very skinny, motivated 14-year-old, but I must have had something, because two of the guys there, Simon Roberts and Ted Remedios, decided to take me under their wing and convert me to road racing.

We would all go mountain biking together, but they would use the time to educate me about road cycling. At first, like so many others before they are seduced by road riding, I was totally against it. I thought the road was a bit effete, old school – the Lycra, shaven legs and boring conservative mentality – but as time went on I began to pay more attention, mainly due to their persistence. I'm grateful to them for that.

Ted was the main protagonist in this brainwashing. He told me stories and loaned me magazines, books and videos. Little by little, I became fascinated by it all. Road racing seemed purer than mountain biking, more mythical, and it made mountain biking seem childish and transient. There were few moments of technical genius, unlike football or basketball or cricket, but what it did have was epic human accomplishment on a grand scale, performances as seemingly close to *super-human* as I'd seen in sport.

One story particularly touched me.

In the 1990 Tour de France, Miguel Indurain was riding as *domestique* to Pedro Delgado, then still the great Spanish champion. Delgado was not at his best, yet Indurain supported him unquestioningly. Indurain lost any personal chances he had during one mountain stage by staying with Delgado and pacing him through the valley to the foot of the last climb. Indurain never claimed that he could have won the 1990 Tour, yet many since have said that he was fully capable of it.

This was new to me, this culture of sacrifice and obligation. In other sports, champions were just champions – they hadn't served an apprenticeship as a professional helper to other champions, before finally getting their own chance. I found this ideal, of working up through the ranks to earn your right to lead and to win, dignified, old-fashioned and romantic.

I read two books that really seduced me, *Kings of the Road* and Bernard Hinault's biography, *Memories of the Peloton*. Both seemed epic, honourable and sometimes tragic. The more I learned about it, the more it seemed that in professional cycling – unlike other sports – winning really wasn't everything. It appeared to be as much about respect and panache as about winning. I really liked that.

I'd never come across a sport like it, and my growing fascination with it – and the secret dream of one day riding in the Tour – was the final nail in the coffin of my mountain biking days.

Yes – I know how this reads now: I was very naive and romantic, but my youth gave me that right. Idealism is a good thing and, at its purest and most passionate, it can take you a long way. The downside is that it can leave you incredibly unprepared for the harsh realities of that world when you get there.

Before leaving off-road behind, I did manage to break my collar-bone again. Out on one of the trails after school one afternoon, I catapulted over the bars, landing badly. I had a long walk back to the road and then a wince-inducing one-armed ride back to the house. That sealed the deal; within a few months I'd sold my mountain bike and, with the help of my dad, bought a road bike. It was a 'no name' frame in green and white, with a Shimano RX100 groupset – the perfect beginner's bike.

Things were changing back in England. Mum and Fran had moved to Maidenhead, in Berkshire. I flew back from Hong Kong, my new road bike with me, for my first school holidays. Mum knew that road cycling was my new thing and had done some research on local clubs, with High Wycombe CC the closest of any standing. Once again, High Wycombe was the centre of my cycling universe: from BMX racing as a small boy, to mountain biking before leaving for

HK – now it would be where I first competed in road racing.

Back then, road cycling in the UK was, at best, a third-rate sport. Funding was minimal, and the sport was amateur and old-fashioned in its attitude. After having my imagination fired by the romance and grandeur of Hinault, Indurain and the Tour, it wasn't what I expected, but it did make it quite easy to jump in as a clueless enthusiast. Local time trials were the lifeblood of the scene and each local road club would have its mid-week evening '10' – a 10-mile time trial – throughout the summer.

Anybody could turn up, pay 50p for a number and a start time, and join the race against the clock. The courses, all with coded names, were on open roads and almost always 'out-and-back' as this reduced the number of volunteer marshals needed and made the whole event logistically simpler.

In mid-summer, within a 25-mile radius of most towns, you could find three different mid-week club '10's. It was strange to find out there were so many when you'd never actually seen or heard of them. But road racing had been forced into near secrecy for many years, after time trialling had become the only way to race bicycles in England following the ban on bunch road racing at the turn of the last century. Its cultural roots were those of a rebel splinter group, and close to a century of practice had turned it into the most staid of disciplines.

My first-ever time trial was the Longwick '10,' or HCC202 to use its codename, another lingering remnant of past secrecy. I rode the course in a time of 23:58 and lost by 2 seconds to Bob Addy, a Tour de France rider from the late 1960s, and a local legend for having even started the French race.

After that debut, the club '10' became a regular Tuesday night feature of my spells in Maidenhead. Mum and High Wycombe's very welcoming club members took it upon themselves to support me as much as possible. I loved the time trials, but above all I wanted to road race, as this seemed like much more fun. The club didn't have any road racers at the time and Mum and I were left to figure out my next move.

After the Easter holidays, I flew back to Hong Kong determined to come back and road race during the summer. And so my double life began. I became an expat fun-loving teenager in HK and a dedicated serious cyclist in the UK.

Life in the Far East continued in the same vein.

Dad acquired a speedboat and many mornings at dawn we would scale the fence into the closed Hebe Haven Yacht Club, launch the boat and head out across the millpond that was the early morning South China Sea.

I'd also got back into skating, only now on in-line skates. There was a small sponsored team that I belonged to (although why it existed I don't know, as we never really did anything). The best fun to be had on the skates was by thrashing around the massive shopping malls late at night being chased by security guards, or by having a good old-fashioned sliding competition on the polished floors.

I wasn't into drinking or smoking. I'd go to the occasional house party and have a couple of drinks but I was having more fun riding my bike and skating. On top of that, drinking wasn't exactly a rebellious act in our household, or in expat circles in general.

Any self-aware drinker will tell you that booze is an easy way to remedy loneliness, alleviate boredom and make friends easily – all syndromes that can burden many people when it comes to living far from home. Dad and Ally were fond of a drink, and they had many British and Antipodean friends who shared their interest.

Sometimes a night out would end with a drunken argument that climaxed with all their wedding photos being taken down off the wall. It became routine for me to put these back up in the morning while they slept it off. I hated them arguing and would just leave the house and then on my return pretend it had never happened. That was how I learned head-in-the-sand problem-solving.

I went back to England in the summer and, at long last, was introduced to road racing. Mum had tracked down the British Cycling Federation calendar and had planned where the nearest road races would be. My new club, High Wycombe CC, even had their own race a few weeks after my arrival to look forward to. So off we went, blissfully ignorant, our only previous experience being the club '10'. We took it for granted that the road races would be much the same.

We tracked down the village hall housing the race HQ and Mum left me to sign on while she went off to get the Sunday papers. As I looked around, two things struck me; first that everybody had better bikes, and second that they all looked really serious. I joined the long queue to get to the makeshift table with the sign-on sheet and the little boxes holding the numbers. When I finally got there, they just looked at me patiently while I stood, fiver in my hand, and told them I'd like to compete in their race.

That was when they asked me for my licence. *A licence?* I had no idea you needed a licence to race, and went running off looking for my mum in a panic. Tantrum over, we found out we could buy a 'Day Licence' and so, finally, I started my first road race.

I didn't win it.

Over the next two races, it became apparent that, although tactically clueless, I was definitely one of the strongest in the field. The week before the Wycombe CC annual road race, Mum gave me a book by a guy called Eddie Borysewicz – or Eddie B, a near-legendary Stateside coach. It was called *Bicycle Road Racing: Complete Program for Training and Competition* and it became my bible.

I read it from cover to cover and the world of road racing opened up to me. When I turned up next time, at the inevitable village hall and makeshift table, in Stokenchurch, for the Wycombe race I was an Eddie B disciple, fired up and ready to test my newly acquired *savoir faire* on my peers. The race was one of the bigger ones in the British calendar due mainly to the higher than average prize money.

The circuit was about 20 miles long, a hilly, demanding course with the finish on the top of Aston Hill, one of the longer climbs in the Chilterns, with a snaking European feel to it. This made the race a little bit more exotic and, along with the larger purse on offer, meant that the peloton was of a high standard.

There was another start-line drama, when I was told I wasn't allowed to wear my favourite red and blue full-zip jersey, so instead

I pulled on a High Wycombe club jersey. It was the first race I had entered with any thought of tactics. Up to that point, I had raced every time with the same goal; go as hard as I could for as long as I could. Now I had a plan.

This time, I'd done some research. I knew who the good riders were and what teams they were on, I'd memorised where the climbs were and pondered whether it was worth going for the climber's prize. I decided it was. I then committed myself to working off the other strong riders and their teams. For the first time since I'd started racing, lucidity and knowledge outweighed my passion and exuberance.

There were three laps of the circuit and I won almost all the climber's points, so by the time we came to the final climb leading up to the finish I was a marked man. VC Venta, the best junior team in the country, were there, and they boxed me in coming up to the sprint, leaving me in the left-hand gutter, with one of them in front of me and another of their riders next to me.

Meanwhile, their teammate Danny Axford, who had won the junior national series that year, attacked from the front of the group. As I watched it all happen, I could remember Eddie B's words coming back to me. 'Wow,' I thought, 'I've read about this. They're trying to box me in – better get out of here.'

I touched my brakes, dropped back a little, pushed the guys behind and beside me out of the way, and launched after Danny. I caught him and won by a large margin. It was a turning point for me not only because it was my first win, but also because I realised how important using my head was if I wanted to be a good bike rider.

As I slowed to a halt, the legendary June Smith – aka 'Auntie June' – made a beeline for me. 'Bloody hell,' she exclaimed, 'you can race a bike, can't you?'

'They tried to block me at the finish!' I protested, adrenalin still pumping.

'Well, you showed them didn't you!' laughed June.

After I'd caught my breath we chatted some more about the race and about my plans. June's enthusiasm for cycling was infectious.

'Now look,' she said, 'I've been speaking to your mum. She tells me that you're very new to all this, and I think I can help. I'm with the Southern Centre of Excellence – we'd love to have you with us.'

I had no idea what the Southern Centre of Excellence was, but it sounded, well, excellent. June explained that each area in England had its own centre that would nurture young talent. I fell under the Southern Centre of Excellence umbrella.

In my mind's eye, I imagined a smart building with a lab and a gym, white-coated technicians, a bank of cutting-edge technology and pages of data and test results. It was actually Ian Goodhew's living room.

The centres had minimal funding and relied hugely on the generosity of individuals who loved the sport and wanted to help. June and Ian were two of these people and they put a lot of time and effort into helping me develop even faster. After less than two months of racing in England, I returned to Hong Kong, a fully fledged road racer. I would have to wait for the following April, in 1994, before I'd be back again to continue racing.

Over the next year, I crossed a Rubicon in my development as a cyclist.

I raced a bit in HK, which involved dawn starts and bus rides out to the country parks for chaotic and very hilly racing. I would destroy myself in these, relishing the challenge to see how much I could hurt myself, and more often than not I would finish cross-eyed and semi-delirious. I was very serious about cycling and it began to be known at school that it was my thing. I couldn't wait to get back to racing in England.

Meanwhile, that intensity earned me a place on the Hong Kong team. I found myself in Macao one weekend in a group of Chinese athletes, eating dim sum the night before the race. We were sponsored by Chinese triads, who – apparently – loved cycling. Our jerseys were purple with big white Chinese calligraphy embroidered on the front and back.

My progress continued and in 1994, I became a part of the Great Britain Junior National Team. But support was minimal. A kind volunteer would give you a ride in his car to Belgium, put you up in a hostel and lend you a jersey for the race. And racing in Belgium, with its deep culture of cycling, was brilliant. Everything seemed so professional and the races were hard and incredibly competitive. I was 17 and I realised that if I really wanted to be a pro cyclist, then I would have to leave the UK.

With another year of school remaining and my A levels to come, I knew that I wouldn't be able to return to Britain for the selection races. So the GB Team made an unprecedented decision to give me a guaranteed place on the Junior World Championship team for 1995, almost a year away. I returned to HK and was surprised to find I'd been selected as a prefect and house captain for athletics and cross-country. I began my last year in Hong Kong with the intention of enjoying it and making it memorable.

School had become a meeting place to organise my extra-curricular activities, and I was now fully committed to becoming a professional cyclist when my A levels were finished. I was quietly confident that this was a certainty, although I hadn't actually admitted it to anybody. Cycling had taken me over but it was still my secret – I'd stopped trying academically and didn't even bother filling in university applications, relying solely on a hopeful art college place, so determined was I that racing was my future.

Dad was spending more and more time away from Hong Kong.

Ally had moved back to the UK and he would return there whenever he could, leaving me alone with the townhouse, car, speedboat, supermarket cards and club memberships.

I was flying by the seat of my pants. I also knew that it was my last year in Hong Kong and I wanted to live it to the fullest. So far, I'd done well to avoid much of the partying that went on, but I didn't want to leave Hong Kong and have any regrets, so I set about making up for lost time. I was still too gauche to have a long-term girlfriend – two weeks was my record – and with cycling so

important to me, girls, in all honesty, weren't top of my list of priorities.

I fancied them, and was intrigued by them, but I didn't want to be tied to one. As for sex, well, it terrified me, despite losing my virginity in a disappointing drunken episode the year before. In fact, the most time I spent with girls was in my art class, as I was the only boy.

As I dived into HK's after-hours social scene, our house became a haunt for my friends. We would hang out there, do bongs in my room, talk shit, go to the yacht club, eat Singapore noodles and drink gunners.

Ruggero Nardone was my wingman in these escapades. We didn't really know each other until arriving in sixth form and finding ourselves in the same small graphics course. Rog is half Italian, half Chinese, a brilliant mix. We became firm friends in our general indifference to school life, bouncing between groups and having fun.

Our weekends would comprise mainly of getting a little drunk, hanging out in the bars before finding other things to entertain us. Most of the time it would mean hitting the *dahgay* (games arcade) and playing Daytona. Soon we were as good as the local Chinese at this game. This was an achievement that had required many lunchtime excursions from school to Mongkok to hone our skills.

Although I was drinking and smoking a little bit, I was quite evangelical about chemical drugs. I found the thought of them disgusting and fundamentally wrong. At one of the parties in my house, I came across a guy chopping up some powder in my bedroom. I flew into a rage, grabbed him by the scruff of the neck and threw him out, telling him never to do 'that shit' in my house. It was one of the only times I have ever come close to being physically violent with anybody and it was over drugs.

Yet despite my immersion in the social scene, I grew more and more lonely. I was living by myself most of the time, with nobody to answer to or to regulate me. There is only so much fun a teenager can have before it starts to go too far, and it was obvious that was the case with me. I lived by my own rules.

As the exams came around and that final year drew to a close, I became brutally aware of the ending of the Hong Kong dream.

The day after the end of year dance, sitting on top of Rog's roof in Kowloon Tong, under the flight path of the incoming planes, I got Rog to cut off my long hair. I was preparing myself to leave for the UK and to start my other life, my cycling career.

I hadn't told anybody I was leaving, as I had no idea when, or if, I'd be coming back. Only Rog knew and we went to one final party on a junk in the harbour, knowing my flight left the next morning.

The next day, Dad took me to the airport. I gave him a 'Thank You' card.

'Thanks, Pater-san, for the last five years,' I wrote. 'I'll be surprised if I ever beat them. Love, your son, David.'

4

CHASING A DREAM

After flying back to England from Hong Kong, I had a few weeks
till the Junior World Championships in San Marino. But with that
guaranteed place in the British road race team came anxiety because
I knew that I hadn't trained enough to ensure I had the form of the
year before. So I panicked and pushed myself as hard as I could in
training and racing in an attempt to try to recover some semblance
of form.

Meanwhile, I had to race in a time trial in the north of England
in order to qualify for the World Championships time trial, as my
place in this discipline was not guaranteed. Mum and I travelled up
north but, under the nose of the British selector, the trip was a
disaster. Rolling to the start line, I punctured and missed my start
time.

In what I considered to be typically petty British fashion, I was
not allowed to start again. I refused to accept this, waited till the
last man had gone, and set off 1 minute later. Unlike most of those
competing, I wasn't on a special bike – just my road bike with clip-
on triathlete bars and borrowed wheels. Despite that, I completed
the course in the fastest time by a significant margin, but it still
wasn't accepted as legitimate and I was not selected. That experience
cemented my desire to get out of the British racing scene as fast as
I could.

After cramming my training, I arrived in San Marino for the
Worlds thinking I had made up enough ground in the previous four
weeks. I was proven gravely wrong. It was a very hard course and
I couldn't even do half of the race distance with the front of the
peloton. I got dropped unceremoniously but stuck with it, riding

lap after lap on my own. It was humiliating, but it taught me a lesson. At one point out on the circuit, there was a quiet area with nobody around. I got off, put my bike down and sat there for a few minutes in despair.

I was so angry with myself. I felt like such an idiot for being given the opportunity and just wasting it by having too much fun in HK. It didn't take me long to realise how ridiculous I must have looked, so I pulled myself together and promised to prove that I was better than this. I'm quite sure that was the moment that gave me the drive to work as hard as I did over the next eighteen months.

The British team rode terribly, yet the results failed to reveal just how badly we performed. Although Charlie Wegelius finished in front of me and I ended up getting lapped, I was somehow awarded twenty-seventh place in the results – making me highest finisher in the British team. We took a bit of a beating in the British cycling scene's traditional mouthpiece, *Cycling Weekly* – more often called 'The Comic'.

I noted the name of the author of the piece, determined that one day I'd be able to exact my revenge on him. But the desire to prove myself was becoming intense and I went back to racing and winning road races and club time trials in the UK.

I was with the biggest British cycling team at the time, Team Energy, and, against my will, they wanted me to ride the National Junior 25-mile time trial championships. Under duress, I acquiesced and travelled up north with one of my older teammates, designated as my chaperone for the day. Once again, contrary to the majority of other competitors, I was on my road bike with time trial add-ons.

It was a classic British open time trial, out and back on one of the busiest roads in England, the A1. This did mean it was very fast, and it was one of the first times I got to race on a far bigger 'senior' gear, a 52 × 12 ratio compared to the 52 × 15 we were limited to as juniors. In the end, I barely used it, but I did use it enough to have a sore knee for the next week. I won, and it remains the only open 25-mile time trial I have raced in the UK, so officially I'm yet to better my time of 52:05.

Next came a GB trip to the Junior Tour of Ireland, a race that at the time was organised by current UCI (International Cycling Union) president, Pat McQuaid. At the last minute, the volunteer manager in charge of the trip was changed to Mike Taylor – a fortuitous moment in my cycling life.

I can still remember arriving in Chapel-en-le-Frith in the Peak District, at the Taylor household, where I was to stay the night before we left for Ireland. Ten years later, when I was the fallen-from-grace British number one, I was given the same warm welcome from Pat, Mike's wife, as on that first meeting.

'Hello, love,' Pat would say. 'Come in. You must be tired – fancy a cup of tea?'

Mike and Pat are two of the loveliest people I've met through cycling, and Mike went on to play a very important role in my future development.

That trip was my first visit to Northern Ireland, and it was shocking to see the armoured cars and fortress-like police stations. Before then the 'troubles' all seemed so distant – far-off events I only saw on the news. Just in case it wasn't overwhelming enough, we arrived in Londonderry on the day of the Orange Walk, a Protestant march that wreaked havoc in the town.

We were kept awake for hours that night as all hell seemed to break loose outside our hostel. When we dared step outside the next morning, there was debris everywhere – windows were broken and there were bricks and other missiles scattered all over the place. Great Britain's junior cycling team were, to be frank, shit-scared.

The race itself went brilliantly. We won the overall classification and, on the day of the time trial, I won the road stage in the morning and the time trial in the afternoon. Mike was a great teacher, but he was also our manager, masseur, coach and cook. I learned more about bike racing in that one week than I had done in all the races up to that point.

Mike and Pat were huge cycling fans and had been travelling to Europe to watch races for years. He was full of stories and he seemed to know all the big British continental professionals well, as he'd take care of them whenever they came back to race in the national championships.

He was good friends with the commentator and ex-pro Paul Sherwen, and I'd seen photos of him with Robert Millar, Sean Yates, and even one with Eddy Merckx. In short, Mike was like a god to us.

We came out of the Tour of Ireland different bike racers. Mike gave me the confidence to believe I wasn't insane in thinking I could just head across to Europe and hold my own. The next step was to tell Mum that I wanted to postpone my art college entry so that I could race on the continent with the goal of turning professional. This took some courage.

I didn't have a place on a team in France – tradition and statistics dictated that France was the best place for British riders to graduate from amateur to pro as, from Tom Simpson to Sean Yates, they'd almost all taken this route. I had very little money, and there was the small matter of having decided a few years earlier, with Dad's backing, that it was pointless to learn French. All of these were mere details however.

Mum was very logical. She listened carefully to me as I explained The Plan to her.

Funded by my winnings from the Tour of Ireland, I intended to leave for Belgium the next week, staying with another British junior with a family in Ieper, in western Flanders, and race against continental juniors for the last month of the season, in order to get results which would add value to my *palmares* – my cycling CV. This would help boost my search for an amateur team for the following year.

While there, my supposed excellent results would supply me with enough money to live. I would return from Belgium, find a coach and train all winter while living at home with Mum in Maidenhead. During this time I would start to learn French in order to make my arrival in France a little easier. I would give myself a maximum of two years as an amateur and if by the end of this I didn't have a contract, I would return and go to art college.

Mum sat and listened patiently. Then she rained on my parade.

'So what job will you get when you come back from Belgium?' she said.

It hadn't even crossed my mind that I'd have to get a job, but I knew she was right. I was fuelled by the self-belief and desire to prove everybody wrong that characterises most teenagers, and was desperate to race in Europe. Once again, I was about to leave the confines of the UK. Sadly, that was how it felt – as if I was suffocated, restrained and held back by the parochial British cycling scene.

Fifteen years on, things are very different and it's a measure of how far British cycling has now come that I am perhaps one of the last riders to have followed this tortuous path. Back then, there was no National Lottery funding, no national team to speak of, no indoor track in Manchester, barely a racing scene and hardly any sponsors.

Everybody meant well, but the British cycling scene, such as it was, only survived because of the goodwill and charity of the people who loved it. Racing at home was light years away from the Tour de France and the continental professional scene. I had to get out.

Sleeping in a bunk bed for over a month in the home of a cycling-mad Belgium family was an interesting experience and surprisingly good fun. Ieper had been the scene of great destruction during the First World War. There were family connections: my great grandma – who was still smoking and drinking whisky at 99 – lost her brother in the final horrific fighting of the battle of Passchendaele in 1917.

There is something very haunting about Flanders. The scars of battle are still evident. On every ride we would pass fields of white crosses, sometimes stretching beyond the horizon. Riding a bicycle through the countryside while surrounded by such tragedy felt frivolous, yet the melancholy of the place was important to me. I never really understood why.

The cornerstone of Flemish racing is the local *kermesse* race. *Kermesses* are the village or town festivals, and these festivals wouldn't be complete without a bike race hurtling through the town, and finishing, at the heart of the *kermesse*, on the main street. We would just turn up to these, jump on and race. The locals would bet on us, and it would all be fun and games. As gung-ho juniors, we'd just smash each other for the full distance, usually about 90 kilometres, and be given our cash prizes at the finish. I didn't finish lower than third in the ten or so that I raced in.

The last *kermesse* I rode was the big one and also the last race of the year, in Koksijde, called 'Keizer der Juniores'. Within two laps, my roommate of the previous four weeks, Paul Butler, and I found ourselves off the front of the race on our own. It was horrible weather – cold, dark, raining – anybody who knows Koksijde will also know that even on a perfect summer's day the place doesn't exactly glow.

With about 100 of the 120 kilometres still to race, it wasn't an astute move tactically. Thirty kilometres from the finish, we came round a corner on the seafront a little too fast and slid off in perfect unison. I got up, Paul didn't. Somehow I managed to hold on for third place. It was enough to seal my reputation in Flanders and to return to Britain, head held high, convinced I had done enough to get myself a ride with a top French amateur team.

I'd got to know one of the *Cycling Weekly* journalists, fellow Scot Kenny Pryde, quite well. Through his contacts, Kenny found me a place with a big team in Brittany. I wouldn't be expected to go over until the following February so I had almost four months to get ready. I found myself a coach, and – as Mum had suggested – got a job stacking shelves in Tesco's at night. But I didn't learn French.

Over the winter, I discovered that there were others in the British scene, who, like Mike Taylor, backed my decision to head over to the continent. They were again ex-professional cyclists and keen lovers of the sport, two of whom were Sid Barras and Keith Lambert. Along with some like-minded others, they had started a small fund in order to help young British amateurs head over to the continent. It was named after a talented young English pro called Dave Rayner, who tragically died very young.

Because Mum and I only found out about it late in the day, my application to the Dave Rayner Fund was sent after the closing date. Fortunately, they were not of the rigid British cycling school of thought, and still read my application and invited me to the interview weekend in Yorkshire.

We stayed at Sid Barras's farm and met all the people behind the fund as well as the other applicants. One by one, we met with the committee members and then impatiently awaited their response. I was lucky enough to be the rider they chose to back, and their financial help and their belief in me was an incredible help. It was also hugely motivating.

I trained ferociously through the winter, regardless of the weather. My coach, Dave Smith, had developed a very technical training programme and I followed it obsessively. I barely stayed in touch with any of my Hong Kong friends and I didn't make any attempt to find new ones. I was extremely determined to arrive in France in the best possible condition. Nothing else mattered.

But then, late in January, I found out the team in Brittany had decided to take another foreign rider. I was devastated and completely lost as to what I should do next. So I turned to Mike Taylor. 'Don't worry, Dave,' he said. 'I'll fix it.'

Ten days later, Mike called asking if I could get down to the Basque Country. I had to ask Mum where the Basque Country was – for some reason I imagined it was in Switzerland. Mike explained that the team was based in St Quentin, in the Picardie region of northern France, but was down in the Basque Country training and competing in early season races. We decided that I would head over to St Quentin to be there when they got back. Mum had sold her car to help me buy a battered Ford Escort. I packed it up and set off for France.

5

'QUOI?'

It was grey and wet when I arrived in St Quentin in the middle of February 1996. The roadsides were dusted with the remnants of the previous night's snowfall and it was a miserable winter's day. The team had a small house, used to lodge foreign riders, in the little village of Morcourt, only a kilometre away from the massive MBK factory (the team's bike sponsor). The factory's canteen was my lunch stop through most of that year.

I arrived at the house and was greeted by the team's other foreign rider, who, luckily for me, was an Englishman – not some oddball Eastern bloc desperado, as might have easily been the case. Andy Naylor was a few years older than me and had raced the final couple of months of the previous season with VC St Quentin, so he knew the ins and outs. He did his best to give me the lowdown.

We were, Andy told me, the only foreigners on the club. They'd decided that British talent was best after Jeremy Hunt had raced for them the season before and cleaned up across the French amateur scene. In fact, Jez, who later became a firm friend, won so many times that he turned professional for Banesto – Miguel Indurain's team – at the end of the year.

British riders were *en vogue* and great things were expected of us, or so it seemed. In reality, we just happened to be infinitely cheaper and far less trouble than a good French amateur. If we did turn out well, then that would be a wonderful bonus for the club and the powers that be would be credited with great *savoir faire* in talent spotting.

The club had increased its budget in the off-season and recruited some of the biggest names on the French amateur scene. I had no

47

idea of this at the time. Unwittingly, I had found myself on the strongest amateur team in France, yet neither Andy nor I had an inkling of this because neither of us spoke a word of French.

Despite that, I was keen to impress. On our first group training rides I was one of the last to get dropped when we tackled motor-paced interval sessions behind a team car. Coming into the first race, just north of Paris, I was confident I could make a good showing, although the long distance made me nervous.

It may sound odd now, given that I regularly race for well over 100 miles as a professional, but at that point I'd *never even ridden* 100 miles – let alone raced that far. For years afterwards, I remained convinced that I had abandoned my first race with VC St Quentin, so bad were my memories of it.

It was only when I bumped into one of my amateur teammates at a pro race years later that he reminded me that I had been in every break from the start, that we were caught about 20 kilometres from the finish, and that I was literally weaving around in the road, delirious with exhaustion. Then I remembered crawling to the finish line, ages after the winner.

The next race followed a similar pattern. But it must have been worse as that evening I made a trip to the village phone box to call Mike Taylor and told him that I thought I'd made a mistake – maybe everyone who'd told me I was too young was right. But as I'd only been there three weeks and had raced twice, Mike wisely told me to hang on to the next weekend and see how I fared.

'Make a decision after that,' he told me.

The next event was a two-day race, with a road stage on the first day and, on the second day, another road stage in the morning and a time trial in the afternoon.

On the first day, I found myself in a breakaway group of about fifteen riders with two guys from my team. With my basic French, I'd picked up that there was a steep and crucial climb about 25 kilometres from the finish. The behaviour of the breakaway riders was also a clear giveaway that a crunch moment was approaching. Everybody was drinking, eating and soft-pedalling in preparation for the 'finale'.

As this lull continued, one of my teammates dropped back to the VC St Quentin team car to speak to *directeur sportif*, Martial Gayant. A few moments later, he rode back alongside and and indicated that Martial wanted to speak to me; I went back to the car wondering what the hell he was going to say that I could understand.

'You!' Martial bellowed at me. '*Attaque! D'accord?!*'

Well no – I wasn't exactly '*d'accord*'. Up to that point, I'd been trying to figure out how I was going to survive when the others started attacking. But Martial – my boss – had given the order so attack was what I would do.

Coming into the next village we turned a corner and were confronted with a dead straight, very steep road. Without a thought, I followed orders, attacking at the foot of the climb as hard as I could. Halfway up I could sense nobody was with me, and near the top I was hurting, but as it levelled out I dared to look back over my shoulder. There were a couple of guys weaving around behind me, but they were no threat, and the rest of the group was in pieces behind them.

On seeing this, the pain faded into the background. I changed into high gear, got out of the saddle and accelerated once more. I rode the last 20 or so kilometres on my own with ten guys pursuing as a chain gang behind me. I finished a minute and a half ahead of them and so won my first amateur race in France. The next day I won the morning time trial with ease, but nearly lost the race in the afternoon when my bike broke and I was forced to borrow a teammate's bike and endure a long chase back on – the local press loved the drama.

I called Mike that evening.

'Hi, Mike,' I said. 'I felt better this weekend.'

'Ahhh, there you go, David, I told you it'd get better. How did you get on?' he asked.

I recounted the story of the race as Mike listened. ' . . . So I got two stages and the overall,' I concluded. 'Anyway, Mike – does that count as three wins?'

'Fuckin' 'ell, David!' Mike bellowed joyfully, shouting down his hall. 'Pat! *PAT!* David just won three races at the weekend!'

And that was it. I'd cracked it. After that, I was unstoppable.

In forty-six days of racing I was in the top three twenty-three times, and barely outside the top ten in the other twenty-three. I loved the racing and embraced the hurting. I would turn myself inside out at every opportunity. I was learning to push myself physically much further than I had ever done before.

While the racing enthralled me, life off the bike was mind-numbingly boring. The social highpoint for Andy and I was to hang out at the big Cora supermarket on the edge of St Quentin. This was as close as we ever got to actually seeing girls. We would walk the aisles grazing off the shelves. I'd always eat a chocolate chip baguette, and Andy would just take bits of it from me, as he'd be trying to 'watch' what he ate.

Our only pressing daily engagement – other than training – was *Star Trek Next Generation*, at 6 p.m. on Sky One. Somehow – and I still wonder how it came to be there – we had a very dodgy satellite dish set up. It was lying on the floor on the terrace and was haphazardly connected to our TV.

Miraculously, it worked most of the time, and was our happy place. Sadly, Andy only lasted a couple of months before heading back to the UK, and it was a shame to see him go as we'd got on really well. But it also meant that somebody else would be moved in, and probably not an English speaker. This I was not looking forward to.

I was paid a very nominal allowance by the team. That, and the support of the Dave Rayner Fund, allowed me to eat properly and fuel my car, which was all I needed. Eating 'properly' was none-theless fairly basic. These days, I'd probably have been given a shelf full of books by Jamie Oliver or Nigel Slater and gone foraging in French farmer's markets. Back then, however, it was *Cooking in a Bedsit*, volume 1. Rice and pasta, made that bit more enticing with cheap tins of Aldi's finest bolognese sauce, were my staple diet.

I'd never cooked before so it was a bit of a steep learning curve, although the curve didn't rise very far before I'd learned enough to survive, and that was all that mattered.

Ruggero was my only friend from Hong Kong that I stayed in

touch with, and, as he was at university in Manchester, contact was rare. Hearing about his new life as a student made our old world feel even further away.

I imagined that they were having the time of their lives at university, working but mainly playing very hard. In contrast, I had an incredible amount of time on my own and that meant a lot of time – perhaps too much time – to think. The only thing that mattered to me was the racing, so if that wasn't going well then my morale plummeted and self-doubt and self-pity took root.

The biggest challenge to overcome was loneliness. I think I was surprisingly good at coping with this and more resilient than most. There's no doubt that most of the young Brits who made the move to the continent cracked mentally before physically. For some of them, it was a little too easy to head up to the Channel and nip home. But I felt my home was in Hong Kong – that was where I missed. I also knew I wasn't going back there. In that sense, giving up on France wasn't really an option.

I was steadily becoming accustomed to the increasing demands that racing at this level put on my mind and body. In junior racing I had been so strong that I controlled the race, and, effectively, I could do what I wanted. On the highly competitive French amateur scene, this was not the case. I had to learn how to manage the longer distances, more astute tactics and greater intensity of racing. I couldn't just rely on being stronger than everybody else.

I couldn't count on doing what I wanted, when I wanted, with relative ease. Often my body would be telling me to stop for much of the race and this was something I didn't understand at first. It was only after pushing myself further and harder that I learned to ignore what my body was telling me. My psychological strength was increasing and I was getting tougher and more capable of managing the suffering.

This didn't mean, however, that I wasn't scared shitless of the race distances. Because of that, I became increasingly obsessive about eating enough, carbo-loading furiously, right up to the last minute. I would take home-made rice pudding with me to the race, sitting in the team car at the start, eating as much of this as I could without being sick. I just couldn't fathom how it was possible to race close to 200 kilometres when you stopped eating 3 hours before the race, as was recommended by all the coaches and magazines. I was still very skinny, almost 10 kg lighter than I would be a few years later, and was built like a fragile junior.

I think this was one of the reasons that Martial Gayant took me under his wing. He could see that I had a lot of progress to make physically and yet, despite that, I was already a dominant force on the French amateur scene. Unknown to me, Martial was also protecting me from what was already a dirty culture.

Martial Gayant had been a very solid professional rider. He had ridden the Tour de France and even, one year, enjoyed a few hours of glory in the yellow jersey. He'd also, unusually for a French rider, worn the pink leader's jersey in the Giro d'Italia. At that point, he was the first person I'd met who'd had such success as a pro.

We had a fairly up and down relationship but he took good care of me. I was very demanding and intense as, unlike Martial, for me VC St Quentin was my life. He would sometimes disappear for days at a time and be completely out of contact. I'd want to go out motor pacing or know what my race schedule was or just ask his advice, and yet he was nowhere to be found. This would drive me crazy, but I'm sure that sometimes his disappearing acts were primarily to get away from me. This never crossed my mind at the time though.

As well as ambitious kids, the team also included several seasoned campaigners. The majority were career amateurs, guys who had never made it as professionals and so raced at the top level for as long as they could as amateurs. In rural France, they could make more money doing this than in the job that awaited them – taxi driving, bar tending, working the land – if they were to retire from the sport.

So deep-seated in French life was the culture of cycling that even being an amateur carried a certain amount of prestige. As the year went on, I learned that it was one of the moments in their lives when they would be respected by their community. To me, amateur status was simply a stepping stone to a professional career, and if you were still an amateur when you were in your late twenties or thirties then you hadn't made it. I didn't realise that for many of them they *had* made it – this was as good as it got for them.

There was one teammate in particular, Eric Frutoso, who took great care of me. Eric had won the Mavic Cup, the most prestigious prize in French amateur cycling. He rallied the rest of the team to ride for me, the 19-year-old foreign kid, and he inspired me to start learning French, so that I could express the respect that I had for him. Eric was 27 and from Biarritz. He would fly to the races, which was unheard of back then (the rest of us were crammed into the team's Peugeot estates and driven far and wide across the country).

From May onwards, these never-ending trawls across France were made even more horrible by the lack of air-conditioning, and we would arrive twisted and tormented at the hostels (or whatever rudimentary accommodation had been arranged for us). This was part and parcel of amateur racing, the rites of passage – and journeys to and fro sometimes matched the races themselves as a test of endurance.

Eric sheltered me from the doping that was already going on within the team. Years later he told me that he had made it clear to the others that I was not to see anything. Eric himself was one of the good guys, on a long-term sabbatical from his job as a postman. But this was coming to an end and he had to decide whether to accept the pro contract that was offered to him or race one more year as an amateur before returning to his job in Biarritz.

Because of Eric, I was totally naive with regard to any doping going on within the team, and I was 100 per cent sure that any whining from the amateurs about widespread doping in the pro scene was only to excuse their shortcomings in not making it as pros; either that, or simple jealousy.

It was at our team sponsor's summer barbecue, at Pascal Cordier's house, just outside St Quentin on a perfect June afternoon, that I spoke to Eric about it for the first and only time. I had received a fax with my detailed training programme and full nutritional plan for the upcoming weeks and was sitting going through it in the garden with the English-speaking Pascal. Eric wandered over and asked what we were looking at. As Pascal explained, Eric turned his nose up.

'Paf, that's not cycling to me,' Eric said. 'All too scientific and complicated.'

His stance didn't surprise me. At first, I just considered it to be one more reason why he was still an amateur at 27. I just shrugged and said to Pascal that I thought it was the difference between us, why I would turn professional, and Eric wouldn't.

Pascal looked at me: 'Oh, Eric can turn pro if he wants. Gan have been in touch with him – he just doesn't want to.'

I was stunned. Why would he not want to ride for Gan, one of cycling's biggest pro teams? I didn't fully understand Eric's response until later, when I had entered the professional arena.

'That's not cycling to me either,' Eric explained. 'David, if you turn professional you will understand.'

'I have my job in Biarritz waiting for me, and a life that goes with it. I'm not willing to sacrifice that to be part of the professional cycling world.'

He knew he couldn't help or look after me, if and when I turned pro. He knew I had my heart set on it and also the talent and drive to achieve it, so he let me keep my perfect world for as long as I could. I'm thankful in a way, because I would have judged him jealous and thought of him differently if he'd told me what he knew. And, back then, I wouldn't have believed him.

In August there was my one and only Great Britain National Team race of the year. As usual it was run on a volunteer basis and, on this occasion, Jimmy Rutherford was the team manager for the trip. The race itself was a big one, the Tour of the Wallonie Region in Belgium. It was a professional race and had some of the top teams competing – Mapei and Lotto being two of them. The rest of the peloton was made up of national teams and lower level pro teams. It was the biggest race of the year for me, and a massive opportunity to show myself in front of the pro teams.

It went well. I was second in the prologue to the late Frank Vandenbroucke – or VDB, of whom more later – and then second in the individual time trial as well, again behind VDB. A strong showing in the road stages only reinforced my status. I was already on the radar thanks to all my results in France. Confirming my talent on a bigger stage meant that I was offered two contracts immediately.

The ball was now rolling. Before I knew it, four pro teams were interested in me. I didn't know where to go or what to do. It wasn't about money, because bidding wars over neo-pros never happened. It was about choosing the team that was going to be the best for my future development. There was also talk of a big new French team starting up with Cyrille Guimard as *directeur sportif*.

Guimard was a legendary figure in the sport and had been one of the main characters in a lot of my reading material in Hong Kong. He was a kingmaker. He had discovered Bernard Hinault, Greg LeMond and Laurent Fignon, and guided all three of them from neo-pros to Tour de France winners.

Now he wanted me. Within a couple of weeks he had come to St Quentin to take me out to lunch with the manager of his new 'super-team', Alain Bondue, another ex-pro.

Bondue had been the final link in the chain of contacts that had culminated in my getting a place at VC St Quentin at the beginning of the year. When the Breton team fell through, Mike Taylor had called his old friend Paul Sherwen, an ex-pro turned TV commentator. Paul had then called Bondue, one of his ex-teammates and a very good friend. Alain had then called Pascal Cordier, sponsor of VC St Quentin and called in a favour – the favour being me. Now it had come full circle and Bondue and I were sitting at a table together discussing my future as a professional cyclist.

My spoken French was getting better, but during that meeting I relied on Alain translating between Cyrille and myself. I'd already met with two other *directeurs* before Guimard, so I was starting to know what questions to ask.

Guimard told me that he'd like to sign me for three years. I'd remain amateur for one more year until I'd matured physically. He planned to place me in the top amateur team in Brittany so I'd be closer to him. At the end of that year I would turn professional and ride some of the smaller pro races so that I would go into the winter with a better understanding of what awaited me. I would start 1998 as a full professional and begin my build-up to my first Tour de France in 2000, when I'd be 23. None of the other *directeurs* I had met had even mentioned the Tour de France, let alone had a plan for when I'd make my debut. That was enough to convince me and I agreed to join Cofidis, Guimard's new team.

Martial invited me over to his house to discuss it all. He too had turned professional with Guimard and had enjoyed his biggest successes with him. Gayant and I communicated as best we could, which was surprisingly well, considering my still rudimentary French. The evening finished with me asking Martial if I could see his yellow jersey from the Tour – his *maillot jaune*.

I'd never seen one before, but instead of having it framed or mounted on the wall, Martial hung it amongst the rest of his clothes in his wardrobe. I thought that was funny, and revealed the sort of unflashy person Martial was. He said I could try the yellow jersey on, but I refused as I thought it would be disrespectful.

'I'd only deserve to wear it if I was leading the Tour,' I said. Martial laughed at that.

'But it's only a matter of time, David.' He smiled.

Latvian rider Romans Vainsteins moved in with me for the final two months of the year. I was thankful for this as the house had become simply a stop-over for French riders coming and going and I'd had things taken from my room more than once. After that, a rider from the Eastern bloc seemed like a wonderful option. Romans spoke good English and was as driven as I was. He had the old school Eastern bloc work ethic. I was blown away that he would do 30 minutes of training on the rollers every morning before breakfast. I'd never heard of such a thing and his energy made me feel like a lazy teenager. We got on well, especially when we raced together, and for almost a month straight we would alternate first and second place between us. Racing with Romans was a lot of fun.

My final objective of the year was the World Championships. For the first time, the new Under-23 category had replaced the Amateur category. I fancied my chances as I'd only done one U-23 race all year and it had felt like a junior race, but I came down with bronchitis and my season was over. So was my career as an amateur. The pro contract with Cofidis was ready to be signed, so Sherwen, Bondue and I met in a café in a nearby village in what was an extremely French scene. After signing, I returned home to England a professional cyclist, with no intention of ever going to art school.

Signing the contract was a relief, but it didn't even cross my mind that I was at the very beginning of the journey. Becoming a professional cyclist had never been an obvious career path and, in truth, I'd always felt a bit timid in admitting my ambitions to people. I felt like a bit of a dreamer; I was embarrassed to say I wanted to become a professional cyclist. So for a long time, I stuck to what everyone else at school was doing, and that was finding somewhere to continue my education.

Art was the obvious choice, as it was where I actually stood out, and it was the only thing I had really enjoyed at school. I was offered an unconditional place at art college, but my heart wasn't in it – I loved cycling too much.

At school, I'd only ever talked openly about cycling with one teacher, Charlie Riding, at an end of year dance.

'So, David – are you really going to do it?' he asked with a smile. I was baffled. 'Do what?' I replied.

'Become a professional cyclist.' He was grinning this time.

With just as big a smile, I told him yes, I *was* going to do it. I've never forgotten that exchange. It was the first time I acknowledged that my dream could become a reality.

Years later, while living in the Peak District, serving my doping ban, Nicole – now my wife and a keen cyclist herself – came back from a ride one afternoon to tell me she'd bumped into one of my old school teachers from Hong Kong, out on the road.

She didn't catch the surname – 'Charlie something,' she said. She'd given him my number, as she was sure I wouldn't mind. He called later on that day and Nicole and I went and met Mr Riding from my old school, in a pub in nearby Hazel Grove.

Charlie's parents lived there and he was over visiting them from Hong Kong. We reminisced and he helped me to remember a time when it was all a lot simpler. He was very proud that I had admitted to my mistakes and that I had decided to return to the sport I loved.

Since I returned to racing from my doping ban, Charlie Riding has been at every Tour de France I've raced in. I rarely see him for long, but every now and then at a stage start, someone working for the team will step aboard the team bus and tell me I have an old friend outside from Hong Kong who sends his regards.

I'll emerge into the sunlight and there, hand outstretched, smiling his big smile, I'll find Charlie Riding, telling me how well I'm doing.

6

THE PROFESSIONALS

After I got back to Britain, I gave myself a break. I visited Ruggero in Manchester for the first time and hung out, pretending to be a student for a weekend or two. I hadn't touched a drop of alcohol in almost eighteen months, so I was easily amused. Rog 'lived' – I use the term loosely – in a dirty student apartment of five boys that looked like it had been created by the set designers on *Withnail and I*.

Contrary to what I'd imagined, they didn't receive endless invitations to amazing parties populated by cool people and hot girls. As for their education, that seemed to be fairly low down on the agenda. It left me feeling a lot older and further ahead of the game than my peers, although I remained a little envious of their fun-loving life.

After a month or so off the bike I began to train again, realising at the same time that I wouldn't be able to endure the life of an amateur for one more year. I knew, now that I had effectively turned pro, I would lack the motivation to train alone through another winter.

I called Bondue and told him I couldn't face going to Brittany and spending another year doing what I'd worked so hard to leave behind. All I could see ahead of me was the loneliness and boredom of living in another little village doing the same shitty amateur races. That wasn't what I'd dreamed about.

At the time, I was the least of his worries. The team had fallen into turmoil with the news that its number one signing, Lance Armstrong, had been diagnosed with cancer. The team had effectively been built around Lance, taking many of the ex-Motorola team riders to Cofidis with him. They were now trying to work out what to do and before long had signed up two of the biggest names in the sport, Tony Rominger and Maurizio Fondriest, both in the twilight of their careers but still forces to be reckoned with.

Maurizio was an Italian superstar and had long been one of my heroes. I'd had posters of him on my bedroom walls in Hong Kong when I was younger. Rominger – 'Swiss Tony' some called him – was as much of a star and had been Miguel Indurain's rival in the Tours de France of the early 1990s.

Guimard didn't object to my change of plan. I think it was a small matter to him and he didn't have the energy or desire to defend his original plan. So, the date came forward and I would turn pro on 1 January 1997.

I carried on training but, in the middle of December, returned to Hong Kong for the first time since leaving the year before. I flew my bike out with me, but didn't touch it once in the three weeks I was there.

I was too busy partying in HK, enjoying a final hurrah. My dad was living the life of a bachelor, sharing his house with another pilot. The pair of them could out-drink me, Rog, or any of my friends, with ease. We had a lot of fun, the highlight being a night out that led to my dad meeting his future wife. Colette's a Yorkshire lass and about the best thing that's ever happened to Gordon, and all because I forced the old man to join us for a drink or two in Tsim Sha Tsui. We had a lot of fun: I forgot about my life as a cyclist, considering it an obligation to be as sociable as I could be before I returned to France. It didn't even cross my mind that I was only weeks away from meeting my new team in France as a full-blown professional rider.

I arrived in Lille in north-eastern France for the first Cofidis get-together, fresh from Hong Kong and shit-scared. It was incredibly cold and I was disgustingly under-prepared. We spent the first few days meeting sponsors, shooting photos and getting to know each other. Our grand team presentation was scheduled to take place in Paris, before we headed south to the training camp.

For two days we hung around a freezing warehouse for the photo shoot, during which I befriended the Americans. There were four of them – Lance, Bobby Julich, Kevin Livingston and Frankie Andreu – all ex-Motorola riders. Despite his testicular cancer diagnosis, Lance was very much the leader and the others were, undoubtedly, his troops.

The only thing we seemed to have in common was spoken English. As it was their first time in a non-English-speaking team, I was the bridge between them and the Frenchies. I remember Lance having the biggest pack of chewing gum I'd ever seen. I didn't like chewing gum, but I took a stick when Lance offered me some.

Lance was battered from chemo treatment, sporting no hair and with a skinnier, gaunter look. He was far from the awesome athlete he had been until recently. Even so, his clear physical degradation had barely dented his personality and he radiated a brashness that only American sports stars can get away with. Yet the more time I spent with him, the more I glimpsed a darker and more thoughtful side.

I didn't know if this had always been there, but it seemed to me it was something new, as it was incongruous in relation to the rest of his persona. Even so, you wouldn't have imagined that he was a man who'd just escaped death by a whisker.

We went out on the bikes and did a couple of pointless rides on icy roads around Lille. Even though he didn't know when or if he would race again, to our amazement, Lance came out with us. Not only did he join us, but he was determined to show that he was still one of the strongest. Everybody thought he was a bit crazy; looking back, maybe he was – and perhaps a little scared too.

The Cofidis presentation in Paris, in a beautiful hall not far from the Champs Elysées, was grandiose. A decade later I found myself back there, celebrating the completion of another Tour de France. I wasn't with my Saunier Duval team at the time, but had gate-crashed the CSC team party. We went on to the Team Discovery party in the penthouse of the Hotel Crillon, where I was to bump into Lance, me no longer the gauche neo-pro, him no longer the gaunt cowboy, teetering on the abyss.

As a rookie, I wasn't exactly in high demand at the Cofidis presentation. Bobby Julich, unknown at the time, was in the same boat. We slowly and deliberately ate our way through tray after tray of canapés while sipping champagne, hardly a bad way to spend the afternoon. There was a small clique of British journalists there and, after a few drinks, I wandered across to pick their brains, in what was probably quite a provocative and confrontational way.

'I don't suppose you guys know Stephen Farrand?' I demanded. They nodded their heads hesitantly.

'Yeah? Well,' I said, 'you can tell him I haven't forgotten about the slagging he gave us after the Junior Worlds in San Marino. The bastard. I hope he remembers, because I won't forget.'

The man on my right extended his hand and smiled: 'I'm Stephen,' he said. 'Nice to meet you, David.'

Typical.

From Paris, we returned to Lille for yet another Cofidis jolly, the company's annual soirée. This was a professionally produced event in the largest auditorium in Lille, which included a bum-numbing 3-hour presentation and then a circus-like extravaganza in the adjacent hall. There were half a dozen free bars, and the team's riders were left to mingle with Cofidis employees, all 800 of them, while performers of all sorts entertained us. It was debauched.

The next morning we finally set off for the training camp. Some of the riders had not slept, were still drunk and stank of cigarettes. The Americans were in a state of shock, having left early the previous evening in pursuit of a good night's sleep, much to the derision of the French.

Lance was flying back to the States while the rest of us were heading down to Amélie-les-Bains, in the eastern Pyrenees for ten days of hard riding. I was still quietly confident that I'd be okay, thinking I'd probably be put in an easy group and allowed to build up slowly, given that I was so young.

An hour and a half into the first ride and I was nearly exploding. All twenty of us were in one group, and it would soon be my turn to hit the front. There was no easing into it and our first ride was going to be 5 hours of hilly riding. I'd tricked myself into thinking that even with my appalling lack of training I wouldn't be in too much trouble. But every time the road went uphill my heart rate would be in the 180s, the level I would expect to hit on the hills in amateur races.

I took my turn setting the pace at the front, watching the clock obsessively, begging for my 10-minute stint to come to its end. The clock ticked down as my heart rate steadily rose. By the time we were in the ninth minute, I was peaking out, using all my concentration to project a façade of tranquillity. I didn't dare look to the side or behind, or betray any weakness. At 9 minutes 59 seconds, I indicated, a little too eagerly, that my turn on the front was done, a *faux pas* that revealed how uncomfortable I really was.

It is the done thing to always impress upon your teammates that you are within yourself. At least that's how I see it and on the slide from the front to the back of the group, I checked out my teammates, convinced they'd all be blowing hard. To my absolute horror they all looked genuinely fine – *all* of them.

Being the best amateur in the world guaranteed you nothing when it came to racing against the pros. Up to that point I'd always raised my game, from mountain biking to road riding, from riding for fun to racing as a junior, from racing regionally to nationally and then internationally. Even the graduation from the junior to amateur ranks had been relatively painless. It had been an upward, linear path of progress with very few hiccups.

This was different. I was standing at the bottom of a sheer cliff face, my past achievements dwarfed by the mountain I had to climb. It was a big wake-up call and after a few days of the camp I was broken. My lack of fitness had taken my body beyond its capabilities and it had thrown in the towel. It was something I would get used to in that first year as a professional.

Cofidis founded its business on selling credit by telephone. Almost anybody could call the free number on our racing jerseys and get a loan. That was the easy part – the comparatively high interest rates made it expensive to pay off. Cofidis had a significant budget to spend on marketing and it was through a marketing study that it concluded that cycling was the best sport to use as a publicity vehicle. Effectively, those interest rates paid for the team.

Cofidis's sponsorship was different to most pro teams. Their *PDG*, or CEO, François Migraine, had built the team from the ground up and the company owned the team outright as a subsidiary of its principal business.

Cyrille Guimard was the biggest name in French cycling, and an appropriate leader for the wealthiest team in France. A *directeur sportif extraordinaire* and French sporting legend, he was a proud Breton.

Physically, he was not a big man. He was a wiry ex-pro and built as such, and although he'd retired twenty years earlier, he had not let himself go as much as some others. He always sported glasses that would have been fashionable in his heyday, the mid-1980s, around the time of *Footloose*. They seemed perfectly in character and by persisting with them, they'd become almost classic when worn by Cyrille.

I remember the first time I saw him stroll into breakfast, sporting a tracksuit with the zip at half mast, revealing a bare chest and gold chain, the finishing touches being bare feet with open-toed beach sandals and his ever-present pseudo-aviator glasses.

My initial shock soon turned to amusement at the complete insouciance with which he wore his 'look'. He had clearly decided that fashion had stopped progressing to his taste in the mid-1980s and opted to single-handedly carry the flame. One day, no doubt, everybody would see the light. I guess there was a deep-seated psychological reason for this, as it was during the early 1980s that he reached his zenith.

Guimard had been a successful pro, but he became an even more successful *directeur sportif*. After retiring at the relatively young age of 29, he moved straight into team management and immediately tasted success at the highest level, winning the 1976 Tour de France with the Belgian rider, Lucien Van Impe. This was just the beginning. Soon after, he took Hinault to his first Tour de France victory, then coached Fignon to two Tour wins, and signed LeMond, who went on to win three Tours. He also discovered two of the biggest names in French cycling during the 1980s, Charly Mottet and Marc Madiot.

But Guimard's intransigent personality was not predisposed to building long-term relationships. Each one of the stars he discovered and guided to the top would fall out with him not long after reaching their peak. Typically, the French would blame Guimard's Breton personality. In fact, I think it probably has more to do with the personality of the newly successful sportsman.

It is very easy to forget how you got to the top once you've arrived. The transition from being an unknown to a star is not gradual. Sometimes it happens overnight, in the space of a few hours. One exploit can make your name; repeated successes can make you famous. That's particularly true of the Tour de France, and particularly true if you're French.

I am certain that Guimard made many cyclists much more successful that they would have been if they hadn't worked with him. But once you were successful he still treated you in exactly the same manner as he had before. He didn't indulge any prima donnas. This went against how everybody else acted around the new star and would hasten the beginning of the end between Cyrille and his latest *vedette*.

Away from the racing, it was possible to have constructive discussions with him. He was a great motivator and always saw the big picture, just as he had done with me when mapping out my next five years at lunch that day in St Quentin. There's no doubt that he knew the psychology of a professional cyclist better than many other *directeurs*.

During the races, however, it was a different matter. He gave the orders; his style wasn't that of co-collaborator but that of a tactical savant who knew what was right and wasn't interested in a debate. This was something he had from day one.

At his first Tour, in his first year as a *directeur*, he ordered Van Impe to attack rival Joop Zoetemelk.

But Van Impe refused, or at least he did until Guimard, at the wheel of the team car, drove up alongside and told him that if he didn't follow orders, he would drive him off the road. Van Impe quickly learned to do what he was told.

And Guimard was right. Van Impe rode so hard that he put half the field outside the time limit, took 3 minutes from Zoetemelk and then went on to win the Tour. Even the great Hinault, one of the most feared men in professional cycling and perhaps the greatest-ever French cyclist (who twenty-five years after retiring is still a physical force to be reckoned with), agreed.

'You don't argue with Guimard,' Hinault said.

Cyrille brought his support staff with him to Cofidis, an old guard of colleagues who had been with him for close to twenty years. These were the stalwarts of French professional cycling, the men you would see in old black and white photos massaging a young Hinault or hanging out of an old Peugeot team car having a cigarette. They had seen it all and were not to be questioned; it was their way or the highway.

But I chose my allies. The *soigneurs – soigneur* is the French word for the carer of an athlete – were definitely the real deal. Their principal job was to massage the riders, but in fact they did much more. They would do everything: pick us up at the airport, transport our suitcases between hotels, organise the kitchens at the hotels and become *maître d'* of any restaurant that wasn't up to the high standards of service they deemed necessary. They were also our medical advisers – our nurse and often our doctor – prescribing whatever they thought was needed.

It was with the *soigneurs* that we would have the quietest, most intimate moment of every day. After the frenzy of racing, lying on the massage table for 45 minutes of relaxation, peace and quiet, was the time when concerns would be voiced and anxieties aired. That was often the case for me during that first year.

My first pro race was programmed to be Etoile de Besseges, the opening stage race on the French calendar. It is only five days long and not exactly tough, but a shock to the system nonetheless, even if you are in a good state of fitness. It's almost impossible to prepare for racing fully in training. No matter how hard you try, what race simulations you attempt, you cannot push yourself as hard and as deep as you can in a race. You need competition that will push you psychologically and physically beyond a level that you or your training partners can attain while training at home on your local roads.

The ultimate training partner is a motorbike, ideally a Derny. Riding behind these motorised bicycles comes about as close as is possible to racing in the slipstream of a professional cyclist in full flight. Behind a Derny, you can ride a bigger gear at a higher cadence and experience fluctuations in pace that are nigh on impossible to generate on your own. Of course, the Derny needs a good driver, preferably an ex-cyclist who knows you very well so that they can read your suffering from a glimpse of your poise on the bike and the look in your eye. If they know you well enough, they can keep you on the edge of collapse and, in doing so, make you race-ready.

But I didn't have a Derny and my training had been further compromised between the end of that miserable training camp and my first race, after I had moved to Nice, to share an apartment with Bobby Julich.

I had heard about Nice, but I'd never been there before. When the Americans were discussing their planned move from their previous base in Lake Como to the Côte d'Azur, I chose to join them. After chilly St Quentin, the balmy Côte d'Azur sounded much more like my idea of France.

Soon after my arrival in Nice, Bobby rented a van and we set off to pick up his final bits and pieces from the apartment in Como. I could see why they'd decamped to Nice. Como is a beautiful place, but it's not ideal for a cyclist. The weather can be quite miserable in winter and there isn't a vast selection of roads to choose from. The Americans had made it their European base principally because their coach lived nearby.

There wasn't much to pick up in Como, but it was worth going if only to visit the storage room they had in the basement. There were bags of Motorola cycling clothing lying around, kit I would have died for only months before. When I was younger, I'd been given an old Motorola plastic rain cape, with a rider's name on it, by Mike Taylor. I thought it was the coolest thing in the world. Bobby was busy looking for something that he couldn't find, so I tried to contain my excitement as I had a nose through some of the Motorola kit bags.

There wasn't any question of me 'taking' anything but it was weird to think that all this kit was to be discarded. I treasured every single bit of cycling gear I owned and here, at my feet, were piles of kit worn by some of the best-known pros in the sport. I opened a bin bag filled with white jerseys and to my weak-kneed astonishment, realised that they were Lance Armstrong's unused World Champion jerseys.

Bobby must have heard me mutter, 'Oh man, oh shit.' Pausing from what he was doing he glanced across to see me reverentially clasping a pristine Motorola-branded rainbow jersey.

'Oh yeah,' he said with a shrug. 'Lance is always leaving shit around. God knows what else there is here.'

'But they're his rainbow jerseys,' I spluttered, still such a fan. 'There's a whole bag of them . . .'

Bobby was unimpressed. 'You should just take one, he'll never know. He's probably never coming back here to get his stuff.'

I was still clinging to the jersey, but I couldn't take it, even though I wanted to so bloody much. I put it gingerly back in the bag and tried my hardest to forget about it. Soon after our visit, the very same storage room flooded and everything was thrown away.

As Bessesges loomed training was going better. I was able to go out with Bobby and not get killed, and although I was getting the bejasus scared out of me by everybody about how hard the racing was going to be, I felt a little more confident. Although not as good as I could have been physically, I was fresh and fearless psychologically. Shockingly, Besseges was even harder than I expected; hills that would have ripped a race to pieces with the amateurs didn't even require the professionals to change out of the big ring. The sprinters, who I'd presumed couldn't climb, would have been able to win hilly amateur races. With the amateurs I barely needed to get out of the saddle to win races, with the professionals

I was having to get out the saddle so much just to stay in the bunch that my arms would lactate and give up before my legs. It was a different sport – I was soon to learn why it was quite so different.

My blissful ignorance about the 'demands' of the European scene was swept away at Besseges, my first pro race. I was rooming with Jim van de Laer, a Belgian rider and formerly a great hope, who hadn't fulfilled the potential that was expected of him. Jim was a great guy, and we got on very well. He told me that the team wanted him to get a result in that very first race of the year and that he'd been offered cortisone in pill form to 'help' him.

He didn't want to do it, and was really pissed off that the team was already panicking about results and acting in such a way when the season had barely begun. I wasn't stupid enough to think the sport was squeaky clean, but I didn't expect my team to be condoning it. Crazily though, the French didn't really think of cortisone as being 'proper' doping.

I learned over the years to come that cortisone was the drug of choice in French cycling. Back then, it was undetectable in doping controls, and although it was on the banned list, its use was permitted if a medical situation required it. Cortisone wasn't exactly hard to get hold of – the local doctor would prescribe it if you had bronchitis.

But there's no doubt it was something of a wonder drug. Boosting the natural levels with a pill or injection can decrease pain and increase strength in the short term. If the stronger forms of it are used it will reduce weight by making your body go catabolic. That's not a bad combo for a professional cyclist, but equally, not good if abused. The very muscles you rely upon are slowly eaten away by your own body as fuel; that's just one of the down sides.

I was devastated by what Jim told me, by the fact that the team was asking – no, telling – one of its riders to dope. Already the choice was there, working on me. After only a few weeks as a pro, I'd been confronted by it. There was no more protecting the young guy: Jim, bless him, was taking me into his confidence, asking my opinion. I told him I didn't even know what cortisone was or what it did.

'Jim, I don't want to know about this shit,' I said to him, a little desperately.

I called my mum later that night.

'Mum, they've asked my roommate to take this pill,' I told her. 'I don't think it's that bad but it's not that good either. He's refusing to take it, but it's clear the team is panicking. He's asking me what I think. It's just stupid – why's he asking me?'

'Oh, David,' she said. 'I'm so sorry.'

'I didn't think it was like this. From what Jim says there's a lot of it going on. I don't know what to do, Mum, I don't know what I've got myself into.'

'Well, has anybody approached you about taking anything?'

'No, I don't think they ask neo-pros to do anything.'

'No? Well, good,' she said. 'Just make sure you stand by what you believe in, and remember, you can pack it in tomorrow and come home and go to art college.

'You have options, David – don't forget that. It's your dream, I know, but it shouldn't make you unhappy, and it shouldn't make you do things you don't want to do,' she said.

'Remember that – and to hell with the rest of them.'

7

CHILDHOOD'S END

I realise now that, despite my age and the fact that I was a raw, new professional, Cofidis threw me in at the deep end. Yet I survived February and was due a couple of weeks off racing in March, during which I would train hard, in the hope of getting back on top of things.

After one 6-hour day training in the mountains behind Nice, I came home to a message from Guimard. He wanted me to race in Tirreno–Adriatico, the tough and mountainous week-long stage race crossing the backbone of Italy, tracing a route from the Mediterranean coast to the Adriatic.

I told Guimard that I didn't think it was a good idea, as I was

tired from the recent big block of training. He didn't listen. Off to Italy I went. So it was at Tirreno, before the race even began, that the scales definitively fell from my eyes.

In 1997, the UCI introduced what they called a 'health check', a new 50 per cent limit on hematocrit, to guard against excessive use of artificial EPO, the red blood cell booster. Hematocrit is the percentage of oxygen-carrying red blood cells coursing through your veins. I'd heard talk of this but had no idea what it meant, what my hematocrit level was or ever had been. In fact, up to that point I don't think I'd ever done a blood test. But I was learning fast and it became clear that, during the EPO era, hematocrit levels were the cyclist's holy grail.

EPO (erythropoietin), like cortisone, is naturally produced, making it very hard to find in anti-doping controls. Prior to the creation of an effective test, during the first ten years of its popularity it was impossible to detect. In essence, its benefits are the same as altitude training – some riders used to call it altitude training in a syringe.

By the mid-1990s, EPO use had become excessive and there were plenty of stories in the peloton of those who'd pushed their hematocrit level to over 60 per cent, and whose blood was like thick soup.

Heart failure had been widely linked to EPO abuse – there were stories, urban legends, of riders setting alarms to wake themselves through the night in order to do sit-ups, or some other exercise, as insurance against their hearts stopping.

The UCI knew that EPO use was rife, but was, apparently, powerless to stop it. The health checks weren't dope tests, because if you tested 'positive' – that is, were over the 50 per cent threshold – you were simply suspended for two weeks. If, after that, your hematocrit was back below 50 per cent, you quietly resumed racing.

Of course, the presumption was guilt if you did get suspended, and in the majority of cases, rightfully so, but for a few it was an undeserved black mark. Some do have higher natural hematocrit, be this genetic or simply because of living or training at altitude. A small percentage of the professional peloton carried certificates demonstrating their high hematocrit but these were not easy to get and required years of supporting data as proof. All in all, it was very basic science, yet the 'health check' did serve to rein in the 'he who dares' attitude towards EPO use.

We had a shitty journey to the start of Tirreno–Adriatico, arriving at Sorrento in the small hours after a late night drive from Rome. We were billeted in a grand but faded old hotel that had seen its best days long ago. The first stage was an afternoon prologue time trial, but because I didn't even have a time trial bike yet, I was using my training bike and wheels that I'd brought from Nice.

I was still unaware of the excesses of EPO, so when I went out for a ride the morning before the prologue, with a group of older pros, I was puzzled by why we were going so hard and so far, when I'd imagined that the ride would be a short 'loosener' after the long journey. I was dropped on the first hill and turned around and went back to the hotel decidedly worried about what awaited me in the race.

Later, I began to understand the thinking at the heart of that manic pre-race training ride. They were trying to ride the EPO out of their blood. Tirreno–Adriatico was likely to be the first race in which the UCI were going to use the new 50 per cent test. There's no doubt that a large number of the peloton were using EPO, but all to differing levels. So, it was impossible to know how many were actually teetering close to the 50 per cent limit.

One thing is for sure, none of them wanted to go over 50 per cent. The word was that it was a good idea to keep training hard right up until the race started, in a bid to keep hematocrit low. I just thought they trained like that before every race and that it had been easy for them and hard for me. But it was a demoralising start to a painful week and I only finished 100th in the prologue.

I worked my arse off at Tirreno, looking after our team leader, Maurizio Fondriest. The stages were all fast and crazy and we seemed to end on hilly finishing circuits every day. I don't think I made it round one of those with the rest of the peloton.

One day sticks firmly in my mind. We had been lined out for over an hour, grappling to hang on to a fierce pace. I was doing everything I could just to hold the wheel in front of me and prevent myself dropping back through the convoy of following team cars. But it was killing me. I was so tired that I was barely able to get out of the saddle after each corner or haul myself over the smallest inclines.

Just as I was about to give up the ghost, I looked up and saw Robbie McEwen, the Australian sprinter, swing out of the line of riders, waving his arm in the air, angrily shouting obscenities. Eventually he looked behind him, by which point he was not so far ahead of me.

Robbie wasn't done though. He put his head down and started sprinting back up to speed alongside the line of riders, only to begin ranting again.

'FUCKING JUST *STOP!*' he screamed. '*THIS IS NOT FUCKING BIKE RACING!*'

I felt better after that. Later, when the pace eventually dropped, I introduced myself. It was the first time I ever spoke to Robbie and he made me realise that I wasn't the only one finding it hard. I'm grateful to him for that.

I also got introduced to 'recovery' – or *récup* –methods at Tirreno. This was the use of injected vitamins to speed recovery from racing and keep your blood levels at a 'healthy' level. I remember, after one stage, lying on the bed, watching my roommate Frankie Andreu opening syringes and breaking ampoules, in front of the TV.

Another rider came in the room, looked across at me and said to Frankie: 'Sure he should be seeing this? Wanna do it in my room?'

Frankie, in his very pragmatic way, simply replied: 'He's gonna see it sooner or later – it's no problem.'

I got on pretty well with Frankie. Yes, he was grumpy, but you knew what you got with him. I asked him later on what he'd been doing.

'What was that you were injecting?' I said.

'Vitamins. Iron and vitamins. The usual, all legal, don't worry.'

'Does it make a big difference?'

'Don't know about big, but you know, David,' he said, 'small things make a difference.'

I was pretty sure I was irritating him, and the bottom line was that I wasn't about to start injecting myself, so what did I care? I tried to be as nonchalant as possible about it all. I was curious though. What exactly was 'the usual'? What did it do and where did he get it? And how the hell had he learned to inject himself?

As the race went on, I realised that most of the guys were doing 'recovery'. They all had their own little medical bags with their ampoules and syringes, and it did not appear to be any different to them than having a protein drink or some amino acid capsules. Injecting yourself was normal.

There were other things that I had to get used to. Ice was regularly delivered to rooms, by the *soigneurs*, in little plastic bags. I'd noticed it a couple of times and thought nothing of it; after all, ice is a sportsman's best friend.

I was picking up on it more and more but not noticing any correlating injuries. I couldn't figure it out. When I was sharing with somebody who received one of these late night or early morning ice deliveries, he'd disappear into the bathroom soon afterwards with another small bag, normally a shoe bag or large toiletry bag, dug out from his suitcase.

Incongruous visits to the bathroom by roommates was one more thing I was growing accustomed to. Most were unlike Frankie and hid everything from me. I would tell myself they were protecting me from knowing too much too young, but in honesty I think they were simply protecting themselves.

There was always an urge to dig around in their suitcase when they were away at massage or elsewhere, but at that stage, that would have been an unforgivable faux pas – a neo-pro, a jumped-up Brit, found rifling through an older pro's suitcase?

I would have been a dead man walking if I'd been discovered. In that world, I was at the bottom of the food chain, a burden to the team, more than likely a dud who would not make it further than my first contract. I had no rights and few expectations.

I had to impress them and to prove myself. It wasn't just my performances on the bike that were being judged. I had to make myself liked in order to ease my acceptance within the team and within the sport. This was especially true as a foreigner in a French team, perhaps the most chauvinistic of cycling nations.

After we got back to Nice, I managed to pluck up the courage to ask Bobby about the ice deliveries. He was straight with me, telling me what he'd seen: that some of the guys were using EPO, and that EPO has to be kept chilled or it's ruined. So they kept the ampoules and syringes in an ice-filled thermos. Twice a day they'd replenish the ice.

If it wasn't chilled, EPO didn't work – and you'd come down with a fever that would leave you pretty damn sick for 24 hours. Then there was the pain of the wasted expense and the stress of sourcing more.

I didn't ask Bobby much more than that. I'd learned that I could really only expect to ask one question, otherwise it all became uncomfortable and reduced my likelihood of ever being able to ask any more questions on the subject.

Bobby was great though. Like Frankie he was open with me and treated me with respect beyond my neo-pro status. He told me about how EPO use had become rife, especially in Italy. I did slide one last question in there, the same as I'd put to Frankie, the one that now interested me the most.

'Does it make that big a difference?' I asked.

'It can turn a donkey into a race horse – from what I've seen,' he told me.

It's hard to describe my feelings after he'd told me that. In a way I was relieved that there was something going on that explained the massive difference between the amateurs and the professionals. It meant that I wasn't doing that badly; I was simply young, lacking experience – and clean.

But it also confirmed that there was some bad shit going on. It wasn't the sort of thing I could just tell my mum or anybody else. My initial shock and sadness on discovering such a degree of doping already seemed a lifetime ago. What I was beginning to learn was too big for me to fully grasp, let alone comprehend. The 'system' was already working on me.

*

I was wrecked for ten days after Tirreno, too exhausted to ride for more than an hour and a half. There was no way I could even contemplate racing. The team wasn't bothered though and I was sent to Cholet–Pays de Loire, a one-day race in Brittany, three days after Tirreno finished. I can't remember it; if I finished then I'd be surprised.

I went back to Nice, skulked around, bought some roller blades, and started skating again in an attempt to remember happier times. That backfired when, after two years off the skates, I fell badly trying to slide along a rail, smashing my leg and giving myself deep tissue damage.

Obviously I couldn't tell anybody, certainly not the team, so I just kept quiet about it and hoped for the best. I visited my mum and Fran back at home and tried to ride my bike there, but it was a lost cause. I returned to Nice to an empty apartment, as Bobby was away racing.

Living in Nice wasn't quite the existence I'd imagined. Although it was much better than northern France, life was becoming lonely. Instead of hanging out in the Cora supermarket in St Quentin, we now had a panini stop down in Vieux Nice.

I started to read more and to listen to music, buying many books – Irvine Welsh, J.G. Ballard, Brett Easton Ellis, James Ellroy and Cormac McCarthy became favourite authors – and numerous CDs. That was about the only thing I spent money on during that first year.

I also started to feel a little ashamed, aware that perhaps being a professional cyclist wasn't something to be very proud of. I tried to develop myself by widening my interests, with music and reading at the heart of things. And reading helped while away the endless hours of nothingness I had to fill.

I realised I was going to need somebody who could be my mentor through these early years. So I contacted Tony Rominger, the elder statesman of the team, as he seemed to be one of the more cerebral – and hugely successful – cyclists out there. Tony lived in nearby Monaco, which made contact a lot easier. I thought if anybody would be able to steer me through all the shit it would be somebody like him, somebody nearing the end of his career and who had seen it all.

Tony seemed almost flattered when I asked him if he could help me out. He was very keen and I flew to Manchester to see him as he was undergoing some tests for an hour record attempt in the new velodrome.

It was the first time I'd ever been to Manchester. The velodrome was quiet back then, in the pre-Brailsford-run Team GB days, and barely used. There wasn't the hustle and bustle of a hugely successful national squad buzzing about as there would be in years to come.

Tony was there with a small entourage. When I arrived he was whirling around testing equipment and positions, so I left them to it and found myself a basketball and started shooting hoops on one of the courts in the centre of the velodrome.

Eventually, as they began wrapping up, I wandered over. Tony was, as ever, excited and happy. He introduced me to the small group, one with his head down over a computer. Tony pointed in his direction and said: 'That's Michele, he'll join us for lunch.' Immediately I realised that this was Doctor Michele Ferrari, a legend in the professional peloton.

In European cycling, Michele Ferrari had become the guru of sports doctors. He was already a controversial figure even before the allegations and scandals that would surround him in the years to come (he was convicted of doping offences but later acquitted following an appeal). At this time, though, his was still a name riders were proud to be associated with. He only coached the best and had been a student of Professor Francesco Conconi, perhaps the first recognised sports doctor in cycling.

I had heard of Conconi as a junior, as any physiological testing I did was based on the 'Conconi Test'. This was a ramp test that measured the point of maximal steady state workload, that is, the highest intensity effort an athlete could maintain for a prolonged period of time – in other words, their threshold.

After Ferrari had finished poring over Tony's results, we all went back to the hotel where they were staying. Tony suggested I got a massage from his personal *soigneur*. Massage was one of the things I disliked most about being a professional, as I could never relax, and whoever was massaging me would have to keep reminding me to de-contract my muscles. It just didn't come naturally to me, but I thought it would be bad form to ignore what Tony said, so I took his advice.

Afterwards, I sat down for lunch with Michele and Tony. I'd never thought about Ferrari having anything to do with my relationship with Tony, and thankfully neither had Tony. But Michele was still curious about me. He asked me about my statistics – weight, height, threshold and power – I was simply a set of numbers to him. At one point, out of the blue, he reached across the table and pinched my biceps. I wondered what the hell he was doing.

'Not bad,' he said. 'Could get skinnier though.'

Ferrari was obsessed by weight. In his world, the lighter you were, the faster you would be. I didn't really understand his philosophy – if I'd got any skinnier I wouldn't have been able to ride my bike, let alone race it.

He was an odd fish, something of a nerd. For a man with the reputation he had, he was hardly imposing. He had an odd rodent-like appearance, accentuated by a skeletal physique and slightly protruding teeth. He topped his look off at the time with some oversized, slightly feminine, spectacles.

What he lacked in physical presence, he made up for in seriousness. Cycling wasn't romantic in Ferrari's eyes, it was simply about numbers: weight, watts – and wads of cash. It was all business to him. I saw that within minutes of this, our one and only meeting.

Over the weeks that followed, Tony took me under his wing. It was Tony who told me the harsh realities of professional cycling in the 1990s.

We were out on a training ride together, just the two of us, an easy ride – and there are very few to be found between Nice and Monaco – of some laps around Cap Ferrat. It was a remarkably beautiful place to learn such ugly truths.

By this point, I understood that most of the top guys were using EPO, and that even those who weren't knew about its potential, but I still couldn't believe that that was the only way to win big races. That didn't seem right and surely wasn't possible. How could it be so prevalent? Did no one care?

'Tony,' I began, 'is it possible to win big races without EPO?'

At first, he was a little taken aback. 'Oh. Uh, well, it's possible,' he said.

'In one-day races, sure, I believe it's still possible. The Classics, if you do everything right, yeah, it's possible. I'm sure of that.'

'What about the Tour de France?' I said.

'Hmmm.' He thought for a moment. 'No, it's not possible. Over three weeks you can't compete against guys on EPO.'

'Really?' I was devastated. 'Shit. Why?'

'EPO allows you to go faster for longer. I mean, you still have to train and diet and do everything else, but with more oxygen you can stay at threshold for longer and recover faster. That's what the Tour is all about.

'It's just the way the sport has gone,' he said. 'It's sad. When I started we used to turn up to Paris–Nice with 2000 kilometres in our legs. Well, *maybe!*' That triggered the classic Tony chuckle.

He continued. 'Now some guys are arriving with 8000 or more kilometres with full *preparation*. My God, we used to race with leg warmers those first races. Now they are treating it like the Tour de France! EPO changed everything. Now everybody thinks they're champions. I'm glad my career is at its end now – the sport's not the way it used to be.'

Well, great – fucking brilliant, I thought. Now I knew.

Strangely, what he said didn't really have that much effect on me. I'd figured out for myself what was going on, but I just wanted to hear it confirmed from somebody who would know.

What Tony told me meant that I didn't need to question it any more. Those were the facts, I told myself. Get used to it.

Preparation was a term I was to hear more and more. It had another more sinister meaning. If you were prepared, it meant you were doped; it also meant you were ready.

'*Il est bien préparé,*' they'd say. If that was said about a team leader at a race, it meant that it was all systems go and that his team would be working their arses off for him.

It is hard to explain how I felt about this and it may also be difficult for some to understand. I had been upset and angry when I'd been confronted with the realities of pro-racing at my first race. But Mum had been right. I could just walk away, pack it all in, and go back to Britain and become an art student.

But I didn't want to do that: I loved racing and I loved my dream of one day racing in the Tour de France. I was young and blindly optimistic. I still had a lot to learn, about the characteristics of the races, the intricacies of the peloton, which wheels to follow and when. I reckoned I had a good few years before I would even reach my physical maturity, and who could tell what I'd be able to do when I was at my peak – so, I left it at that.

Doping was not for me; what the other guys did, well, that was nothing to do with me. If the riders, governing bodies, teams, race organisers and media weren't doing anything about it, then what the hell could I, a 20-year-old neo-pro from Scotland, do about it?

And that was that. I had to live with it going on all around me.

David Moncoutie, a young Frenchman who joined Cofidis when I did, was of the same opinion. We did our thing and kept our heads down. It was amazing how well that tactic worked. The need to dope wasn't foisted on us because in many ways the idea was to see how far we could progress *a l'eau claire*, on simply bread and water. That would gauge what sort of talent we had and hint at what sort of future lay in front of us. So both of us just trained hard and turned up to races where we would systematically get our heads kicked in. And race we did: I had over eighty days of racing in that first year as a pro.

I had to quit most stage races due to exhaustion, climbing into the *voiture balai* – the broom wagon (so called because it brushes up the weak and sick who can no longer ride their bikes to the finish) – on the last day. Yet I don't think there was one race where I wasn't in a breakaway on one stage or another. I could always get in a break if I wanted to, but I wasn't really strong enough to survive in it and, come the finale, I was too tired to actually race for the win. The next day, still tired from the effort, I would be on my hands and knees and could barely finish the stage.

I didn't confront my first 'recovery' moment until a few months into the year. It was at the Vuelta a Asturias, a five-day stage race in north-west Spain. It was my first race in Spain, and it was very different from racing in France or Italy.

In France, there was no rhyme or reason to the racing. Sometimes, it was almost amateurish the way in which everybody just smashed themselves from kilometre zero to the finish line.

The Italian scene, on the other hand, was pure finale racing. The days followed a predictable scenario; start fast, get faster, finish at warp speed. I never really experienced warp speed, as I was generally out of the picture before then.

In Spain, there was a very civilised feel to it all; a calm to the racing. There was little other than stage racing on the calendar and these followed an unchanging pattern. Flat stages finished in mass sprints won by sprinters, although a kamikaze breakaway would slip away early on, and usually be controlled by the chasing peloton until the final 10 kilometres.

Summit finishes were won by climbers, their teammates controlling the day's racing until the bottom of the decisive climb. If there was a time trial, then the team with a general classification rider strong enough against the clock would control the race and the outcome would be decided in the time trial. Each day, when we rolled away from the start, we knew what awaited us. It was refreshing and more akin to what I had expected of professional racing.

But the shock came when we hit the mountains. The climbing speeds were like nothing I had encountered in France or Italy. The Spanish are primarily great climbers, and this stems as much from nurture as nature, as most racing in Spain, from junior level up, is hilly.

In order to be a successful pro in Spain, you have to climb fast, in much the same way as in Belgium all racing is flat, windy and cobbled, breeding hard northern classic riders. The Italian scene breeds a combination of the two, as the majority of their racing is hard, tactical one-day racing.

I was considered something of a climber with the amateurs, and my time-trialling ability meant that I was expected to be a general classification rider in the future. In theory, Spanish racing was made for me. But in Spain, the climbing stages were ridiculously fast and once again my weakness riding out of the saddle was exposed, as my arms gave way before my legs. I was out of my depth, a minnow in a sea of big fish.

Tony Rominger was using that Vuelta a Asturias to lose weight and fine-tune his condition for the Tour de France. His *soigneur*, Torron, was on 'making-sure-Tony-had-no-chocolate-duty' and also focused on ensuring that his pre-race morning meal was pasta with olive oil, nothing else.

Tony was a clever man; he spoke six languages fluently and was very dynamic, but when in the team environment he was cared for like a little boy. His big thing at this time was PlayStation football, which he loved and took very seriously.

Meanwhile, I was expected to room with a young French pro who wasn't a renowned talent or even a key member of the team, but seemed to have been in the right place at the right time to fill the quota of French professionals required on ours, a French team.

When we'd all met at the gate for our flight to Spain, everyone was relaxed and jovial except the young French rider, who kept to himself and looked a little on edge. Once he started talking, we couldn't stop him bragging about how hard he'd been training. On the flight I sat with Laurent Desbiens, who was in his first year back racing after a doping ban. He and Philippe Gaumont, also in Cofidis, had served a ban together after testing positive while on the same team the year before.

Both Laurent and I had registered that there was something up with my future roommate.

'I can see it in his eyes,' Desbiens said, as we chatted on the plane.

'What do you mean?' I asked.

'He's *allumé*,' he replied. 'Lit up . . .'

When we got to Spain, it became clear that 'lit up' was an understatement. The young Frenchman didn't speak to anybody on the way to the hotel, only glancing at Desbiens nervously as we sat on the bus.

I wasn't overjoyed when I got to the hotel and saw that the two of us were sharing, but there wasn't anything I could do about it. I dropped my stuff, ate and had a massage. When I came back from massage, my roommate wasn't there. About half an hour later, one of the *soigneurs* came in and asked angrily what I'd been saying about him because he'd apparently complained about me saying things to the others. I was completely taken aback, annoyed even, and roped in Desbiens to back me up. By this point, my roommate was avoiding me, and when he didn't turn up to dinner we were starting to get a little worried.

When I got back to the room he had locked me out. Eventually, thanks to a spare key, we got in.

He was in there, looking completely deranged. He started whispering, saying that the room had been bugged with microphones and telling us that we were being listened to. The *soigneur* didn't hesitate; he immediately told me to pack up my stuff, as I'd be sleeping in another room.

Desbiens wasn't at all surprised to learn that the kid was amphetamined up to his eyeballs. He'd obviously taken it to panic-train before the race and had ended up 'cooking' his brain, a condition otherwise known as speed psychosis.

This, it turned out, was standard practice. 'Pot-Belge', a concoction of drugs, was used to underpin big training sessions and there was certainly a type of pro who loved the *allumé* training session. They used to say that if you were *allumé*, it didn't matter if it was raining, as there'd be sunshine in your head.

That was perhaps not a bad thing for those tackling their early season 6-, even 7-hour rides in the cold and wet. Often, however, they didn't even really need to light up – it was seen as just good fun. Taken in the wrong doses or abused – yes, even amphetamine users can be responsible – you could not only destroy your body but also your brain, just like my friend. That was the last we were to see of him.

His plight demonstrated the risks riders ran if they 'experimented' on their own. It was usually the *soigneurs* who dealt with rider medication. Any self-respecting *soigneur* would have their own comprehensive medical bag and, if the doctor was not at the race, which was often the case, then the *soigneurs* would assume the role – often with relish. The team truck would also have a sort of mini-pharmacy, nothing illegal, just a comprehensive array of pharmaceutical supplies.

The big fad at the time was for Italian 'recovery' products. This was what I'd seen Frankie injecting. Prefolic acid, Epargriseovit and Ferlixit: prefolic acid, vitamin B and iron. These were all supposed to help keep your blood healthy and to maintain your oxygen-carrying capacity at its highest. Up to this point, it was all I had seen.

It was common knowledge that I didn't do 'recovery' and I think it was beginning to annoy some of the staff in the team, especially the *soigneurs*. They could see that I was a talented racer, but they also knew what I was competing against. I think they thought I didn't understand, that I was naive, perhaps stubbornly idealistic, that I hadn't grasped I was now a professional in a world in which where there was no room for idealism.

My *soigneur* took it upon himself to explain, as he had done previously, that there was nothing 'wrong' with 'recovery'. It was not illegal and, far from doping, it was a simple injection that gave my body the vitamins it couldn't replace through eating alone.

I'd spoken to Tony about it during the week, and he'd said that the combination of prefolic, Epargriseovit and small doses of Ferlixit could actually boost your blood values by a point, completely naturally.

I thought about it some more. Maybe they were right; maybe I was just being stubborn. After all, this wasn't doping. If I was going to take a stance against doping, then I needed to make sure I did everything else within the rules that might help my racing.

So when my massage was over at the penultimate stage in Asturias, and my *soigneur* asked if I was sure I didn't want to do recovery, I finally said:

'*Bon, allez, je vais le faire.*'

'Okay, fine, let's do it.'

I sat on the massage table and watched as he got out the ampoules and the paraphernalia required to inject it intravenously. Everything was new and disposable, the syringes and needles were all individually wrapped in plastic and he carefully opened all of these. There was one bigger syringe and one smaller, one needle and a butterfly; such a lovely name for such an ugly tool.

The butterfly was the little plastic-winged needle at the end of a thin tube, used to make the IV junction between the vein and the syringe. The prefolic was in two ampoules. One was like a mini jar with powder in it, the other was a little standard ampoule with clear liquid; this liquid needed to be siphoned out and mixed into the powder. This was then shaken and left.

He broke the top off the pinky-red Epargriseovit ampoule and drew that out into the bigger syringe, then the dissolved prefolic mixture could be siphoned out into the same syringe. This was put to one side, while he snapped off the top of the Ferlixit ampoule, a very dark brown liquid and exactly what one would expect iron to look like. He drew half of the ampoule's contents into the smaller syringe and laid it carefully down next to the other syringe.

It was strange watching all this, taking it all in. Once the two syringes were lying there, side by side, it was hard not to question what I was doing. I felt uncomfortable, but I was now too embarrassed to say, 'No – stop.'

So I sat there as he put a tourniquet on my arm and told me to clench my fist, my veins bulging out like the roots of a tree. He joked about how hard it was to find a vein. I smiled, trying to find it funny.

The butterfly was now brought out and he wiped down the vein he'd chosen in the crease of my arm. I didn't like needles. I'd been avoiding my tetanus booster for years, as I hated the idea of being stabbed with a needle. And now this . . .

And then it was in.

The butterfly gently pierced the skin and the wall of the vein and laid its wings down upon my arm. A couple of centimetres of blood pumped up through the tube before stopping, the pressure of the tourniquet limiting blood flow. He then connected the bigger syringe to the end of the tube and deftly removed the tourniquet. With one hand holding the barrel and the other gently pulling back on the pump, my blood flowed smoothly up and entered the syringe with a tiny little exploding cloud.

'*Ça va?*' he asked me. I answered, '*Oui.*'

And, slowly, he began to empty the syringe into my body.

He told me that I should tell him if I felt it burning. He emptied the syringe completely and pushed air through the tube till there was just a drop of liquid at the tube's end, near the butterfly wings. Then he smoothly disconnected the empty syringe and reconnected the smaller darker one. This was the iron, and he said he had to pump this through much more slowly.

'*Pourquoi?*' I asked.

'Because that's what you have to do with iron,' I was told.

Once again, my blood was sucked back up through the tube till it met with the barrel of the syringe, only this time there was no pretty little exploding cloud, as the iron was darker than the blood.

We sat there in silence apart from the occasional '*Ça va?*' as the syringe was emptied.

And that was that. A line had been crossed. I now did 'recovery'. I didn't like doing it and would only do it after the hardest days in stage races. I was a light user for no other reason than I didn't like injections.

My season progressed. I began to adapt to the racing and finally to get some results. I was close to the top ten in time trials, began finishing stage races and, unlike most other neo-pros, actually made it into breakaways.

These were all big achievements for me that first year. I had high hopes of success in the Tour de L'Avenir – literally translated as the Tour of the Future, a mini-Tour de France, organised by the Tour de France promoter, ASO.

There was a prologue and a time trial before it headed off into the mountains and I'd fixed my sights on winning both. The prologue I won with relative ease, but in the time trial, I was swept aside by French rider Erwann Mentheour.

I finished the race and was being congratulated by everybody on what seemed an inevitable victory when Erwann came ripping through the finish taking my 'fastest time' and pummelling it.

It was my first experience of having a win taken from me by a guy who was clearly doping, something he subsequently admitted to. But to his credit, Erwann didn't really hide it and effectively apologised to me the next day. That didn't stop me from quitting the race and going home though.

I ended the season racing for Great Britain in the World Championships in San Sebastian. I was excited at the prospect of being able to spend some time with the British team, which felt like a safe, friendly place compared to where I had spent most of the rest of the year.

I didn't know at the time that Tom Simpson had won the World title in San Sebastian 32 years earlier. But then, when I was 20 years old, I didn't really know much about Simpson's story.

Robert Millar was team manager that week and we got on well. Chris Boardman and I were the two riders entered for the time trial. Chris took bronze in the TT, and I ended up in the middle of the field, but struggled in the road race and didn't finish. But one of the key moments of that week in the Basque Country was meeting Harry Gibbings, a charismatic Irishman who was working for Oakley sunglasses at the time.

Harry and I hit it off straight away and my first pro season ended with us partying the night away together, post-road race on Sunday evening. At some point I dropped my phone in the harbour, Bjarne Riis took a cigar out of my mouth and stuck it down my shirt, we both lost our jackets and went body surfing in the freezing sea. I woke up the next morning 30 kilometres away in Harry's hotel, fully clothed apart from one bare foot. It was to set a precedent for our times spent together over the next eight years.

8

TOUR DE DOPAGE

By the start of 1998, I'd had enough of Nice. The Americans were a strange bunch, bitching about each other incessantly, and, with Lance making his comeback after his cancer treatment, it was all getting too much. Cliques were forming and it was very hard to tell where you stood with anyone – plus, they weren't really that much fun.

So together with Jeremy Hunt, a fellow British pro, I decided to move to Toulouse, where a small group of Aussies – in fact, Henk Vogels and Stuart O'Grady, a freckled ball of energy who became a great friend – were based. This seemed like a good idea at the time.

I was left in charge of all logistics, so after packing all my things into a rental car and saying farewell to Bobby, I drove to Toulouse. Unfortunately, however, neither Jez nor I had ever been there before.

I went to some estate agents but quickly came to the conclusion that I didn't want to be living there. I was in a no-man's land now. I couldn't go back to Nice, so I decided to continue on to Biarritz.

I'd been there once before and had been struck by how beautiful it was, yet it had never crossed my mind to live there, probably because no other pro cyclists lived there. As my disillusionment with the sport grew, however, this became an appealing characteristic.

I called Eric Frutoso, my mentor two years earlier at St Quentin, and he kindly offered to put me up while I decided what to do. I found an apartment in the nick of time before heading off to my first races. I lived there for the next seven years. That was how Biarritz became home.

I'd saved up some money for furniture and I loved getting my own place together. I was nesting, and for the first time in a while it felt like I had found somewhere I could be happy. Biarritz affected me in much the same way Hong Kong had done.

It's a soulful place, precariously built on a rocky, wild coastline. The architecture is eclectic: the town is a nineteenth-century folly, built for wealthy and aristocratic Europeans. For a while, it was the only place to be in summertime, if you were rich.

When I moved there, the town was a faded version of its once chic self. The shoeless surfers outnumbered the Hermès-carrying *mesdames*, and no longer was Coco Chanel to be found gallivanting with fallen Russian princes. Instead, there were numerous VW vans and groups of stoned, drum-playing students. That didn't mean there weren't a few remnants of la belle époque, and when one did see them a perfect juxtaposition was created, of two worlds colliding, fur versus neoprene. I loved it.

Biarritz offered me an escape from a world I was beginning to hold in ever-greater disdain. I loved racing, and I loved being a cyclist, but I struggled with the people and the environment. The world of doping and the law of silence – the *omertà* – that went with it were eroding my self-respect.

I started to distance myself from the people, and from some of the classless idiots who were considered as great champions. I was a mere apprentice yet I was already losing respect for my profession. Even so, I still believed that I'd be better than the dopers when my time came and I was confident that I could do whatever I wanted to, if I put my mind to it.

As I separated myself further from the ethos of professional cycling, I read more and more. From McCarthy and Ellroy, I bounced on to Graham Swift and Niall Williams, and then to a biography of Victor Hugo, which helped me understand why I had seen his name in every French town I'd ever ridden through. Reading felt like the only way I could be different, more cerebral. I wanted so much to be different from the archetypal pro.

Most of the time, when I raced, I got my head 'kicked in', as they say. But the rest of the time, things were better. I could actually be part of the race, and that made up for all the pain. Winning remained almost impossible, but I was better than most when it came to time trialling. I took it more seriously than others and I took great pride in my bike and in achieving the best and most aerodynamic position.

That said, I didn't have good equipment and I spent my first five years as a professional battling for bits for my bike. But because I cared, the mechanics did their best with what they had. I also took every time trial seriously, because of what Guimard had told me once, when I was particularly exhausted and I asked if I could take it easy in the time trial.

He'd stared at me. 'You are a professional – you do every time trial at 100 per cent,' he said. 'One day it will serve you well if you find yourself in the leader's jersey.' I have stood by his advice ever since.

That spring, I won the time trial at the Three Days of De Panne, a brutal race held in Flanders and finishing on the grey Belgian coast. Feared by every professional, the general rule of thumb is that if you make it through without crashing you've had a great three days. Coming into the last day I wasn't expecting much. After a 110-kilometre morning stage, we tackled the time trial, a simple affair out and back along the coast. I was 14 seconds faster than the next guy, Italian Michele Bartoli, the best one-day rider at that time, and I also broke the course record. To say it was a surprise would be an understatement.

We went straight from there to another race in France, the GP Rennes, and soon after that I had another little stage race, Circuit de La Sarthe. The Italian contingent of the Cofidis team flew in to compete and I raced with Francesco Casagrande, our Italian leader and widely seen as one of the sport's big stars, for the first time.

I was on a high, largely because of the results of the blood tests the team had run on us all the day after De Panne. In theory, this was to make sure that nobody's hematocrit was over the 50 per cent limit. When the results came through the day before La Sarthe started, I was a pitifully low 40.1 per cent.

But instead of being disheartened by this I felt vindicated and excited, as it demonstrated that it wasn't necessary to be near 50 per cent in order to win. I knew I'd raced against guys in De Panne who were fully *prepared* for the one-day Classic, the Tour of Flanders, a couple of days later. The blood test result made me realise that anything was possible.

In my youthful exuberance, I was telling anybody who would listen that I'd won in De Panne and broken the course record with a hematocrit of only 40 per cent. I went to see Casagrande and his roommate, whom I'll refer to as l'Équipier ('the teammate'), so that I could show Casagrande the test results.

I stood there, a big grin on my face, expecting Casagrande to congratulate me and say something morale boosting. But he didn't. After a pause, he handed the result back to me and then turned to speak to his roommate in Italian.

'*Perché non è a 50?*' Casagrande asked l'Équipier, puzzled.

'*Why isn't he at 50?*'

L'Équipier knew that I'd understood and that it wasn't what I wanted to hear, so in his accented French he tried to say something more congratulatory. It was too late though. I was crestfallen by Casagrande's reaction. The damage was done.

Many of the guys I raced alongside considered it their professional duty to be as close to the limits as the rules would allow. In their world, it had nothing to do with ethics, or what was right or wrong, and certainly had nothing to do with cheating. It was simply medical preparation.

To riders like Casagrande I was a fool, a naive young foreigner who had yet to understand the true nature of his profession. He was right in thinking I was a naive young pro but he was wrong on one count: I wasn't a fool.

After that shattering meeting with Casagrande, I recognised – perhaps even accepted – what I was up against. But it didn't make me upset like the first time I'd encountered it with Jim van de Laer the year before. Instead it made me angry.

Fuck them, I thought.

Fuck them for thinking they could judge me, or my choices. I wasn't a fool, and I was no longer naive. I took it upon myself to prove to them that I was better than they were. I had no respect for them, these stupid men, these 'professionals', uneducated athletes who took drugs because they had no other option in life. If anything, I pitied them.

It was this attitude that would allow me to survive clean for so long in such a deep-rooted doping culture. I had no outside help and it wasn't something I could talk about or share, because everywhere I turned people seemed to have their head in the sand about it.

It was a dark world that existed behind the technicolour caravan, a world that most in the sport knew about but none would challenge. It was all a big lie. And there was nothing for the clean guys to do but to carry on and stick to their guns.

I didn't race in the 1998 Tour de France, when that dark world was finally exposed for all to see. The Festina affair was triggered when a Festina team car, searched as it crossed the border from Belgium to France, was found to contain a substantial quantity of drugs.

The Festina team was filled with the French darlings of the time –

Richard Virenque, Laurent Brochard, Pascal Hervé, Didier Rous and Christophe Moreau. It was the biggest doping scandal to ever hit cycling and dramatically revealed what had been hidden within the professional ranks for years.

If the customs officials had not stopped that Festina car, and if the French police had not made arrests and begun investigating the Festina team, there is no doubt in my mind that nothing would ever have changed. Professional cycling had reached a point at which it was incapable of confronting or fixing its own problems; the sport had failed, monumentally. The enforcers of criminal and civil law had to act in order to begin the long and difficult clean-up that has been going on ever since.

That year's Tour became a farce, as arrests, raids, interrogations and overnight stints in cells punctuated the race. That led to rider strikes and team withdrawals. It was all very dramatic, but it also meant that many guys then had to race without their usual drugs – which may have been the main motivation for some of them to quit the race.

The 1998 Tour had started in Dublin – there were tales of drugs being dumped overboard from the ferries taking the convoy across to France and I've since heard of other innovative transportation methods – unmarked cars, motorbikes, even friends in the publicity caravan – being used by teams who dared try to outwit the French police.

How true these stories are is debatable, but there's no doubt that it would became the least-doped Tour in years. Ironically, it was Marco Pantani who won the race overall, the same Pantani whose cocaine addiction led to a premature death and whose huge talent was ruined by drugs.

But for young, clean riders the grand exposé was wonderful news.

Watching riders get arrested, hearing about the dope-dumping from the ferry and imagining the panic that most of the riders would be feeling at the prospect of racing for three weeks without their usual medical stock, tickled us.

It was a revenge of sorts on the dopers, whose charged-up performances had made our lives hell.

In our naivety we thought it would change the sport overnight. Surely now that everybody knew what was going on, the powers that be would be forced to act? Unfortunately this did not happen.

The initial joy of what this meant for clean riders was quickly replaced with resignation and despondency, as we realised what the Festina affair had done to the image of the sport. The shouts from bystanders, when we were out training, usually of '*Allez, allez!*' were now replaced with '*Allez les dopés!*'

It hadn't crossed our minds that we would be tarred with the same brush as the riders who had been caught doping. From then on, as far as the public was concerned, being a professional cyclist meant you doped. It didn't matter who you were – a 20-year-old neo-pro or a 32-year-old Tour winner – they saw the same person.

Now, we were all dopers. Not only were we fighting the world in which we lived and worked, we were on the defensive when confronted with a member of the public. It was around this time, when I found that I had to defend myself on an almost daily basis, that I decided it was best not to tell people I was a pro cyclist, unless it was absolutely unavoidable.

Even so, many people just assumed I was doping. Back in Biarritz I went to see my neighbours, a very sweet retired couple who looked after my mail when I was away. We had the now inevitable conversation about drugs in cycling and the drama of that year's Tour. Yet I didn't expect them to be so supportive, almost apologetic, for the way in which cycling was being vilified. The lady treated me almost like a grandson, and when her husband wasn't in the room, she took me to one side.

'David,' she said, 'we've always known that you dope – we know it's impossible to do it without it. But promise me you'll be careful and look after your health, won't you?'

I was lost for words.

The elderly in France, who'd grown up with the Tour, understood that it was a preposterous sporting challenge. In their pragmatic manner, they didn't see it as being humanly possible, and considered it part and parcel of the job to do what one had to do in order to survive and to perform.

That didn't mean they believed doping was right, but for them professional cycling was a brutal sport that only desperate or crazy men would become part of – a 'peasant sport', because there was no way a member of the bourgeoisie would choose to become a professional cyclist.

This was a far cry from the romantic and ultimately naive perspective held by the modern generation of Tour fans. There's no doubt that the older generation's view, no matter how pragmatic, was wrong, but was it better to be naive and to believe in what was essentially a corporate-funded fraud?

Before heading off to the Tour de l'Avenir that autumn, I hooked up with Jay Sweet – another Australian cycling buddy – and enjoyed the final days of the summer party season in Biarritz. We were a little delicate by the time we got to the race. I came down with bronchitis prior to the prologue, but somehow I still managed to win it. Then I avenged my time trial defeat of the previous year before finally pulling out of the race, due to illness.

That was my season done and dusted. In the aftermath of the

Festina affair, it had been hard to gauge the feeling in the peloton but among the younger pros there was a feeling that what had happened was perhaps going to change the sport for the better. Our optimism proved unjustified.

9

THE VDB SHOW

I spent the winter of 1998 training alone in Biarritz. While the sport came to terms with the aftershocks of Festina, I clung to the belief that it was all going to be different in 1999.

New anti-doping measures were being introduced, the most important of these being the longitudinal testing programme. The plan was to test each rider's blood four times a year in order to create a rudimentary profile that would supposedly reveal who was manipulating their blood. The thinking was that dopers were specific in their doping and that the majority of them would target certain events, such as the Tour de France. In theory, their blood profile in the summer would bear little resemblance to that established in the periods of the year when they weren't 'prepared'. These quarterly tests would make it possible to spot who was doping and – just as importantly – who wasn't.

Initially, this sounded great. In reality, it meant nothing. There were no sanctions attached to an anomalous longitudinal test, and, even if a rider's profile suggested doping, there was no way to target them with specific anti-doping controls as a ratified EPO test didn't even exist at that point. Nor were there tests for many of the other products that were used.

That problem was compounded by the fact that there was no previous experience of blood profiling among professional cyclists – there was little understanding of what was 'normal.' After a while, I realised that it was not much more than a PR exercise, to appease the people who needed appeasing, rather than being the cure that it was proclaimed to be.

Yet my belief that things were changing was reinforced by my start to the '99 season. In my first race, Etoile de Besseges, I was fourth overall, and from there I was thrown into the Tour of the Mediterannean. Cofidis needed an expert time triallist to lead the team in the team time trial stage and – much against my will, as I'd lined up a date with a Swiss girl – I was that man.

I missed the date and rode my frustrations out in the team time trial stage at Besseges, powering around the course with zero consideration for my teammates. Instead of shepherding my flock, I blew them all away. Single-handedly, I dragged the team to the finish, but also dropped five of them in the process.

L'Équipier, my teammate, on the look-out for another leader to ride for – Francesco Casagrande had been banned for a positive testosterone control the year before – was impressed.

After we'd recovered a bit and were rolling back to the team bus, l'Équipier came alongside me and said the first flattering thing I'd heard from him.

'David, that was incredible – I didn't think you were so strong,' he said. 'I've never seen anybody do that in a team TT before – and I've seen a lot of riders. Where are you racing next?'

I knew that, without Casagrande, l'Équipier was a bit lost. He needed a raison d'être and I sensed that he was mulling over his options, probably with our teammate Frank VDB Vandenbroucke at the top of his list. But after that conversation, I realised l'Équipier had also made me an option.

Up until then I hadn't raced alongside VDB. That was about to change at my next races, the Trophée Luis Puig and Vuelta Valenciana, in Spain. I would be joining the guys who had been out there for a while, a group that included VDB and his sidekick, Philippe Gaumont. Those of us racing on the French programme had already been hearing stories of their shenanigans in Spain. Word got back to us that Gaumont had been living on the edge since the training camp in January.

Before Luis Puig and the Valencian race, the whole team had got together at the Cofidis annual party following our presentation in Paris. The next morning, we flew to Spain. As we left Paris, it was immediately obvious that Gaumont was still on a high from the night before. When we got to Madrid, where we had a 2-hour wait before our connecting flight to Alicante, Gaumont disappeared. When he finally returned to get on the plane he was in an even worse state than before.

'What has Gaumont been up to?' I asked a teammate as we waited to board the flight. 'Jesus, he looks a mess.'

Gaumont was a strange character, the most alpha of males in what was very much a man's world. He was physically imposing, especially for a cyclist, but also quite charismatic to match. Philippe was also articulate. He could be the most charming and thoughtful person, but also the most intimidating and cruel. The best policy with him was to keep a low profile and avoid attracting his interest. If he decided to intimidate you, he'd never let go, and if he chose to like you he would do his utmost to drag you into his world.

I first came onto Philippe's radar in one of my earliest races, the Tour du Haut Var. The team had missed the breakaway and had been chasing for most of the race. I was completely wrecked, couldn't do my turns at the front any more and slid back through the peloton. Soon after that, I saw Philippe drifting down the side of the bunch looking angry. Eventually he spotted me and unleashed all his fury on me. It was scary as well as humiliating.

Off I went, back up to the front, riding hard until I was cross-eyed and almost falling off my bike. When we hit the decisive final hill, I was dropped immediately. Then, once again, I saw a Cofidis rider ahead of me, going very slowly looking over his shoulder. As I got closer, I realised it was Philippe.

'Oh shit,' I thought, 'now what have I done.'

But his mood had changed. As I got up alongside him he smiled and patted me on the back, telling me I'd done well. He then rode with me all the way to the finish, chatting. That was typical Philippe, enraged one minute, considerate the next.

The Gaumont who boarded that short flight to Valencia was clearly the raging Philippe. I was told he'd drunk two bottles of champagne while waiting for the connection, and also tossed in some sleeping pills for good measure.

I was stunned when I was told this. 'He's taking sleeping pills?' I said in disbelief. 'But it's lunchtime ...?!'

Gaumont was a mess, but like the rest of us, he was in his Cofidis team suit and so was allowed onto the plane. More than once, he tried to light up a cigarette. Fortunately somebody from the team was able to stop him before it got totally out of control, but it was clear that he was a loose cannon.

Things didn't get any better when we landed. We watched with nervous hilarity at the baggage carousel, as he rummaged through bags, piling them up around him, muttering: 'My bike, I need my bike. I've got to get to the hotel.'

Still nobody intervened. Eventually, Gaumont found his bike bag and suitcase and marched out to the waiting bus. Once outside, he opened up the bike bag and started struggling to build his bike, while the bemused bus driver looked on.

By this time, it was about six in the evening and the hotel was still 90 kilometres away, not that Philippe would have had the motor skills or wherewithal to change into his cycling clothing, let alone to put his bike together and actually ride it.

Eventually one of the team *directeurs* did what should have been done hours before: he talked Gaumont down until they managed to get a semblance of control over him. Once on the bus, he promptly passed out.

Philippe didn't turn up for dinner, but his odyssey hadn't finished. Later that night, he was seen wandering the hotel corridors, dragging his suitcase, sobbing, saying: 'I want to go home ... Where am I? I need to speak to my wife ...'

A couple of the senior riders who knew him well stepped in. They tied him to his bed and stripped the room of anything that could get him into trouble – wallet, phone and sleeping pills.

The next day, the management sat the team down and told us it was unacceptable behaviour and there would be consequences if anything like it ever happened again. But I don't believe that Gaumont was ever reprimanded.

It was the first Stilnox-fuelled mess witnessed collectively by team personnel. During that year we were to see such excesses at their most extreme. Stilnox was often behind this wild behaviour.

Stilnox, or Zolipdem, is a sleeping pill. If you take it when you're in bed you won't notice any real side effects; if you take it and try to stay awake then the side effects are quickly noticeable. Thirty minutes after taking it, you'll start to feel a little strange, almost a little drunk, and you might find yourself bumping into walls or walking into doorframes.

Your brain still feels like it's operating normally, but the rapid decline into total loss of control has begun. If you don't fight it and just go to bed there are no problems. But the longer you try to stay awake, the greater the loss of control. I learned that the ticket to getting maximum 'side effects' was to take more than one pill and have a couple of alcoholic drinks with it. Within an hour or so you could find yourself acting and feeling the same way as if you were completely drunk.

On Stilnox, however, you wake up feeling rested: that's because at some point the pills can't be fought any longer and you pass out into a deep sleep. There's still the memory blackout to deal with but, in a nutshell, it's like waking up after a big night of drinking without a hangover.

Stilnox and other sleeping pills had been used for years in European cycling. The life you lead on a stage race, such as the Tour, Giro or Vuelta, affects people in different ways, but contrary to what people might think, deep sleep is not the easiest thing to achieve when your body is as drained as that of a pro rider after a long day of racing. For some riders, after a big stage in a long race, Stilnox was often the only way to get a good night's sleep.

So many things come into play; you may not cope well with constantly sleeping in different rooms with different beds, with differing lengths and different mattresses. There's also the comfort of pillows and sheets – in fact, I always take my own pillow on the road with me. Then there's the efficiency of the air-con, or the lack of air-con; maybe it's too noisy or too quiet – and there's also how you cope with sharing rooms with a teammate. It's not exactly conducive to a good night's stress-free sleep, and sometimes the worry about sleeping badly and not recovering well for the next day is enough to make sleeping pills seem attractive. That's why, for a long time, taking sleeping pills was considered quite normal – in fact most of the older riders didn't think anything of using them.

At the World Championships in 1997, we were staying in a hotel that ticked all the boxes for a bad night's sleep. A couple of days after I'd arrived, I ended up chatting to a member of the old guard when I was out training on the course.

'The hotel's terrible,' I told him. 'I'm sleeping like shit.'

'Take Valium,' he responded. 'I use it all the time, you'll sleep like a baby.' I ignored his advice.

Of course, if used responsibly – not beyond the recommended doses or frequencies – sleeping pills are fairly harmless. Unfortunately, responsibility was not a characteristic of the pro scene at that time. The recommended doses were seen almost as a challenge by some pros. This was particularly the case with the Cofidis team of 1999. Gaumont and Vandenbroucke, in particular, took this to levels that most doctors would doubtless deem impossible.

I didn't really know the scale of what was going on inside the team when I got to Spain. Gaumont and VDB could be charming when they were in the mood, but there were continuous rumours that they were out of control, running amok in hotels late at night. There was a story doing the rounds in the peloton of them 'borrowing' the team camping car late at night and taking it to a local brothel. Like many other tales of excess, this seemed pretty far-fetched. Of course, it turned out to be true.

I continued my good form in Valencia. Lance Armstrong, now with the US Postal team, had returned to the sport after his illness. I had been sitting at the back of the bunch on the first climb of the first stage, chatting to him, when all the attacking started. He was in a bad way and told me that if I was feeling as good as I looked I should go with the break, so taking his advice, off I went.

I ended up attacking, then moving clear on my own and building a 3-minute lead. ONCE and Kelme, at that time Spain's two best teams, joined forces to chase me down, which seemed to me an overreaction, as we still had 80 kilometres, the final 40 of which were flat and far from in my favour. But that reaction did show that I was beginning to earn respect from the peloton. They were not taking any chances with me taking time on the opening stage of a five-day race – that revealed that they feared me.

The scenery around Valencia is beautiful and it was a pure joy racing alone ahead of the peloton. I raced up the climbs, bagging all the mountain points, and then ripped down the technical descents using every inch of the road. I was 22 and pretty fearless, oblivious to the consequences of making just one mistake. That gung-ho attitude caught up with me, with about 50 kilometres to race.

I came roaring around a blind switchback bend to find the road kicked on, through almost 180 degrees. All that stood between me and the other side of the valley was a protective barrier. At high speed, I T-boned the barrier, took off and saw that it wasn't a sheer cliff, more of a very steep drop.

That season, we'd just started using shortwave radios, linking the riders and the team cars. The big heavy receiver, tucked away in my back pocket, took the impact as I slammed onto my back and began sliding down the hillside. I started grappling for something to hold on to. Eventually I came to a halt.

In the post-crash stillness, I lay there, gripping onto bushes and rocks, trying to understand what had just happened. Above me, up on the road, the team car that was following me down the mountain had slid to a halt alongside the barrier I'd just flipped over. Meanwhile far below, my bike was bouncing down the mountain.

Before I knew it, our team mechanic was with me, roughly pulling me back up the hill. I sat on the barrier for a moment, my head in my hands, realising how lucky I'd just been. After peering down at the tangled remains of my bike, my team *directeur* asked me if I was okay, and within seconds I was being put on a spare bike and pushed off.

Despite my tumble, I was still hyped: as soon as I got back on the bike I felt fine again; so fine in fact, that a couple of hundred metres later, when I saw photographer Graham Watson on the next

hairpin bend, readying himself to take a shot, I yelled: 'Graham –
you just missed the most amazing crash!'

The race in Valencia was a great success for me. I claimed the
mountains jersey that first day and, after deciding to defend it, found
a new confidence in my climbing ability. I was playing with the big
boys, riders like Laurent Jalabert, Michael Boogerd, Michele Bartoli,
Alexandre Vinokourov. I finished fourth overall and won the mountains classification.

I was really beginning to think the sport was changing – it didn't
cross my mind that I was.

After the success of Spain, I was flown to Switzerland for two
races, GP Chiasso and GP Lugano. They weren't very high-
profile events, but Chiasso was renowned for being physically
extremely hard. Roland Meier, the Swiss rider on our team, told
us: 'Normally out of the 200 who start, 50 or so will finish. If it
rains, maybe 15.' This was not the most motivating of pep talks,
but it proved very accurate.

Chiasso went straight up one side of a mountain valley, dropped
down a bit further along, did a loop and then repeated the climb
and descent. It was a savage course. It began to rain about halfway
through – cold, icy rain – and as Meier had predicted, half of the
field dropped out. I wasn't overly motivated as my big objective was
Tirreno–Adriatico, a few days away, but l'Équipier, my new-found
loyal *domestique*, took it upon himself to get me to the front and
string the field out into the climb.

His was the classic teammate's kamikaze effort, riding himself
into the ground as he set the pace on my behalf. I've done it myself
and gone down in flames in the process. So, inevitably, the exhausted
l'Équipier finally sat up. I remember thinking: 'Off to the showers
you go – you bastard. Now I'm out here on my own and I've got
to race ...'

Soon after that, as we approached the top of the climb, it began
to snow. There were about fifteen riders left and we still had over
an hour of racing ahead of us. After a brief hiatus, we all dropped
back to our team cars to get what little warm weather clothing we

had left. I was fully clad in thermal gear by this point, yet still couldn't feel my hands or feet.

As I looked around it was clear that the few guys who were left were not only the strongest, but the hardest men in the race. We rode over the summit in a blizzard and faced up to the fast descent.

It was a horrible experience. After only a couple of minutes I was chilled to the bone, shivering everywhere, and the finesse needed to brake in the wet was lost. I could barely move my fingers, let alone feather the brakes, as I'd normally do.

As we slid into the hairpins, it was simply a case of braking in time and making it through the corner. We weren't racing on the descent – we were fighting to survive. It was an epic experience and I loved it. Some riders missed bends and disappeared into the sleet. I stayed upright to finish third but I collapsed as I crossed the finish line and was carried to the showers in a hypothermic state. But it had been a classic day of bike racing, the kind that had enraptured me when I fell in love with the sport in Hong Kong.

The next day was a rude awakening. My disillusionment with Cofidis deepened, as instead of recognising that I'd gone deep into my reserves 24 hours earlier, they told me that I had to race in what was essentially an amateur event.

'Think of your teammates,' I was told. 'Do you want them to see you sleeping in, while they're out there racing?' That was all it took for me to feel guilty. I caved in and raced.

We started at 7.30 a.m. and the course was over 200 kilometres long. I finished, but it meant I had raced over 400 kilometres in 24 hours. Within a day, I developed a cold that turned into bronchitis. I was still driven down to Sorrento in Italy where I was expected to start Tirreno–Adriatico.

We stopped at Pisa for the night but I was coughing my lungs up and knew there was no way I was going to get better in time for Tirreno. Once again I protested. Once again, nobody wanted to listen. I knew it was useless.

'There are still two days to the start,' they said, 'and then you can just ride yourself into the race. We'll see how you are on the morning of the race.'

It was no surprise, after the workload of the previous five weeks, that I was ill. It was obvious that I should go home and rest. But the team needed me – there was nobody else who could lead in Tirreno. With Vandenbroucke leading the team on one front, Cofidis had become reliant on me elsewhere. They were better off gambling that I might miraculously recover than they were going into a major race without a leader.

I started Tirreno, but didn't even make it through the first day. I was so angry. They'd forgotten that I was 22 and that I was being stretched to my absolute limit. They risked wrecking me, burning me out, and it felt like they didn't care if that happened. I could have just refused to race, and now, older and wiser, I would have done, but I was still desperate to impress.

I recovered in Biarritz and started training for my next race, the two-day Criterium International in the south of France. Despite having been ill, my form held and I finished second overall, only 0.002 seconds behind final winner Jens Voigt. But I should have won.

My time trial bike for the final afternoon was a joke. I'd waited a year for specific handlebars, but still they were not ready. We had so few time trial wheels that I was using the same front wheel as I'd used in the road stage. It would have taken the tiniest detail on my time trial bike to have closed that 0.002 seconds deficit. It was a lesson that I didn't forget.

In some ways my good results worked against me, because even though it was clear that I had already raced too much, Cofidis kept me racing. The quick recovery I had made for Criterium International disguised the underlying fatigue that had set in.

In the meantime, VDB and his clique were dominating every race they entered. There were suspicions about those successes and Cofidis was getting a reputation within the peloton, especially the French peloton, which, in the aftermath of the Festina affair, was doing everything it could to eradicate doping.

At Paris–Nice that spring, VDB and his cabal had raced how

they wanted, without any other teams being able to live with them. I'd heard stories of them actually laughing and joking about how easy it was. Some said that they were exploiting the reluctance of others to use EPO as an opportunity. There were more and more tales filtering back of extreme nocturnal activities, fuelled by sleeping pills and alcohol. Cofidis was getting a very bad name within the world of cycling; in 1999, only a few months after Festina, that was no mean feat.

Then Vandenbroucke won perhaps the toughest one-day race of all, Liège–Bastogne-Liège, in a manner never seen before.

Before the race VDB had told whoever would listen where he would make his decisive attack. Yet the night before he had taken eleven Stilnox and could barely talk or walk before passing out. Within ten days of his win in Liège, he and Gaumont were arrested by the French police, over amphetamine possession. They were interrogated for 24 hours but nothing, other than thousands of column inches and the exposure of their relationship with an infamous 'horse doctor', Bernard Sainz, came of it. Sainz – nicknamed Dr Mabuse – was an oddball character from Paris, a guru who coached riders and gave them little-known homeopathic treatments.

The team suspended them for a short while, but then, things simply carried on as normal. I was outraged and decided that I had to talk to François Migraine, the president of Cofidis. I needed him to intervene for me. I wanted nothing more to do with VDB and Gaumont. We met at his office in Lille. We shook hands and sat down. I took a deep breath and then all my rage came spilling out.

'François, everybody is talking about how it's not normal that our team is so strong,' I told him. 'Everybody thinks Gaumont, VDB and the rest are still doping. I've been told that in Paris–Nice they were laughing at people, showing off how much stronger they are. It's not right.'

Migraine looked at me. 'Have you seen them doping?'

'No, our schedules are different so I don't usually race with them,' I explained. 'Anyway, I think anybody doping hides it well now after last year.'

'It's surprising that anybody would be so stupid to risk it after Festina.'

I carried on. 'But they're crazy, François – they just don't care. Things in the peloton have changed since last year, yet VDB and Gaumont have seen it as an opportunity to get an even bigger advantage.

'The team lets them get away with anything as long as they're winning. They've been taking sleeping pills, drinking at night and intimidating the riders who aren't with them.'

Migraine looked pained. 'Does Alain [Bondue] know about this?'

'It's difficult to imagine him not knowing,' I said. 'I think he's just happy they're doing so well. I don't think they'd get away with it if their results were shit.'

He got to his feet. 'I will have to speak to Alain about it, but if this is true then I am sorry and I will make sure it no longer happens. I can understand why you're so angry, David – thank you for telling me.'

Then Migraine walked across his office to where a large framed photo of Gaumont, winning Belgian classic Ghent–Wevelgem, was hanging in a prominent position on the wall. He turned and looked at me.

'David, I have had enough of Gaumont,' he said, 'and I will show you how much.' Migraine reached up and took the photo down, turning it to face the wall.

'That will no longer ever hang on my wall,' he said. 'I'll make sure he does not cause any more destruction.'

Philippe Gaumont may have had his photograph removed from Migraine's office wall, but Frank Vandenbroucke was still the golden boy.

Frank's incredible results from the early season put him in the number one world ranking position and the team was now excited about him finishing the year in the top spot. They genuinely didn't seem to care about what may, or may not, have happened earlier in the season; they certainly weren't putting any measures in place to prevent it happening again.

VDB had long been pushing the envelope on what was possible within the rules and more than once he had just scraped in under the 50 per cent UCI blood control. He was so far over the 50 per cent limit the day before the 1999 World Championships in Verona that he had used two bags of plasma, brought to his hotel by a Cofidis teammate, to increase his blood volume and reduce his hematocrit – even then, he was still right on 50 per cent. That, along with the painkillers and cortisone he was using, meant that when he fell off and fractured both his wrists early on in the race he was able to get back on and ride a further 200 kilometres – and, despite being unable to get out of the saddle, to finish seventh. He was then taken to hospital where he had both wrists put in plaster. His performance was hailed as 'heroic'.

Meanwhile, I was finding it very hard to get the condition I had had at the beginning of the season and increasingly felt like I was banging my head against a wall. I decided I would race in the Isle of Man week in late June, partly for fun, partly because I needed an ego boost.

Even then, it didn't quite work out. Chris Newton smashed me in the National Time Trial Championships. After the race, I was heading out to train on two laps of the Isle of Man TT course as prep for the Manx International a couple of days later, when a cocky little Manx kid came up and asked me for my autograph.

'Awrright?!' he said. 'You must be disappointed . . . !'

'I am a bit, just not fit enough at the moment,' I said. 'Are you from here?'

'Yeah,' he said, 'we live here. I'm a cyclist too. So's me brother.'

I was impressed. 'You race at all?'

'Not that much yet,' he said, 'I'm too young.'

'Ah, you've got plenty of time, just have fun, don't take it too seriously till you're older.' I signed a racing cap for him.

His eyes lit up. 'Me pals are gonna be *sooo* jealous . . . !

'And, erm, can we get a photo please? Sorry to ask, I know you must get this all the time.'

'It's no hassle,' I said. We posed together. I put my arm around his shoulder.

The same cocky kid knocked on my hotel room door when the 2007 Tour de France started in London. He gave me a framed copy of the photo of the pair of us, arm in arm, taken on the Isle of Man that day.

'Thought you might like this, David,' Mark Cavendish said, a sly grin on his face.

10

19:03 MILLAR TIME

The road climbed sharply once more. I wearily lifted my backside out of the saddle yet again and cursed. Bobby Julich, riding alongside me, sensed my disbelief.

'Are you having a fucking laugh?' I spat, at nobody in particular. 'This is *nothing* like what it looks like on TV.'

Bobby shrugged. 'It's not called La Doyenne for nothing.'

Bobby and I were riding in the Belgian Ardennes, reconnoitring the route of the brutal and unrelenting one-day Classic, known as the Doyenne–Liège–Bastogne–Liège. I was on the back foot, struggling for form, after losing most of the second half of the 1999 season to injury.

I'd lost ground the previous summer, when those of us not racing for Cofidis in the Tour had been sent to an altitude training camp in the Pyrenees. Having spent weeks looking forward to the summer season in Biarritz, I found myself locked away in a miserable mountain-top town. It put me in a petulant frame of mind, and after our part-time mechanic had wrecked my very expensive SRM power training cranks, my mood worsened. I was trouble. I'd never partied during a camp or a race before, but now I did. In fact, I partied like it was 1999 . . .

It was my teammate Janek Tombak's birthday on the last night of the camp and, despite the dead-end atmosphere, we made an effort to celebrate. We found ourselves in some empty, shitty disco drinking vodka. Janek had some Stilnox and offered me one. I paused, and then took it, more out of curiosity than anything else, but it didn't take long for the effects to hit me.

I don't remember much after that, but I do remember trying to break back into the hotel by climbing over the roof and going through a window. When that didn't work I decided to jump off the roof, ending up in a crumpled heap, having hit the ground with such impact as to explode the air bubbles in my Nike Max trainers.

Janek and I both thought it was pretty funny, but I wasn't laughing the next morning when I woke up with a massively swollen ankle that I couldn't put any weight on. I hobbled around and tried to pretend it was fine, but it was a lost cause. After X-rays, an ambulance took me back to Biarritz.

The team manager at the camp told everybody that I'd simply fallen down some stairs. In fact, we covered it up so well that even Alain Bondue refused to believe me when I told him the injury was really bad. I even got sent to a race while I was on crutches.

It took six specialists to figure out what was wrong. After more X-rays and an MRI scan, I went to a doctor in Monaco who diagnosed it from the first X-ray that had been taken. It was a clean fracture of my heel.

I lost the second half of 1999 and was unable to ride properly until November that year. But after losing so much time, I was hyper-motivated and locked myself away in Biarritz on a comeback mission. Returning from injury is hard, though that's not really due to the injury itself, but more to do with your head coping with the total inability it has to make the body do what once came easily.

More often than not, injuries occur when you're close to your peak fitness, so the last memories you have – the last performance markers you have – are of elite performance. Comebacks are at the opposite end of the scale, which is humbling for a professional athlete, but it also makes coming back an interesting and affirming experience.

The best thing about a comeback is that expectations are low. It's one of the rare times that you live without that constant white noise of expectancy, be it external or internal. There's only one goal, and that's getting back to top fitness.

Pro cyclists face up to an obligatory 'mini comeback' at least once a year. It's called December. As soon as the professional season ends at the beginning of October, most of us take a month, maybe more, completely off the bike. For the majority of my career I've taken two months off the bike and done zero exercise – no cross training, nothing. I'd just travel around seeing family and friends, meeting up with the people I didn't see the rest of the year, catching up on all the good times I was convinced I'd missed.

So after four months off, starting again wasn't that much different from going through December. My right heel was permanently swollen and the injury had changed my foot position. When I was riding, the heel began to kick out more, so instead of having my feet perfectly aligned they were now slightly off centre. I didn't like that. I have always worked very hard on the bike to make sure everything is perfect, what we in cycling like to call 'form'.

Perfect 'form' is judged on everything from the pedalling action, the position on the bike, the attire that's worn and the style with which it is worn, to the way one carries oneself. The list goes on, but once you know how form is defined, you can judge it with a mere glance at a passing cyclist. For me, cycling has always been about form, so having my right heel kick out annoyed the hell out of me. It was a lingering reminder of the damage sleeping pills and booze can do to a young man.

Yet I was obsessively committed to getting back to top condition. I'd been waiting for the 2000 season ever since Cyrille Guimard had mapped out my career over lunch in St Quentin three years earlier and announced that I would make my Tour de France debut when I was 23 – in July 2000.

Guimard was long gone from Cofidis, a conflict with François Migraine and tax problems leading to his departure after only a year with the team. This meant that, although there were other managers, Bondue and Migraine had overall control over the team, although neither of them were ever at the races or knew much about what was going on beyond our results.

By the time I got to the 2000 Ardennes classics, Flèche Wallonne and Liège–Bastogne-Liège, nine months after breaking my heel, I was struggling for form and very much out of my depth. I was taking a hiding and the problem with that is that you begin to think negatively. Before then, I'd believed I could beat the dopers, but now I felt like I couldn't do anything against them.

Bobby 'J' and I had remained friends after I'd left Nice, and were rooming together for the few days we were in Belgium. After racing in the Flèche Wallonne, we were so demoralised that we had emptied our mini-bar and commiserated together that evening. Taking on the riders on EPO seemed like an impossible task when you were clean.

That customary Liège 'recce' – the one that had me spitting and cursing – involved riding the final 100 kilometres of the 268-kilometre race. Liège was considered the hardest one-day race, the only one where the Grand Tour contenders came out to play, and the final 100 kilometres were the hilliest.

When you watched the race on TV, it didn't look *that* bad. Riding it was hell though, which was why the recce was such a shock.

'I should've stayed at the hotel,' I moaned to Bobby as we tackled yet another climb. 'I'd have been much better off not knowing about this.'

'Dave,' he said, 'just relax. Do what you can do. And don't think about the course or what the other guys have or haven't done.'

'Come on, Bobby, you of all people should know that's not going to happen. We're fucked.'

'Well, yeah,' he said, as we pondered the numerous climbs. 'Probably . . . and wait till see you see La Redoute, that'll blow your mind! And St Nicolas – remember VDB went up it in the big ring last year? You won't be able to do that even in training. That'll make you realise just how fucked up it really is.'

'Thanks, man. How far is that?'

'40k to La Redoute, 70k to St Nicolas,' Bobby intoned.

'What . . .? So that's 230k and 260k into the race . . .?!' I was disgusted. 'This is just stupid.'

When it came to the race itself, I got dropped and didn't even finish, pulling out at the second feed zone, not far from where we'd begun our recce three days earlier. I was already on the ropes in the first few kilometres and I simply couldn't comprehend that we had over 260 kilometres of racing ahead of us. With that final savage

100 kilometres yet to come, mine really was a lost cause.

Things weren't going well for me and it became easy just to blame it on the fact that I was clean and too many of the others were doped. But I wasn't alone. In the post-Festina era, many French teams and riders found themselves off the pace.

That may have been because they had, in the majority, cleaned up their act in the aftermath of Festina. Teams like Marc Madiot's Françaises des Jeux and Roger Legeay's Gan squad were genuinely doing everything they could to prevent doping and had a proactive anti-doping stance.

But some of the other French teams were less dynamic. I know that Cofidis turned a blind eye to their riders' preparation, not caring which coach, trainer or doctor their leaders used, or where you went to train. (Location was a surprisingly obvious indicator of a tendency towards doping – France was a no-go because of the new doping laws, which led to Italy and Spain becoming doping havens.) Sadly, suspicious training habits and regularly anomalous longitudinal blood values weren't of great importance to the team – results however, were.

By the middle of the 2000 season, the French had grown increasingly pessimistic. So dark was their mood that they were beaten before they even got to the start line. The '*peloton à deux vitesses*' – the two-speed peloton – they called it. One group of riders doped, the others alongside them racing clean.

You can work out for yourselves which group was fastest.

I had signed with IMG in 1999. Tony Rominger, my mentor at Cofidis and now retired from racing, had been with the global sports marketing company for many years. My mum and I met Tony and Marc Biver, boss of IMG Suisse, for lunch to discuss what IMG would do for me. As we talked they told us they would take care of everything in my financial life, from contracts to tax issues.

Following my stellar start to the 1999 season, Marc had wasted no time in negotiating a new contract with Cofidis that doubled my initial two-year contract of €80,000. Despite everything, I was happy to stay with Cofidis. I was growing up with the team and François

Migraine's promises that things would change reassured me.

So I signed one of the longest contracts in cycling, a four-year deal, that ran to 31 December 2003. I had a fixed contract of €160,000 a year, €80,000 of which was paid in France and the other €80,000 into an image contract through Luxembourg. Although the structure of it was completely beyond me, the bonus system was the most lucrative in cycling.

But I didn't really understand what an image contract was. I had no holding company through which I signed the contract, I had no bank accounts outside of France, and to that date I hadn't even realised that I had to pay more tax than the French were already taking from me at source. I was, to put it bluntly, incredibly naive when it came to money.

There were two reasons IMG signed me to a four-year deal. First, if I continued in my development and fulfilled all the bonus criteria, it was an amazing contract. Second, it meant that I was tied to IMG for four years and was legally bound to pay them 10 per cent of all earnings (before tax) from that contract until it ended.

At the time, this didn't seem like such a big deal as the contract appeared well negotiated. They had taken full responsibility for arranging my finances, which was something that I desperately needed guidance with. But I look back now and it's my firm opinion that IMG never really fully guided me, and I didn't escape the mess this contract created until a decade later.

The deal IMG negotiated with the team meant that I was in for the long run with Cofidis. Yes, there were problems, but I was convinced that François Migraine wanted things to move on and the team to develop. Cofidis wanted me and needed me and I was quite sure that one day the team would be built around me.

There were negatives. I didn't like the fact that the team was tarnished, but I clung so strongly to my beliefs and ideals that I felt incorruptible. David Moncoutie and I had already survived the previous three years without doping. We didn't plan to change that. Doping was around us, but it was never forced on us.

The riders who doped were fully responsible for their actions, sourcing their own products and paying their own coaches and doctors. The team did not play an active part in doping, but it facilitated it by never asking questions or being proactively against it in any way.

There's no doubt that it was a demoralising environment for clean riders and it bred contempt towards the senior figures within the team, but at the same time we didn't know any different. As far as we were concerned, that was how the world of pro cycling operated.

I had grown used to getting a pat on the back and being told after a good result: 'Well done, David – you should be happy, you're the first clean rider.'

Initially, I was proud of that, but it was becoming increasingly frustrating. I wanted to win clean, and I knew that, if everything went to plan, it was possible.

I hoped it would be possible at the Tour that year.

Winning at the Tour would be the ultimate 'fuck you' to the dopers and the fulfilment of a dream that had sustained me through thick and thin.

Bernard Quilfen's hangdog features wore a frown.

'What's going on, David? You're not yourself – I know you're a much better rider than this.'

I sat on the edge of my bed, listening to my *directeur sportif* pull me apart. 'You've only got two months until the Tour – there's no room now for relaxing. You can't go to the Tour if you carry on like this . . .'

We were at the Tour of Romandie in Switzerland and Quilfen had decided to give me a talking to. It was a good call – I needed it.

I tried to explain.

'I've lost control a bit, Bernard,' I said. 'I wanted to take it easy for the first part of the year so that I could peak for the Tour. Maybe I relaxed a bit too much. But two months is a long time for me – I can change completely in that time. I just need the pressure to do it.'

Quilfen shook his head. 'Well, you've made it harder for yourself now. You need to be going better by the Dauphiné Libéré or we'll have to rethink things.'

The Dauphiné Libéré, an Alpine stage race in early June, was a dry run for the Tour.

I knew he was right. 'Bernard, I'll be good at the Dauphiné. But I'm not going to be good here, I can tell you that right now. Look – I know what I have to do. If I'm not better at the Dauphiné, then I don't deserve to go to the Tour.'

Sure enough, I rode like shit at the Tour of Romandie, but a switch had been flicked in my head. I suffered through the five-day race, not feeling self-pity, but seeing it as the first step in my grand plan. I started dieting properly and, when I got back to Biarritz, I kept training hard and looking after myself.

A month later, at the Dauphiné, I was chomping at the bit. I had lost weight and was back in the race. I was focused solely on what I had to do in order to be at my best for the start of the Tour.

That included paying attention to the details, like the set-up on my time trial bike. The custom handlebars I'd been promised for almost two years were obviously never going to get made, so I found myself some old cow-horn style bars and some clip-on tri-bars and built them to the specification I wanted. I badgered our clothing sponsor incessantly to make my skinsuit tighter and better fitted. I got maps of the 2000 Tour's first stage, a 16-kilometre time trial, and studied them, memorising it all. I was determined that by the time the opening day came, I would have ridden the time trial a dozen times in my head.

After riding well at the Dauphiné, I headed back to Biarritz, living like a monk, my only treat being an evening walk and an ice cream. There was just one last date before the Tour, the Route du Sud, a small race in the Pyrenees.

The night before I left for the race, Jeremy Hunt arrived in Biarritz. Jez and I were planning to drive over to the start of the Route du Sud together. I hadn't seen him in a while so we went out for dinner and, for the first time since that April, I had a drink – and then I had another. The next thing we knew it was five in the morning and we were stumbling back to my apartment.

There was no air-con in Jez's battered VW Golf and we sweated our way across the Midi to some backwater provincial town north of Toulouse. We barely talked during the 4-hour drive, as each blamed the other for the excesses of the night before. Jez dropped me off at the team hotel and we went our separate ways.

Two days later, in the race's 20-kilometre time trial, I was flying. I caught the rider who'd started a minute ahead of me, Dutch pro Leon van Bon, but then I lost concentration and he came right by me again. It woke me up and I switched on the power once more, winning by almost a minute. I even eliminated a rider – my Biarritz booze buddy, Jez. He didn't think that was very cool.

It hadn't been a stellar field in the Route du Sud, but that didn't take away from how strong I'd felt and how fast I'd gone. I'd responded to Quilfen's scare tactics. Now I was ready for the Tour.

My mobile rang.

'Hello, darling!' I immediately recognised the familiar cheery tones of my mum . . .

'Mum – how's the drive going? Not too windy is it?'

'No wind at the moment, but then we're not moving,' she told me. 'We're a little stuck – I'm not sure if we'll be making it down there this afternoon . . .'

The thought of my mum missing my debut ride in the Tour de France certainly took my mind off my nerves.

She was coming over to France with my friend Harry Gibbings in an open-top sports car.

Caterham had lent Harry one of their 7s, and he was driving mum the hundreds of miles from England through France to Poitiers. I had an uneasy feeling it would end in tears.

Harry decided they should visit his uncle's house in Surrey on the way – God knows why as they were already on a tight schedule. They pulled up to the house just as a car was leaving through the gates. Harry didn't recognise the occupants, but gave them a cheery wave and drove in.

It was only after umpteen rings of the doorbell that he realised nobody was at home. They clambered back into the Caterham and drove towards what he assumed were automatic gates. When they steadfastly refused to open, he realised he was in a fix. The gates, it seemed, did not open for any Tom, Dick – or Harry.

Harry couldn't get hold of his uncle or anybody else that could help, so all they could do was sit and wait. He tried to be cool about it when we spoke on the phone, but I could tell he was concerned. Eventually, Harry and my mum got out, but I spent the next few hours absolutely convinced they'd never arrive at the Tour in time. But maybe it was a good distraction in that it did stop me worrying about the race.

The 2000 Tour de France started in the Futuroscope theme park, outside Poitiers. The Tour was much bigger than I had ever dreamed it would be. I had grown used to the professional racing scene and had ridden some of its biggest races – the Belgian Classics, the Dauphiné Libéré, Paris–Nice, the Tour de Suisse – but nothing prepared me for the Tour.

The sheer scale of it was overwhelming. There were thousands of people working on it, hundreds of cars, dozens of motorbikes, numerous helicopters – even planes – and all of that was just within the race organisation. Then there was the mainstream sports media: for most of them, it was the only cycling event they covered all year. Suddenly, the British press, TV and radio journalists all wanted to speak to me. I had been doing interviews during the build-up with newspapers that had never shown an interest in me before. For the first time, I was doing TV interviews in English and this was much more fun than doing them in French. This interest was boosted by the fact that I was the only British rider taking part, as I would be for the next few years.

There was also a documentary crew filming me. Five 'players' from the race would be followed: the director of the Tour, a retired champion, a super fan, the start and finish line commentator, and a neophyte – or debutant – in other words, me. It was as if I'd stepped into some mad alternative cycling world. Everything I'd done before seemed like it had been a rehearsal for the Tour. I was finally in the Big Show.

The course for the opening time trial suited me well. It was not pan flat, but it wasn't too hard either. There were only four corners, and none of those were very tricky. The physical demands of it bore an uncanny resemblance to the High Wycombe CC '10' time trial I'd raced on Tuesday nights during my school holidays.

I was still badgering the team, in an effort to get all my kit just right. My bike was as good as I could get it with the equipment available and my aerodynamic skinsuit was supposed to arrive that day – but as usual it came at the last possible moment. I wanted it to be tighter and completely wrinkle-free, but it was shit, barely any different from the standard one I had.

I flipped. I'd been asking for it over and over for months and was promised repeatedly that I'd have it in time. When that didn't happen, it caused a near nuclear reaction in me. But my tantrum had an impact, and the mother of one of our office staff spent that night stitching up the suit so that it was absolutely skin tight. I was euphoric because I knew that the aerodynamic advantage it gave me could prove to be critical.

The riders set off one by one and the director of the Tour, Jean-Marie Leblanc, who could have followed any one of the leading stars, chose to follow me. Tony Doyle, the former professional rider, was there working with Nike and managed to wangle a place for my mum in Jean-Marie's car.

It was my mum's first visit to the Tour de France but she found herself in the best seat in the house, sitting alongside the race director following her son making his debut in the race he'd dreamed about for so long. If it was all a bit weird for me, then it was much weirder for my mum.

I felt incredibly good during the time trial, relaxed and confident. I avoided getting carried away in the opening kilometres, kept calm and caught the three riders who had set off in front of me, overtaking the third with a couple of kilometres to go. That is one of the benefits of not going with the final wave of riders, usually the stars, among whom there are no catches to be had. Overtaking the third man, just as I was at my limit, was enough to give me the boost I needed for those final very painful minutes.

I rode the last kilometre very fast, at over 60 kilometres an hour, thankful for the fitted skinsuit, modified bars and my ability to pedal faster than most. I knew I was going to get the best time and when I crossed the line I was 11 seconds faster than Laurent Jalabert. It took me a few minutes to recover and return to the team bus where we all watched the last riders come over the line. They were all slower than me and it became clear that the only person who could better my time was Lance Armstrong.

I couldn't watch as Lance came around the last corner and flew into the final kilometre, our times neck and neck. I had convinced myself that I wasn't going to win in an attempt to avoid disappointment, and when the massive cheer rose up around me I couldn't really grasp what was happening.

Everybody started hugging me and before I knew it, I was crying. Bondue was hugging me too, tears in his eyes, telling me how he'd always known I'd do it. Then I was pushed out of the bus into the throng of fans, photographers, TV cameras, and race officials, who acted as bodyguards as I was shepherded through the crowds. As I walked to the podium, trying to pull myself together, I realised that the Tour was now revolving around me, the new *maillot jaune*.

I wasn't prepared for winning. I hadn't visualised beyond the finish line, so stepping up onto the podium and putting on the yellow jersey was an overpowering experience. I was a blubbering mess. But it was good fun being the main man at the Tour and

I quickly grew to like it. I felt special, and the nice thing was that everybody seemed genuinely pleased for me. I was floating on a cloud, I was so happy.

Three hours after the race ended, after the presentation protocols, doping controls, press conference and TV interviews were all over, I arrived back at the hotel. The mechanics were all still on a high and I went around the team and saw as many of the riders and staff as I could. Even though it was late, I was still wearing the yellow jersey. I kept it on for the rest of that night.

11

LA VIE EN JAUNE

When I woke up the next day, the first thing I saw was the yellow jersey hanging over a chair in my hotel room. I couldn't wait to start racing in it, to be the *maillot jaune* at the Tour de France.

I was told to wait in the bus until as late as possible before signing on at the start village, but of course I couldn't do that. I wasn't really prepared for the chaos that surrounded me when I finally did emerge.

I was mobbed. Everybody was calling out, '*DAVEED! DAVEED!*' shaking my hand, taking a picture or stopping me for a chat and an autograph. I tried to satisfy as many demands as I could, although I realised that just wasn't possible or I'd never make it to the start line. In the space of 24 hours everything had changed; I was no longer a young *espoir*, I was now *le maillot jaune*.

Out on the road, racing with my peers, I was able to appreciate the value of the yellow jersey. Almost all the big hitters came and congratulated me. Their words were heartfelt and they seemed genuinely pleased for me. Lance spent a little time joshing with me but was genuinely happy that I'd won, which made me proud.

The notable exception was Marco Pantani, winner of the Tour in 1998. Not once did he congratulate me, which I found a bit strange. It was almost obligatory for a past Tour champion to congratulate the young pretender. It didn't change my view of him as a rider, but his cold attitude did separate him from the others.

Riding in yellow totally changed my experience of moving through the peloton – a living organism, in constant flux – a breathing, kinetic, noisy, colourful being. In order to hold your position, particularly in the front half, you must be constantly moving up. The moment you relax you'll find yourself losing position, simply because when there are two hundred elite cyclists racing along a road the majority want to be at the front. If you're not at the front, you're not in the race.

The more important the race is, the more nervous the riders are, and the more time they want to spend at the front. This puts the peloton in an aggressive mood which means mistakes are made and crashes caused. If you're at the back of the Tour peloton, there are two hundred chances of crashes in front of you; the closer you are to the front, with an empty road ahead of you, the less chance there is of crashing because there are fewer riders in front of you and so less chance of being brought down.

I had been told that the Tour peloton was one of the most stressful in cycling, a bastard to hold position in, very fast and dangerous. So I was prepared for the worst. But I hadn't realised how different it would be when I was wearing the leader's jersey. Normally there is no chance of somebody letting you into a gap in order to move up the peloton, but in the *maillot jaune* this is not the case. I found myself being let into every single gap and riders happily moved out of the way for me. Wearing the yellow jersey gave me an 'access all areas' VIP pass, a *laissez-passer* through the peloton. And this wasn't about me being respected – it was the *maillot jaune* that was respected. I wasn't wearing the yellow jersey; the yellow jersey was *gracing me.*

I was in yellow for three days. There was one near miss when I crashed in the final couple of kilometres of the stage coming into Nantes, but I was up so fast that I was back in the safety of the peloton in no time. I finally lost the lead in the 70-kilometre team time trial on the third day. We were never renowned as a team time trial squad, but our performance was better than normal and we defended the jersey with pride.

Those three days had made me the darling boy of France – one local paper christening me '*Le Dandy*' – and the public had warmed to the young Scot leading the big French team and wearing the yellow jersey. It helped that by this time I spoke French and also lived in France. The French like nothing more than a foreigner who has chosen their great *république* as their home, and being Scottish helped as well, as the auld alliance lived strong in French memories. I learned that much during the Tour.

'*Vous êtes Ecosse?! Ah oui! Ça, c'est complétement different! Bof, on aime pas trop les Anglais non plus!*'

'*You're Scottish?! Ah, yes. That's completely different. [The French] We're not too keen on the English either!*'

The race continued, moving inexorably towards an Armstrong victory. One day, a while after the yellow jersey had moved on to another rider, I was sitting at the back chatting to Stuart O'Grady and a couple of the other boys. The US Postal team was coming up the right side of the peloton, bringing Lance back up through the riders. As Lance came by he looked at me and called to his team to wait.

I turned to Stuey: 'Here we go,' I said.

'*Dave! Come here!*' Lance gestured for me to move across to him so he could speak to me.

I pedalled over to his side. 'What's going on, Lance?' I said innocently.

'Dave, what are you doing back here?' he asked. I may not have been on the same team as Lance, but I think he still considered me to be his little protégé in some ways.

'Chatting to the boys, just a bit of a calm moment,' I said.

'Dave, this is the Tour de France,' he said sternly.

'I know, Lance, I know.'

'Well, Dave, at the Tour de France *you have no friends*. Ride at the front.' It wasn't a suggestion. It was an instruction.

'Yeah – er, okay, Lance.' I looked back at Stuey and shrugged. 'See you later.'

It was a classic Armstrong moment, capturing both how expert he had become at always being at the front and exactly how he saw the Tour de France. It was war for him.

I wanted to finish my debut Tour but I had no intentions of just taking it easy in order to get to Paris. I wanted to go as hard as I could, for as long as I could. In the first mountain stages, in the Pyrenees, I buried myself and realised just how much better I needed to be if I wanted to stand any chance of racing for the overall standings at the Tour. It was a rude awakening, although a couple of days later I was fourth on a stage finishing near Toulouse, which lifted my morale again.

By the time we got to Mont Ventoux I knew a lot more about Tommy Simpson and had a feeling there would be a lot of British fans on the mountain. I wanted to do my best, but I crashed early in the stage, coming down on a spinning back wheel, with my neck taking the full impact. It hurt like hell, left a big gash on my neck and popped my collarbone. I grovelled up the Ventoux and was embarrassed to be right at the back of the race. So many people knew my name now and were cheering for me, something I'd never experienced before. I wanted to tell every fan that I'd crashed and was in pain and that's why I wasn't nearer the front.

The final week included three stages of around 250 kilometres and the first of these was a mountain stage to Briançon. It was a mammoth day and we ended up racing for over 8 hours. The route was nonsensical and went against all the talk of changing cycling and of eradicating doping. I was fuming with the race organisers and didn't hide my feelings, especially when we got stuck in a traffic jam on the way to the hotel.

'It was bullshit,' I told journalists. 'They want to clean up cycling and then after two weeks of racing they put on a stage like that. They must think we're robots. Jean-Marie Leblanc needs a slap.'

Most riders – let alone Tour rookies – might have thought twice before suggesting that the Tour director 'needed a slap' . . . not me.

But Jean-Marie and I made up the next day; I regretted my outspokenness while he was very honourable and apologised for the length of the stage. I was beginning to realise that people – or at least the media – listened when I talked. Unfortunately I hadn't yet realised that this meant I had to think before I spoke.

```
it's millar time...
   @ les bains


stage 22 - sunday 23rd july 11:30 - 5:00am



       7, rue du bourg-l'abbe - 75003 - paris
          vip and guest list entrance only
                dress - chic & cool
```

My sister France had been amazingly supportive prior to the Tour, and she became even more so after I won on the first day. She had become the go-to person when it came to 'David Millar', taking care of everything, but then she'd always looked after her older brother. She had become much more professional about her role now that I was in demand. We were also having fun though, and we wanted to finish the Tour with a bang, so we – well, she – set about organising a party for the final night in Paris.

Fran managed to get one of the most famous nightclubs in Paris, Les Bains Douches, to open especially for us on the Sunday evening after the finish on the Champs Elysées. She had invitations printed up with 'It's Millar Time – Stage 22' emblazoned on them. I intended to hand them out to everybody on the Champs Elysées stage. I even got Jean-Marie Leblanc to take a handful so that he could give them to the podium girls; there was one in particular that I had a crush on, although unfortunately it was unrequited. Fran was only 21 and I was 23 – yet we were planning on ruling Paris for a night. Rather than being daunted by the Tour we already felt it was part of our lives.

I was tired during the last week, but such was the excitement about making it to Paris that I couldn't sleep. I was like a 6-year-old

kid, waiting for Christmas. All my family and friends were coming to the finish, my best friends from Hong Kong had come over, my mum and dad were both going to be there, albeit on opposite sides of the road, and lots of others had also made the trip. It was brilliant having my family and friends there to share it.

Yet I wasn't prepared for my feelings when I arrived on the Champs Elysées. Being part of the Tour peloton and racing up towards the Arc de Triomphe was an overwhelming moment. Every rider who makes it to the Champs Elysées has had a different experience getting there, but I think we all feel the same when we hit those cobblestones and take in the magnificence of that setting.

I knew where my family and friends would be standing on the Champs Elysées and I told them I would get into the standard breakaway so they could see me. Somehow, I did manage to get into the obligatory kamikaze attack and every time I passed the 'It's

Millar Time' group I clenched a fist to my heart and saluted them. It was a bit cocky, I suppose, but I didn't know any better, and it was all done in celebration.

I really didn't want it to finish. The team organised cocktails in the penthouse bar of the Concorde Lafayette, and by the time I got there I was already a bit drunk. Harry gave me a beautiful yellow-faced watch and a bottle of whisky that, a decade later, I still have.

We had dinner in the restaurant of Les Bains Douches. Harry and I were last out of the club, immersed in deep, drunken thoughts while the cleaners brushed up around us. We stumbled out into the dawn light of a beautiful Parisian morning. I think I slept for about 3 hours before heading to a lunch rendezvous at the Trocadéro.

Lunch was even better than the night before, but it had to end some time and, sadly, Monday drew to a close and everybody returned to their lives and jobs. I wasn't looking forward to the journey back to my flat in Biarritz. The bubble that I'd been living in for a month had burst and I was on my own again.

Arriving back at the apartment was a big comedown. I dragged in my bike bag and suitcase and dumped them in the small entrance hall. In the kitchen an empty bowl, with the remnants of the cereal I'd wolfed down in my last-minute rush out of the door, a month earlier, lay in the sink.

I went through to the living room, turned on the TV and collapsed on the sofa. I sat there blankly, watching French television. Everything had changed, yet nothing had changed. It was a rude awakening. I'd just made my boyhood dream a reality, yet I felt lonelier than ever.

12

THE FALL OF DUNKIRK

There was a cure to my loneliness, which was to leave the apartment. As soon as I went out and about in Biarritz, I discovered I had a lot more friends than I'd had a month earlier. People came up and congratulated me.

I was no longer simply, '*Daveed, le coureur.*' I was now '*Daveed, maillot jaune du Tour de France.*'

Biarritz felt like home. I was getting to know so many people that I'd have never met before. If I was out at night, I no longer had to queue to get into restaurants, clubs or bars. I was being called to the front and given VIP treatment. I loved it. I didn't really see any problem – I could see what was going on and knew that it was predominantly bullshit, but I still enjoyed it.

I had many nocturnal friends – the owners and staff of cafés, restaurants, bars and nightclubs – people with whom I was great pals after nine at night, but never saw during the day. Some of them became best friends. I even gave Jean-Claude, the owner of Biarritz institution Le Caveau (a gay club that in winter had the most amazing Sunday night cabaret shows), a yellow jersey on his 50th birthday. This was the same nightclub that, only a few weeks earlier, had refused me entry.

Even so, I was still uneasy in my own company and spent as little time as possible in my apartment. I was beginning to think that maybe this was just the way of life for a pro cyclist, or at least for me. I couldn't balance my life – it was split, separated. I was either the obsessive professional cyclist or a Biarritz social butterfly. When I was the social butterfly, I'd have no contact with anybody in the cycling world. I would disappear and be impossible to get hold of.

The reverse would be true when I went back to obsessive pro cyclist mode; there was no crossover. The only person who could get hold of me in both worlds was my sister.

David Millar a offert son maillot jaune à Didier Borotra qui s'est empressé d'enfiler la mythique tunique.
(Atomic photo)

In the aftermath of the Tour, thinking that I should rest so I'd be good for the Sydney Olympics that September, I had turned down several criteriums – lucrative exhibition races in Holland, Belgium and France – in August. Despite that, I didn't see myself as an Olympian. This, remember, was long before British cyclists dominated at the Olympic Games. To me, the only thing that really mattered was the Tour – the Olympics were simply a footnote.

Nonetheless, I knuckled down and started to ready myself for Sydney, even though it held no real goal for me. I knew deep down that the course didn't suit me, as I'd stand little chance against the favourites in time trials over 30 kilometres. I didn't possess the power needed to compete against the older guys in those longer time trials. I was more excited about the prospect of going to Sydney, meeting other athletes and hanging out with the British team.

I trained hard, despite my pessimism about my chances of winning a medal, but I lacked focus and this became apparent once I'd arrived in Australia. I was sent to the holding camp on the Gold Coast, 1000 kilometres north of Sydney, but was devastated to find that there was only a skeleton team of athletes and staff there. Everybody else had already left for Sydney. The time trial was scheduled for the penultimate day of the Games and I was to be held for as long as possible in the holding camp so I could train on quieter roads, far from the chaos of Sydney. I was crestfallen.

There were other truths to face up to. I'd become a regular user of sleeping pills, something that had begun in the last week of the Tour when I was in a similarly excited state of mind and couldn't sleep. I was forced to go to the British team doctor for more pills, and it was only then that I realised how removed my world was from that of other athletes.

At Cofidis, I was seen as a 'good' boy, somebody the team doctors trusted implicitly, but now, talking to the Team GB doctor, I felt that he didn't trust me, or my habits. In a way he was right not to – I was a Tour de France rider, and we were all tarnished by our sport's reputation. Even though I was clean, I was a walking example of how troubled and confused my sport had become.

I took it for granted that I could just ask for sleeping pills and that I could be trusted to use them correctly. I'd learned my lesson the year before with my roof-jumping incident and now used them only to help me sleep. But it wasn't easy to get what I wanted from this doctor and it annoyed me. Because I didn't dope, I believed I had the right to do anything that *wasn't* doping – that was how the Cofidis team doctors treated me, and also how I'd learned to survive in recent years. In the build-up to the Tour I had even learned to inject myself so that I could carry on with *récupération* at home, in order to recover properly and train harder. I was not a doper, I told myself – I just injected myself to recover and needed pills to sleep.

I knew it wasn't good to need sleeping pills, but my sleeping patterns had become so chronically bad that at times I relied on them completely. I had even taken Rohypnol on occasion, when my insomnia had become unbearable and untreatable with Stilnox. Sitting down with the Team GB doctor, I realised this wasn't normal behaviour. Yet such was the culture of my pro team that it was seen as completely normal – pills were even offered before I would ask for them. With Team GB, I felt like I'd entered a different world, a naive and uneducated one, far from the harsh realities of the European professional scene. It woke me up: I was clean but already corrupted by the world I lived in.

At the same time, I was wobbling, melting down, becoming a problem. I demanded to be sent to Sydney as I was going stir crazy in Brisbane. I argued that I'd be better off staying in the Olympic Village. It was a bad idea. When I got to the Village, I was even more manic. I was too excited and barely touched my bike. I chose not to ride in the road race as I had only been training for the time trial, which was three days later. I watched the road race, then that evening, when I couldn't sleep, left the Village and went into the centre of Sydney to the after party. Obviously everybody knew that I shouldn't have been there, but nobody said anything. Looking back, I think it was quite obvious that I was a little unhinged. The time trial came and went and I got fourteenth place – not exactly what was expected, but precisely what I merited. Afterwards, I started a 48-hour bender.

The next day, I met my mum, dad and some friends who had come to watch the Games, and had a drink with them. At one point, my dad took me outside to speak to me in private, telling me he was worried about me. I didn't really understand what he was worried about. I recognised I was in a manic state, but I wasn't going to tell him about the realities of the world I was living in.

The bender continued right through to the closing ceremony. I borrowed a loudspeaker and ended up on the Australian team bus to their post-Olympic party. At that time, I had more friends on the Aussie team than I did on the GB team, so being with them made sense. I didn't sleep that night and wandered back to the Village the next morning to find the British team buses waiting and Jez Hunt and myself the only two athletes not on board. I ran and got my bags but Jez decided he didn't want to go back to the UK and didn't get on the bus.

The European pro cyclists had made a bit of a name for themselves.

*

When I got back to England, I shut myself away at my mum's house and didn't get out of bed for 24 hours. I didn't want to go back to Biarritz, and I didn't want to even look at my bike. I'd turned my phone off and intended to keep it that way for a while. I couldn't think about going to the World Road Championships, yet instead of telling the team, I just put my head in the sand and waited for them to find out through some other channel. I'd closed down. I'd pushed myself to breaking point and was now in a depressed mood, one that would become increasingly familiar in the coming months.

Dad was so worried about me that he flew over to the UK from Hong Kong. It was a bit of a wasted trip for him, because after a couple of days I started to feel better and couldn't really understand why I'd been so down in the first place. I didn't know why I was so manic-depressive and I convinced my dad that I was fine, as I didn't really know any better.

After more time in the UK, Biarritz and then Hong Kong, far away from the world of cycling, I headed off to Australia in November to keep a promise I'd made to Stuey O'Grady. I'd told him, at both the Tour and the Olympics, that I would head down to Australia for a criterium in November, in a place called Noosa Heads.

Noosa had become a legendary party week, incorporating one of the world's biggest triathlons and an hour-long circuit race in which the pros and local riders mixed it up. Unexpectedly, it was one of the most fun weeks of my life, as Stuey proved once again that he is in a different league when it comes to burning the candle at both ends.

Stuey is one of the greatest cyclists of his generation. His career to date spans five Olympics and he has achieved success in most of the biggest races in cycling. During all that time he has always been the same ball of kinetic energy: a moody bastard at times, but one of the funniest at others. He is one of my most loyal friends and we sealed our friendship in Noosa that week. We have been very close ever since, through the best and worst of times.

On the first night in Noosa, I met a girl called Shari. Within a week, we'd fallen for each other and become an item. Because of that, I stayed in Australia for two more blissful weeks. I had come to the conclusion that I needed somebody in my life and Shari seemed just perfect to me. Until then I had been too focused, lacking the energy for anybody else. Selfishness had worked to a point, but although I didn't see it at the time, my falling for Shari was directly linked to my increasing instability. Love is blind as they say – even when it's selfish.

It wasn't the perfect situation. Australia really did feel too far away from Europe, but all obstacles seemed surmountable. We started planning her first visit to Europe. It got me through the next couple of months of training. I rediscovered my drive and got down to business, putting my worries behind me.

I stayed in Biarritz on my own throughout Christmas, shutting down my social life and living like a hermit. To remind me that I had another life, I started sticking photos on my living room wall and, over time, this turned into a massive mural. I enjoyed my monastic existence, watching the transition in my body as training took me over. It was hard, but as soon as I started to get some physical condition and could feel progress being made, I loved riding my bike again. It was hugely gratifying to see the dieting and training have such quantifiable results as my weight dropped and my power increased.

Alain Bondue and I had bonded a lot since my success at the Tour the previous year. Until that point, I had been seen as 'difficult'. Unlike some of the other pros, I wasn't very scared of authority and had been questioning him since day one of my professional career. Also, Alain spoke English, which ensured that I'd always had a closer relationship with him than with anybody else on the team's staff.

We had history. We'd fallen out over his handling of Gaumont and Vandenbroucke and then when he'd sent me to a race on crutches, but I really liked Alain and saw him as one of the smarter guys in the sport. He had found me the place on my amateur team in France, he'd been there when I'd first met with Guimard and also when I'd signed my first pro contract. So our relationship was closer than that of most riders and their general managers.

At the brief December team get-together we'd had a late-night drinking session and put all our differences behind us. After that night and following my success in the Tour, I'd become his golden boy. It also meant that I was now the main man in the team: I started the 2001 season as leader of Cofidis – then the biggest team in France.

My monastic existence paid off that New Year. At the January training camp, I was on another level to everybody else and was able to ride away from the rest of the team. I would often get back to the hotel well ahead of the others. I wanted to be ahead of schedule with my training as Shari was arriving a few days later and I was sure that things would fall by the wayside during her visit.

We had a great time together, although by the time she headed back, there were the first seeds of discontent. Things weren't as perfect as they had been in Australia, even though my feelings for her were undiminished. But it was the first time I'd been in love and, as someone would later wisely point out, maybe I was more in love with being in love than with the object of my affections.

By the time of my first race, the Tour of the Mediterranean, I'd lost my training camp condition. I finished dead last on the first stage, but my strongest memory of the race is of a conversation David Moncoutie and I shared with l'Équipier.

'Moncout' and I were rooming together and one day l'Équipier was in our room chatting. He may have been an old school cyclist, with a different ethical stance to us, but he was also good fun and an asset to have out on the road during a race. He knew everybody in the peloton and was a brilliant road captain.

We were chatting away, when l'Équipier paused and then said: 'You two are incredible. You're never going to dope, are you?'

Moncout and I looked at each other.

'No,' we responded almost in unison. 'I don't think we are.'

L'Équipier seemed genuinely impressed, as if it was a stance he admired, but fundamentally couldn't understand.

He was from a hardcore world where doping was simply part of the game. He was a good guy who took care of the lesser riders and was universally liked, but he inhabited that parallel universe. Nobody within our team ever asked direct questions – doping wasn't even a point of discussion within the team. Clean or doped, the sport shrugged off all the accusations of malpractice; the *omertà* – the law of silence – was as strong as ever, and there was no stance taken on anti-doping within the team. There was nobody there to tell us that we were doing the right thing, that we should be strong and believe in ourselves.

In fact, there was no anti-doping support or leadership whatsoever. The UCI and the team bosses considered their job done because the riders had signed meaningless charters pledging not to dope. Meanwhile, the dopers carried on doing what they were doing, while the non-dopers raced alongside them.

Yes, there was the longitudinal blood testing and, by 2001, an EPO test that apparently worked. But the word on the street was that EPO was out of the body within three days, so the test served little purpose as EPO was used in training before races – when we weren't tested.

Cycling had cleaned up in some ways since 1998, but only the French had radically changed their mindset, and that was out of fear of the real consequences that now existed. An anti-doping law had been passed making it a criminal offence to dope in France. Arrest was a real possibility if you failed a doping control or were in possession of banned products.

There were only two French teams, those managed by Roger Legeay and Marc Madiot, that had managed to shift their mentality right across even their international riders, and those were the same two teams that had acted immediately after the Festina affair. Cofidis lived in a grey area; the team had some clean riders, and some doped riders.

After Guimard's departure, Cofidis had lacked a proper boss, and Bondue and François Migraine effectively ran the team. Migraine was a lovely man, but he was an accountant at heart and he only saw the riders as names that accumulated points, and races as events that offered points. He was a fan, and he was playing the ultimate game of manager.

Bondue, the firewall between Migraine and the team, was too concerned about maintaining the influence he had. On the ground we had no real direction or leadership. We were made up of two types of rider, *fonctionnaires* who were simply looking to maintain their contract and renew, and mercenaries, foreign riders, signed to score UCI points, make their bonuses and guarantee a future bigger contract. At Cofidis, almost all riders had a bonus system of some sort based on UCI points. We were all driven to look after ourselves.

We were held 100 per cent responsible for our actions. This was made clear on many occasions and was in keeping with how the sport as a whole treated the riders. If a rider was caught doping, then the buck stopped immediately with him. He would be fired and disowned as the management of the team expressed shock, disgust and disappointment, while his teammates would be surprised and appalled that he'd cheated them. The team held zero liability, just like the UCI and the major race organisers.

Although cycling may have appeared cleaner from the outside, it was essentially as corrupt as ever. Nothing was being done to help the non-dopers, to encourage or support them. Even the clean riders like myself and Moncout knew how easy it was to cheat the tests.

You would take some time away from racing, travel to Spain – or maybe Italy where it was easy to obtain EPO – and turn off your phone to avoid an out-of-competition anti-doping control. You'd dope for the necessary period of time and then come back to racing, having given your body enough time to rid itself of the traceable banned drugs.

You didn't even need a doctor to do this. There were stories of EPO being sold over the counter in Spain and of riders, without guidance, just injecting themselves, basing their techniques on hearsay and tips from others. It was all still a mess.

When I told l'Équipier, with conviction, that I wasn't going to dope, I surprised myself a little. Perhaps a part of me wasn't sure any more. Did I really still believe that I could hold out?

I avoided thinking about it too much. Everybody knew that Moncout and I were talented, and we were also known for being strong-willed and for doing things our way. It had taken us both a long time to embrace injectable recovery and we were both quite fragile, yet we had survived our first four years as professionals. The only encouragement we got on a regular basis was: '*Putain, vous êtes des premiers propres, ça c'est sur!*'

'*Shit – you're the first clean riders to finish, that's for sure!*'

We stopped enjoying that after about the fourth time we heard it.

Moncoutie came from a very provincial area of France. His parents worked for the post office. That was probably where he'd have spent his working life if he hadn't been so amazingly gifted on a bicycle, particularly when it came to climbing mountains.

He has a tousle of dark hair and a wide smile, and lives in his own world. Material possessions, and fashion, seemed to have no hold on him whatsoever. He wore the same team-issue trainers for about three years. His great passion was cartography. Quizzed on most areas of France, he could cite road numbers, distances and place names.

In many ways, David was a bit of a hippy. He renounced chemical drugs and ensured that everything he took was homeopathic. If he did get ill, which he did quite often, he would be urged to take antibiotics. He'd take one pill from the course and pronounce: '*Ça suffit*' ('*That's enough*'). This, of course, is exactly what *not to do* with antibiotics, but there was no telling him. He was infuriating.

Moncoutie's racing style was to sit right at the back of the peloton, waiting for the road to climb. Once the field thinned out, he was left at the front with the strongest. Physically, he was one of the best climbers in the world, and therefore something of a loner. That was where we differed. I had lots of ambition, an absurdly loyal sense of duty towards my teammates – and I'd always finish a course of antibiotics.

Perhaps it was because we were both talented and stubborn that we'd escaped doping. We were young and we were able to survive and, on occasions, excel. We'd still not even reached our physical peaks, dope or no dope; we were considered works in progress.

Yet what it eventually came down to was the environment you were in and the personality you had. For some, doping was almost inevitable, while for others it was simply never going to happen, even if every single rider around them doped.

When l'Équipier asked us the question, Moncoutie and I seemed untouchable. For Moncoutie, it was unthinkable. Yet deep down I was beginning to wonder why I still felt so strongly about *not* doping.

Shari's next visit came during the Circuit de La Sarthe, a small, but prestigious four-day stage race in France. The time trial fell on the afternoon of the penultimate day. I won it convincingly and took the race leader's jersey. Shari arrived that night, so for once I had somebody to give the presentation flowers to.

Her visit coincided with the hardest stage of the race, which included a demanding finishing circuit. Lance, although not in contention for the race overall, had made it known that it was a stage he wanted to win. Contrary to being worried about how tough this was likely to make the stage, I was excited.

But there was a problem – our team wasn't strong enough to control the peloton during the race. Because of this we had no option but to fall back on one of the conventions of the pro scene –

we struck a deal with another team to help us keep it together until the finale, when I'd look after myself. Our team *directeur* looked for a team that had no chance of winning and that wouldn't mind making a bit of cash in hand.

As it turned out, there was a Polish team racing there that was perfect for the job. This was, and remains, a fairly standard practice in professional cycling, and ad hoc alliances – sometimes as a favour, sometimes paid for – have long been commonplace. We relied on a financially induced alliance that day.

As I'd expected, all hell broke loose on the finishing circuit. The first time up the steep climb, I was at the front and scanned the crowd to see if Shari was there, cheering me on. I couldn't see her anywhere and so went back to concentrating on the job in hand. I followed the attacks going off the front, but I was, as expected, isolated and had no teammates to protect my position.

Lance was using his team to make the race as hard as possible and whittle the lead group down before he made his decisive move. With two laps to go the attacks started going again, and as I saw everybody suffering, I realised that I was on a different level. One rider was a hundred or so metres ahead – deciding offence was the best form of defence in this precarious tactical situation I put my head down and sprinted across the gap, leaving the others behind.

The lone escapee was Nicolas Vogondy, a rider I knew quite well as we'd turned pro in the same year. As I reached his shoulder, I told him: '*Nico – on y va.*'

Lance had his team chasing hard behind us, but we kept putting time into them. With a couple of kilometres to go, Nico asked if I was going to let him take the stage, a done thing if you're in the race leader's jersey. But this was the last stage and I wanted to win. I wanted Shari to see me cross the line with my arms in the air, triumphant.

I won the sprint from Vogondy, taking the stage and the overall victory. After the finish, I rolled back to the team bus, amid much hand-shaking and back-slapping, proud as hell of a big win. More than anything I wanted to see Shari, but I still couldn't find her.

I assumed she was somewhere in the finish area and asked the *soigneur.*

'Shari?' He shrugged as he wiped the dirt from my face. 'She's gone for a look around the town.'

I was devastated. I tried to tell myself that it didn't matter, that it was cool she wasn't interested in my racing, that I had no right to expect her to hang around at the finish line, but I was hurt.

After the podium presentation, I showered at a friend's house and that was when I realised how upset I really was. I just stood in the shower, letting the water wash over me. Finally, we got in the car and began driving down to Biarritz. Pissed off and confused, I barely said a word the whole way.

Harry was waiting in Biarritz and we partied for most of the weekend, finally grinding to a halt late on Sunday night. On the Monday, I flew out to compete in Paris–Camembert, a one-day race in northern France, but I didn't get to the hotel until late that evening. At the start of the race I felt terrible, but as it went on I got better and better.

Once again there was a hard finishing circuit, and before long there were only about twenty riders left. Moncoutie and I started attacking one after the other, taking it in turns to exhaust them. I kept attacking, then getting caught and dropped, then chasing back and attacking once more. My last chase back came with about 5 kilometres to go, but Frenchman Laurent Brochard was already clear and heading for victory. The rest of us were racing for second.

I looked around the group, picked Scott Sunderland as the fastest guy and glued myself to his back wheel. It turned out to be a good call. Scott was the fastest, and gave me such a good lead out that I came around him in the sprint and took second. I won a ton of Camembert cheese and a shitload of admiration from Harry.

By the Tour of Picardie, two weeks later, Shari had returned to Australia. We were having problems again, and I was on the phone arguing with her even before the start of the first stage. I was so angry when I got to the start that I was first to attack on a long, flat and windy stage – hardly the best tactic, yet my anger made it work.

I was off the front of the bunch all day with different moves and finally finished third on the stage. Never before had I raced in an angry mood and I couldn't believe how powerful it was. Now I understood why Lance used anger so effectively and why he hated the people he had to beat at the Tour. But I'm not very good at being angry – it wasn't something that I was able to tap into at will.

More and more, I was proving myself as the leader of the team. I was a presence in all the races I started, but I was getting so wrapped up in what I was doing, and the team had become so dependent on me scoring points, that I hadn't thought about taking it easy and peaking for the Tour.

I was going to every race and slaughtering myself. I needed somebody to tell me to take it easy, to tell me when to back off. After the Tour of Picardie, I rested for a few days, and then planned a big training block before my final pre-Tour de France racing programme.

That training block was horrible. I did three 6-hour days but felt rotten and had no idea how, only a couple of weeks earlier, I'd been so strong. But, convinced I'd rested enough, I kept on training.

My only goal in my next race, the Bicicleta Vasca stage race, was to win the time trial. Once again, Lance was there and he was aiming for the time trial as well. I wasn't too confident as I'd suffered in the previous day's mountain stage, yet I won, beating him into second place. I seemed to be the only person surprised by this result and it was clear that I was no longer the young hopeful. Results were expected of me now – surprises were a thing of the past.

The classic Tour de France preparation race, the Dauphiné Libéré, in the mountainous south-east of France, came next. Although I'd felt terrible in training since finishing the Bicicleta Vasca a week earlier, I hoped it was simply a bad patch that I'd push through. The first indications at Dauphiné were that this was the case. After three days, there was a stage that climbed the less famous northern side of Mont Ventoux. I was surprised to find myself only a few hundred metres behind the front few riders as we went over the summit.

Christophe Moreau and I were riding together and we attacked the descent like complete lunatics, catching up with the front group well before we got to the bottom of the mountain. On the road to the finish, more riders came together, but I won the sprint for third on the stage, which made me a contender. The next day's stage was a 50-kilometre flat time trial. It was assumed that I'd win and take the leader's jersey.

Sure enough, I took the leader's jersey, but I was beaten into second place by Jonathan Vaughters, an American rider. Jonathan was only a couple of seconds in front of me, while the eventual GC winner Christophe Moreau was in fourth place, almost a minute further behind. I was so tired on finishing that I wanted to go to sleep (in hindsight, not a good sign), but my result on the Ventoux and in the time trial had made me the man to beat for the general classification. It appeared I was coming of age.

Just 24 hours later, those illusions were shattered. Drained and completely empty, I was one of the first to drop behind on the day's final climb. It was humiliating, as I had almost the entire Cofidis team riding on the front of the peloton, yet I could not even stay with the bunch.

I tried to act unbothered as the race convoy passed me, although I didn't really understand what was going on. A few kilometres further, I was immensely relieved to see a similarly wrecked Jonathan Vaughters crawling up the road ahead of me. Obviously we'd gone a little deeper than most in the previous day's time trial and failed to recover.

Two days later, unable to continue and totally exhausted, I quit the race. Yet instead of being rested in an attempt to recover for the looming Tour de France, it was decided that it would be better if I kept racing. So, five days later, I was sent to the Route du Sud. I didn't finish, getting unceremoniously dropped on the final mountain stage in what was my fifty-eighth day of racing since February.

I was wrecked and needed total rest, but I knew I stood little chance of recovering for the Tour. All I could do was rest up and gamble that I'd freshen up enough to come good for the Tour prologue.

The Tour's Grand Départ was in Dunkirk, home ground for Cofidis, as their company headquarters was in nearby Lille. All the expectations were of me repeating my success of the previous year. Deep down, I knew I just didn't have the condition. I was nervous and lacking confidence and I hadn't felt good in training for weeks. I couldn't have been further from the mental state I'd been in a year before. I wasn't ready, and yet I was pretending to everybody I was.

Shari had arrived from Australia and, in an attempt to keep me calmer and more relaxed, she came up to Lille with me. This backfired as I became even more stressed, thinking I had to look after her. I was resentful for not having been more assertive and doing what I wanted to do, which was to rest and not go to the Route du Sud.

But it was the same old scenario – I was blaming the team for not having seen what was happening and telling me to rest and relax. This had become a vicious circle, as I'd then blame myself for being so easily manipulated by the team's needs. Behind my confident façade, I was in turmoil, feeling angry, scared and desperate.

I did everything right for the Tour's prologue. I recce'd the course more than anybody else, visualised and strategised my race, and made sure everything was perfect with my equipment. I was going to lose time on the fast sections, as my lack of top form simply wouldn't allow me to develop the power I needed to go at the necessary speed. It wasn't a very physically demanding course, and this meant my good aerodynamics and bike handling would compensate for what I lacked physically. But I had only one choice if I wanted to win: I had to take risks in the corners.

It was the first time Harry had ever sat in the team car and followed me in a time trial. I didn't tell him beforehand what my tactic was – although I had discussed it with the team's *directeurs* – so when I was literally touching barriers and clipping kerbs, he began to regret his decision to follow. It was quite clear that I was on the ragged edge. Sure enough, on the last corner, I came crashing down at speed.

My whole left side was ripped to pieces, with deep cuts and grazes, bruising and muscle damage. I got up to finish, and immediately after I wheeled across the line I was fairly upbeat about what had happened – after all, I'd known what the risks were. But I hadn't thought about the consequences.

Falling off in a time trial is often bad. They are high-speed crashes and, more often than not, cause much more damage than a crash in the peloton, where there is a little bit of warning, braking time and some cushioning. But I'd never fallen off in a time trial before and the next ten days were to prove what a dire mistake I'd made.

With so much damage to one side, sleeping was nigh on impossible without sleeping pills. It was not a good way to begin the Tour de France, especially considering I was already in a state of fatigue. Now I was starting the Tour's road stages hoping only to survive. I no longer had to live with expectations or pressure.

The team, oblivious to my physical and mental state, told the media that I'd probably take a few days to recover from my injuries then I'd be able to fight for a stage win in the second half of the race. Meanwhile, the realisation of what I'd got myself into was hitting home. I was starting the hardest bike race in the world tired and injured. I knew the team would not send me home or tell me, 'Do your best and don't worry.' Yet that was all I wanted to hear.

As the days went by, my condition got worse. By the fifth stage, I was the '*lanterne rouge*', or last man in the classification, almost an hour behind the yellow jersey. By the end of the first week it was quite clear that I wasn't getting better, although the team still chose to ignore this. I had never suffered so much in a race and all I wanted was for it to be over. Yet the team kept telling me to hang on and that eventually I'd come good.

Funnily enough, if they'd just used a little reverse psychology on me I'd have been much better, because I felt as if none of them understood what I was going through.

If I'd been told: 'David, we know how much you're suffering, so if you want to stop then we will completely support you.' If they had said that, then I might have found a renewed desire to fight on.

The reality was that that wasn't going to happen, because if I went home the team stood little chance of winning a stage. The Tour had evolved into a complete disaster for Cofidis, the only ray of light being Andrei Kivilev's high placing in the overall classification.

As the race arrived in the Alps, it was clear that I was going to be in for a tough time. Bondue and another manager came and saw me after another torrid day and we discussed how I was doing and also what awaited me. Bondue knew that Shari was in Biarritz, and he asked if I'd like the team to fly her in so she'd be waiting in the Alps.

At the time, this was unheard of behaviour from a pro team, as wives and girlfriends were still not really welcome. I thanked Alain and called Shari to ask if she'd like to come to the race. But she didn't want to, reasoning that she didn't want to watch me suffer as she'd already lived through the previous nine days with me. She was amazed I hadn't already been sent home, and I don't think she felt like being used as a pawn by the team. In a way, I understood, but I was still disappointed and her decision to stay away weakened my resistance to quitting.

The next day's stage was from Aix-les-Bains to Alpe d'Huez. I started knowing I wasn't going to be able to finish. It was simply beyond me, and any fight I had left was gone. I didn't want to have anything to do with the Tour any more. I'd grown to hate the suffering and the humiliation of always finishing so far behind the front of the race. Worst of all, I'd given up on my team sending me home or telling me they understood.

I'd let the team down, and, although there was a part of me that thought they should have been more caring, I also finally accepted I was a professional. It was my job to race; they weren't my family, they weren't my friends. They didn't worry about me – I was paid to do a job. It was my responsibility to fulfil that expectation and to get results.

A few kilometres from the foot of the Col de Madeleine, I said my goodbyes. I battled my way to the front so at least I'd actually be starting the climb at the head of the peloton and not be seen to be throwing the towel in so obviously. I searched out Lance.

I spotted him and rode up alongside.

'Lance – I'm out,' I told him. 'I can't do this any more.'

'Shit, Dave,' he said. Then he looked at me. 'You should have gone days ago though. You all right . . .?'

'Yeah, just fucking over it. Good luck for today.'

'Don't need luck, Dave! It's a pity you're not going to see it – I'm gonna destroy it.' He looked across and smiled. There wasn't even the tiniest hint of doubt or arrogance in what he said: it was merely a statement of fact.

And he did destroy it – bluffing that he was struggling all the way to the bottom of the Alpe, before unleashing a shockingly vicious acceleration that left his closest rival Jan Ullrich stunned. It was classic Lance.

Meanwhile, far behind, I found myself alone on the Madeleine, a horrible 25-kilometre climb. That's a long way on your own, as last man on the road in the Tour de France. I had a whole flotilla following me – team car, police escort, *voiture balai*, recovery truck, photographer, TV motorbike, and *commissaire*. It was a death march and they were the hovering vultures. I made it over the summit and then pulled over at the side of the road, a few kilometres into the descent.

The flotilla pulled over with me, and the TV cameras and photographers got the images they were waiting for – a broken and distressed team leader having his race number removed before shamefully climbing into the *voiture balai*. It was about the most soul-destroying experience a cyclist can have. This was the Tour, the race you're not supposed to give up.

I didn't have to spend too long in the *voiture balai*. Jacky Dubois, one of our *soigneurs*, was waiting at the roadside in a team car to pick me up and take me back to the hotel in a slightly more dignified manner. But our hotel was at the finish on the Alpe and we had to drive up the mountain behind the race.

At times, we were going so slowly through the crowds that people knocked on the window and called my name.

'Putain, c'est Millar . . .? Il a abandonné . . .?!'

'Shit, it's Millar . . .? He's given up . . .?!'

After a while I just slid down into my seat and pretended to be asleep. Ahead of us, Lance obliterated the race, just as he had promised.

It was very quiet at the hotel, as if there had been a death in the family. When you have quit the Tour, nobody really knows what to say or do. I went to my room, turned on my phone and started calling the people that mattered. My family and friends were all pleased it was over as I had genuinely started to lose the plot in the previous days. While it was a massive relief, there was now also a gaping hole in my confidence. Everything I'd previously achieved meant nothing; all I was now was a pro rider who couldn't finish the Tour de France.

The Alpe is pretty quiet on the evening after a Tour stage. The sun eventually drops behind the peaks and there's a chill in the air. The thousands camped out on the mountainside head down the descent, the brake lights of camper vans and people carriers illuminating the twilight. All that's left is the race convoy, the clearing-up process and some out-of-season hotels filled with weary cyclists.

Later that evening, the manager who'd been with Bondue after my torrid day in the Alps – I'll call him 'le Boss' – came to my room and asked if I'd like to talk. I was sharing with another rider, so we left to find somewhere quieter. We ended up in l'Équipier's room. It was good to see him. He gave me a big hug and I collapsed wearily onto the spare bed. It was just le Boss, l'Équipier and me.

'Are you okay?' le Boss asked me.

'I'm disappointed,' I said, 'but I just couldn't do it any more. There's no way I'd be winning any stages in the final week. As soon as we started climbing the Madeleine I knew it was over. The last ten days have been so fucking hard – too hard.'

'The most important thing now is that you recover. Go home, see Shari, relax and allow yourself to get better,' he said.

L'Équipier backed him up.

'David, there's still a lot of racing left in the season, you'll be fine, don't be too disappointed. You're talented – you just have to find yourself another goal now. That's why we've been talking about the Vuelta.'

I was interested in the prospect of racing in the Spanish national tour. 'That would be perfect,' I said. 'I just need some rest now – I've been tired since May. I'm sure if I rest I'll come back stronger than ever.'

'Well, we weren't too sure about the Vuelta, but the race organiser will take us if you go,' le Boss added. 'They seem very keen on having you lead the team there.'

I perked up. 'Really? There's a prologue there, isn't there?'

'Yes, there is. In fact it's a time trial.'

'How long?' I asked.

'Thirteen kilometres, I think. That's right, isn't it?'

He turned to l'Équipier, who nodded: 'Yeah, better for David than a prologue.'

'That's perfect. So what races would I do in August? I'll need a stage race. That's the only way I can get good enough.'

'Well, we've had a look,' the manager continued, 'and think maybe Tour of the Wallonne Region and the Tour of Denmark. So you'd then have about three weeks till the Vuelta.'

'That's quite a long time,' I said. 'Are there no more races?'

'We thought you could go to Italy, stay with . . .' he turned and gestured to l'Équipier. 'Stay at his place there. Get out of Biarritz in August.' There was a pause. 'That would allow you to . . . *prepare properly.*'

Initially, I was a little angry that he suggested I get out of Biarritz, as if I couldn't be trusted to behave. I wasn't really in a position to fight though, as all I was interested in was getting back to my best. What was now going through my head was the phrase le Boss had used: '*prepare properly*'.

I knew what that meant.

I looked across at l'Équipier.

'It will be perfect for you, David,' he said. 'You'll be part of the family – beautiful home-cooked Italian food, local dishes, amazing training, and there's a guest room so you'll have your privacy. We'll make sure you start the Vuelta in the best possible condition. Nobody will be able to beat you in Spain.'

'So I wouldn't race after Denmark?' I asked.

I thought the response to this would be a clear indication of what was going on, because normally the team would want me racing as much as possible before a major objective. But if I was going to be doping – taking EPO – then that would mean not racing in order to avoid anti-doping controls.

'No,' le Boss said. 'You'd finish your racing in Denmark, then the two of you would recover and train. You won't need to race, it's better you arrive fresh.'

It was clear to me that I had understood the meaning of '*prepare properly*'.

As I took it all in, something shifted in me. I was being asked to go to Italy to take EPO. I would then go and win the Vuelta prologue, thus redeeming the team with the sponsor. It boiled down to professionalism.

I was weary – too weary to fight any more. All that resistance – all the fighting I'd been doing, all the idealism that at first came so naturally and had slowly grown into a futile and isolating stance – was now behind me.

I had done well – bloody well – as a clean rider. I had stood my ground, done my bit, but now it was out of my hands. The team needed me to accept my obligations, and now it all made sense. The tired young dreamer had been waiting for this moment. The background white noise of the struggle to fight doping finally subsided. I opened my mind and let it in.

I walked into that hotel room an anti-doper; I walked out of it a seasoned professional ready to do what was required of me. There was no torment or confusion in my mind. I now knew that in a few weeks I would be doping for the first time. It felt as if a massive burden had been lifted off my shoulders. I was now a professional through and through with bigger responsibilities than my own personal belief system.

I headed back to Biarritz. Shari, my sister and some other friends were there. They'd been planning on following me through the Pyrenees, but instead we just hung out and I tried to fix myself.

My body was a wreck. I had bronchitis, an upset stomach and some of my injuries from the crash in Dunkirk had still not healed. I spent ten days off the bike and didn't watch the Tour once. Nor did I tell anybody about the decision I'd made. There was never any question of sharing it.

13

2001: AN ODYSSEY BEGINS

My last race 'clean' before I left for Tuscany was the Tour of Denmark. I won the time trial and the general classification. On the last night, I toasted my success with runner-up Jaan Kirsipuu, an Estonian *rouleur* who taught me the merits of vodka. One of the last things I remember is standing at a bar with a range of vodkas lined up, as Jaan explained their differing characteristics in loving detail. They didn't come much more hardcore than Jaan Kirsipuu.

And then, there I was, with l'Équipier, in Tuscany. It was ridiculous really: I had just won a major race, despite not being in top form, yet I was going to dope. After winning Denmark, it would have been reasonable for me to think that I didn't have to go to Italy, that if I worked hard and put my head down and believed in myself, I could win the Vuelta prologue – clean.

Perhaps if I'd had people – somebody – around me who I could have talked to about it, then that might have been the conclusion I'd have come to and I'd have cancelled the trip to Tuscany. But back then, that person simply didn't exist for me.

I had long realised that there was nobody I could speak to about the world I was living in. Since that first encounter of doping at the Etoile des Besseges, when Jim van der Laer had found himself in a corner, I had to accept that pro cycling had a dark and secret world. I had no choice but to adapt to it – or leave.

Mum had put it perfectly when she said: 'You can come home whenever you like.' That was true but I was never going to walk away, even with the shit that was going on around me. I was too in love with the sport. Cycling was still amazing to me and racing as a pro was still my dream. I thought it would be pathetic to throw the dream away, simply because I knew that others were doping.

There was a harsher truth. I knew that any life I had outside of cycling wasn't going to be as good as the life I had carved out within the sport. I had been lucky enough to discover something I excelled in and loved, and to be paid well for it. So few people get that opportunity in life.

I had believed that I could exist in a morally corrupt world as long as I was strong enough to stand my ground and respect my value system. I thought that position would win me respect. I also thought that things inside the sport would eventually change and that I'd never actually have to confront the lure of doping. But change failed to come and, little by little, my idealism soured, my resistance faltered and I grew cynical and resentful.

The decision to dope didn't happen in the time it took me to walk in and out of l'Équipier's room at Alpe d'Huez: it happened over several years. I had been at my tipping point for longer than I knew. When I got to the hotel that night after quitting the Tour I had reached the endgame – it seemed as if there was no longer any choice.

My responsibilities as team leader contributed because I felt that the team's existence and continuation depended on my per-formances. I had a loyalty to Cofidis that in many ways was mis-placed, but was also totally necessary for me to operate. The manager and l'Équipier knew that; they understood my sense of obligation. They chose the perfect time to nudge me gently and ease me to the other side.

Circumstances may have driven me to it, but that didn't mean I wasn't fully in control of my destiny. I had made a decision in that room at the Alpe and it had not crossed my mind to go back on it. It was now professional obligation rather than youthful idealism that dictated my choices. Finally I'd accepted that it was easier to dope than not to dope.

L'Équipier lived in a beautiful old house – it was the archetypal Tuscan villa, on the top of a little hill, in the middle of nowhere, beautiful, and so serene. His wife and children couldn't have been more welcoming and hospitable. They made me feel very much at home.

It was such a happy place, the most incongruous environment to be doping for the first time. This was not some dark, dirty changing room or seedy doctor's office, but a family home filled with laughter, bathed in Tuscan sunshine. I suppose that made it all seem so much easier.

After I'd settled in, l'Équipier and I went out for a short spin on the bike. I broached the subject for the first time.

'Listen,' I said. 'I don't really know much about EPO. How much am I going to have to do?'

'As it's your first time,' he explained, 'not so much, because your body will respond to it very easily. Probably I'd say about 10,000 units over a week. That's nothing really – shit, some guys need to take 4000 units every day for ten days in order to get an increase. That's not good. I've seen a lot of guys end up like that.'

'I don't intend to end up like that,' I said.

'Me neither, I've always managed to be careful and limit the use. It's the only way.'

'So – I guess you have some?' I asked.

'Of course! But we may need to get some more before the end of the week. That's no problem though, I know some people.'

I was worried though. 'How long do I stop before the start of the Vuelta? I don't want *any* risks.'

'David, don't worry. We are going to be working on a *zero* risk policy! You're stopping ten days before the Vuelta. That's the latest . . .'

'So when do I start?'

'Tonight,' he said. 'We'll do it in the evening, it's better.'

I was curious. 'Why?'

'Well, I don't know,' he replied, 'we just do it in the evening.'

And that was that. There wasn't really much else for me to ask. I knew about EPO from everything that had been said or written in the post-Festina years. The grey area in my head was dosage and cut-off time, but l'Équipier seemed to know what he was doing. I honestly believed he wouldn't do anything that would harm me.

That evening we had a wonderful meal prepared by his wife. Once dinner was over, she took the children up to bed, leaving l'Équipier and myself alone at the table. He stood up, went to the fridge, and took out what looked to be a normal can of Coca-Cola, but with a screw lid.

Inside were some small syringes, smaller than I'd seen before. They were different colours and were branded with the EPO manufacturer's logo. All the syringes were the same size but contained different quantities. This was the first time I'd actually seen EPO.

I took a closer look. 'No shit – it actually says "EPO" on the syringe . . .?'

L'Équipier sat down again.

'There are different manufacturers,' he said, 'and you're best getting the brand name syringes, because that way you know exactly what you're getting. It's also possible to get it in a separate ampoule – then you have to get diabetes syringes separately and measure out each dose. This is better because the quantities are clearly indicated on the syringe.'

'Where do you get it from?'

He shrugged. 'It's pretty easy,' he said, 'either the pharmacy or I have a friend at a hospital. It's much harder than it used to be though. There was a pharmacy here that used to make most of its money from professional cyclists! The laws are much tougher now, so they don't risk it. Luckily, I know some people.' He gave that big grin.

I was so accustomed to syringes by now that the sight of them didn't perturb me in any way. I'd been injected scores of times, mostly intravenously, which I was accustomed to and could quite easily do myself. I hated intramuscular injections – considered the best way to take iron. I'd tried a few times but ended up chasing my arse around with the needle, until finally giving up and getting somebody else to do it for me. I knew that EPO was injected subcutaneously, but I'd never had one of these injections.

'Where do you inject?' I asked him.

L'Équipier was completely at ease. 'Anywhere really, but the top of your arm is best. Roll up your T-shirt.'

He pinched my arm, pushed the needle through and under the skin and carefully pushed the EPO out of the syringe. Then he pulled out the syringe quickly and smoothly, while rubbing where he'd injected. There was a little bump where the liquid was sitting under the skin, and a prick mark like a mosquito bite. It was probably the easiest and most anti-climactic injection I'd ever had. It was less like the stereotypical idea of doping than the injectable *récup* I'd grown so used to.

L'Équipier then injected himself with the other syringe, replaced everything in the fake Coke can, screwed the lid on and put it back in the fridge. It had all been done in a couple of minutes. It was a tiny process for what was supposed to give such massive gains and for something that had tormented me for so long. If I hadn't been so conditioned to syringes and injections I'm sure it would have made much more of an impact on me.

The consummation of doping was not the defining moment people might expect it to have been. I can remember vividly the first time I was injected with legal recovery products as a neo-pro, whereas my first doping experience I remember for no other reason than I consciously told myself I should. It was so relaxed. I might as well have been handed a cup of tea, there was so little emotion involved.

We slipped into a rhythm in Tuscany. We'd wake up, have breakfast with the family then head out on the bikes. We didn't have a training schedule, as such. We'd simply head out and do between 3 and 4 hours. The longest ride we did while I was there was four and a half hours.

L'Équipier was of the *laissez-faire* school and there was little real science to our training. We'd ride hard on some climbs, easier on others. He said the most important thing was to keep our bodies ticking over and remind them occasionally that we were racers, which would be when we'd go hard on the climbs. The most important thing was to allow our bodies to adapt and use the EPO. This meant doing the standard combination of injectable recovery, which fuelled the EPO dose with the necessary ingredients to make more red blood cells.

But the impression that I wasn't really doing anything wrong was shattered the day we had to go and get some more EPO. This involved us going for a drive and making two stops in far less idyllic surroundings than my teammate's household. I drove us to a cash point before we pulled over and parked outside an apartment block.

L'Équipier told me to wait and then disappeared for 10 minutes with the cash before reappearing with a small plastic bag. My unease increased when we went to a hospital and another guy came out to the car park and met l'Équipier with a package. Evidently, the first contact hadn't been able to supply enough, so we had to use two sources. The perceived innocence of the Tuscan villa and the happy family slipped away.

We did blood tests the day after I arrived and the day I left. Even in that short time, there was an increase of a couple of percentage points in my hematocrit. L'Équipier was very thankful he'd erred on the side of caution with my dosage, as he said I was reacting amazingly well to the EPO.

He was used to seasoned dopers and had forgotten just how big the effect could be on a first-timer like me. But I was becoming nervous that, once I started racing, it would be very noticeable that I'd taken EPO. My last injection was twelve days before the start of the Vuelta, so we'd be able to monitor my levels, but there was now very little to be done to stop the EPO stimulating growth in my red blood cells.

I was in an odd place, aware that change was happening, but not experiencing any significant physical benefits. Back in Biarritz, I trained for a few days on roads I knew well, but I was no superman. I was beginning to wonder what the big deal was. I'd expected there to be an instant effect, that I'd be powering up climbs in much higher gears. But it wasn't like that. I started to think it had all been a waste of time, that maybe there had been no point in doing it. I left for the 2001 Vuelta more nervous than ever.

14

LA VIDA DOPADA

I was scared shitless before the start of the 2001 Vuelta a España.

I was worried not only that my blood levels were going to be too high and that it would become common knowledge that I'd taken EPO, but, more importantly, that I was going to lose.

We arrived in Salamanca in Spain three days before the race. I spent most of the time, day and night, sleeping. L'Équipier was the opposite. He was nervous too and far from sleepy. I suppose we had our different ways of handling the stress.

As usual, the team ran their pre-Grand Tour blood test on the Thursday morning. L'Équipier and I anxiously awaited the results. Thankfully our levels weren't as high as we thought they might have been. I was only a couple of points higher than usual, a result that could easily be explained by simply being rested and fresh. It didn't look suspicious. I was able to relax a bit more.

Although the three Grand Tours of France, Italy and Spain have similar formats, they have their own distinct characteristics and the Vuelta is very different from the Tour.

The Tour is a well-oiled machine. Wherever it goes, it takes over; villages, towns and cities have to adapt to the Tour's requirements. At the Vuelta, there is little to suggest the race is coming until a couple of hours beforehand, and normal life continues until the last possible moment. The two races typified their cultures: the Tour is a flagship of the République Française and for that reason all-powerful and somewhat arrogant, while the Vuelta is more relaxed and takes itself less seriously. As riders, we were tiny cogs in the Tour machine, whereas at the Vuelta we were integral parts of the race festivities and could enjoy it as such.

Because of this relaxed attitude, it was hard to scout the time trial course before the race began in Salamanca. Nobody even knew where it was. There were no route arrows, barriers or even a clear map indicating the route. So I just slept.

When I did finally see it, my worst fears came true. I had become a nervous bike handler since the crash in the Tour and this course was very fast and technical for the first few kilometres. My cornering had been laughable in the two time trials I'd ridden since Dunkirk, in Belgium and Denmark.

The last few kilometres of the course were hard, so I decided that was where I could make the difference. I had to keep calm through the first time check, as I was sure to have lost time, then make up the lost seconds in the finale.

As predicted, I lost time in the opening kilometres, but then rode out of my skin all the way to the finish line, beating the fastest time by just one second. In contrast to my Tour win the previous year, all I felt was relief – unadulterated pure relief. I'd fulfilled my professional obligations – I couldn't have imagined doping and not winning. But it was all business now. It didn't feel like sport any more. Winning this way had never been part of my dream.

I lost the race leader's jersey three days later in a crash in the final 10 kilometres of the stage. I bruised my lower leg quite badly and one of the *soigneurs* covered it in an anti-inflammatory cream, without knowing the cream was photo-sensitive.

The next day was hot and sunny and the part of my leg that had been covered in the cream began to burn from the inside out. This then spread and was causing me ridiculous pain as it burned my skin off. That mistake has left me with an allergic reaction to direct sunlight ever since.

It didn't hamper my form though and I won stage six, escaping in the finale with one other rider before beating him in the sprint. Although I didn't really notice any marked physical difference due to doping, things were becoming easier for me. I still felt like I suffered as much, but now I could suffer for longer and then recover faster. It was like having the form of my life, day in, day out.

Before the stage to Zaragoza, a rumour spread through the

peloton that the Spanish team ONCE had fitted 55-tooth chain rings on their bikes. Clearly they knew something we didn't.

But as I'd barely slept the night before, due to my skin burning and itching, I was neither worried nor concerned about what ONCE had or hadn't planned. I was not a factor in the overall classification and my two stage wins meant that the team basically had *carte blanche* for the rest of the race, so it wasn't as if we had much to stress about.

In howling winds, that stage to Zaragoza became one of the fastest bike races in history, as the peloton averaged 56 kilometres per hour over 180 kilometres. It also opened my eyes to the power of doping.

When we began to hit the crosswinds in the final stages of the race, I was sitting too far back in the peloton. Within a kilometre I found myself in the third echelon of riders, watching the front of the race disappear at speeds nudging 70 kilometres an hour.

Partly due to the adrenalin rush of riders getting physically blown off the road and partly due to the absolute panic surrounding me, I was motivated by the situation and spent the next 30 kilometres of racing bridging on my own between groups. I wasn't that surprised that nobody could or would work with me, but I began to think it was strange when nobody could even hold my wheel.

It only took me a couple of minutes to recover from the first bridging move. I thought it was a bit odd that I felt so good, but I was beginning to have fun. Without even trying to take anybody with me as support, I went off in pursuit of the front group that was, by now, out of sight.

It was an absolutely ridiculous move, and in the unwritten rules of cycling an impossible one. I spent the next 20 minutes riding at over 60 kilometres per hour, with a cadence in excess of 115. I closed most of the gap in the first 15 minutes and was then able to see the front group, only 100 metres ahead.

They were within reach when I started to fall apart. I was way over my limits, my breathing was out of control and my whole body was starting to lactate. Unable to get closer, it was only because one of the riders at the back of the group saw me, and then told l'Équipier, that I finally made the junction.

L'Équipier dropped out of the safety of the group's slipstream, came back and towed me on to the tail end. I was in a mess, but my lone ride between the groups went down as legendary, a ride that nobody apart from the professional peloton knew about. Yet it also showed what EPO could do. My body was responding in an unprecedented way to the demands of racing.

That experience had an impact on me. I began to think of myself as two separate entities: mind and body. My body was a tool that was capable of things that I previously hadn't thought possible. Now I knew why Frank Vandenbroucke was always pushing the envelope and seeing how far he could go. It was a game, in which he played God with his own body. And in the process, Frank lost his mind.

As the Vuelta went on, my sleep patterns worsened due to the incessant burning and itching from my allergic reaction. We'd set a deadline for me going home if it didn't improve, but the only immediate solution to the problem was cortisone, although cortisone was illegal unless it was for tendon treatment.

Cortisone could sometimes have been used to good effect. There was a famous example of this when Jonathan Vaughters was stung on the face by a bee during a stage of the Tour de France. His eye became so inflamed that he couldn't see. A simple cortisone injection would have quickly treated this, but because Jonathan and his team followed the rules so honestly, he ended up having to quit the race.

In my case, we found a less honest, more pragmatic, solution. The team told the world that I had tendonitis in my ankle and that I'd been given cortisone for this. In fact I'd been given an intra-muscular cortisone injection in an attempt to calm the allergic reaction.

All that was needed to satisfy the UCI was for us to note this in my medical records. Then if cortisone appeared in an anti-doping sample, they would look back at my medical record and see that I had a legitimate reason. As long as the right product was listed in the medical book, and was allied to a legitimate use – in this case tendonitis – it didn't matter if the reason given was accurate or not.

The team doctor and others had been saying I should take cortisone since the rash first showed itself. Yet, even as an EPO user, I held off for a week on taking cortisone. I didn't want to take it. I knew it was a powerful drug, but I also knew it was a catabolic drug that consumed the body. It was probably the most potent drug out there, yet with the right prescription it could be used legally. There wasn't any great resistance to cortisone use within Cofidis, a stance replicated by most pro teams at the time. Even now, cortisone is abused by some, its use being hidden behind the TUE's (Therapeutic Use Exemption certificates) which can be easily acquired.

A few days after the cortisone injection I began to lose weight. I was skinnier than I'd ever been. There were veins appearing all over my legs and my torso as the last bits of fat left on my body were eaten away by the cortisone. Once the fat was gone, it began eating into my muscle, causing my weight to drop continuously.

By the time I got to the World Road Championships in Lisbon, ten days after the Vuelta had finished, I was skin, bone – and a little bit of muscle. Logic would dictate that I felt weaker, and yet I'd never felt so strong. I felt like I could suffer more and push myself harder than ever. And that was exactly what I did in the individual time trial.

Competition in the men's time trial that year was fierce. Santiago Botero, Levi Leipheimer, Jan Ullrich and I were all in contention, but I led through every time check and on crossing the line it appeared that I was world champion. I was chaperoned to the podium, receiving congratulations on the way, not really knowing anything about where I stood, but assuming that I probably wouldn't be beaten.

But Ullrich was still out on the course. As I was taken through the crowd barriers towards the presentation, he and Hungarian rider Laszlo Bodrogi crossed the line together and I sensed the mood change around me.

Ullrich had finished 6 seconds faster than my time, demoting me to second place. It's against the rules to be paced by another rider during an individual time trial, yet this appeared to have happened on the last lap.

Ullrich had been behind Bodrogi, then had caught him. He had overtaken him only to have Bodrogi pass him. Then Ullrich caught and passed Bodrogi once more. Effectively, they paced each other to the finish. This helped Ullrich, not only aerodynamically but also psychologically, and gave him the necessary boost to move from fourth place at the last time check to fastest time at the finish.

I was devastated. I couldn't believe that this could be allowed to happen and wanted the *commissaires* to act. But the result stood. I sat in the press conference with my head in my hands, in a state of shock. It took me a good hour to pull myself together.

Later, sitting in the doping control, I said hello to the UCI anti-doping *commissaire*, the same guy who had also been responsible for the anti-doping procedures at the Vuelta.

We got chatting and at one point he asked if he could see how my ankle was healing. I stared at him, a baffled look on my face.

He repeated the question.

'Your ankle, David . . .? How is it?'

He bent down and looked directly at the burned skin and the rashes, now healing, that had covered my legs.

Finally, I twigged.

'Oh, *my ankle* . . .' I said. 'Yes, much better thanks. It healed quite quickly after we treated it.'

He was very thoughtful and seemed genuinely interested in how I was. Yet he also made it obvious that he knew exactly what was behind my supposed cortisone treatment for tendonitis. He wasn't judgemental, but was simply making it clear to me that, even though he knew the truth of what had gone on, there was nothing he could do.

15

MY PERSONAL JESUS

Despite the problems we'd been having, I spent the winter of 2001 with Shari, in Queensland, in a rented house in Noosa. After everything that had happened during the season, I was looking for an escape. It became a winter of excess and indulgence, during which I lost my way.

I partied far too hard in Australia and there was nobody to blame but me. During one particularly late night, I asked Shari to marry me. I had been thinking about it for a couple of months and had even had a ring made in Biarritz. I proposed to her one night when sleep proved impossible and when, for once, we were alone. It wasn't romantic, but I believed that it was what I wanted to do. Amazingly, she said yes to my proposal and we became engaged. Somehow, I thought marrying her would stop the bad times and leave only the good.

I had gone to Australia hoping to come to terms with the decisions I'd made, but instead I became more isolated and mired in denial. Even if at times I wanted to, I couldn't tell people I doped. Perhaps they would have understood, but I didn't want to share because I was ashamed. As a successful athlete, I was held in some regard, which made me feel even more ashamed. My guilt over the deception crowded in on me so then I'd launch into another bender, in a desperate effort to forget what I'd done.

My recklessness and excesses alienated most of the people I'd become friends with – and then Shari and I broke up. I returned to Europe in early January a shadow of myself. I was still at racing weight, even though I hadn't touched my bike since the World Championships in Portugal, and I was so tired from sleep deprivation and emotional turmoil that I could barely walk between my flights when I transferred in Hong Kong.

As I sat there, between lounges, lost in transit, I realised that I blamed cycling for the mess I was in. I should have been more than a little concerned about the fact I was heading to our January training camp with no kilometres in my legs at all, yet I didn't give a shit. I had no desire to ride my bike at all.

Because I'd become team leader, I was rarely, if ever, taken to task. So when we arrived in the south of France for the training camp, and I was only doing short rides because I was too tired to do more, it was accepted without discussion. By the third day, I was barely getting out of bed, and it became apparent that I was suffering from more than just jet lag.

After a series of blood tests, I was diagnosed with glandular fever. Told to rest, I headed back to London briefly and then returned to Biarritz. I'd only spent a few days there in the previous six months, but when I got back, it felt like home. Maybe the trip to Australia had opened my eyes, but I decided that after all the years as a nomad, Biarritz was a good place to put down roots. So I started looking for a house.

I had finished in the top fifteen riders in the 2001 world rankings, which had massively boosted my bonus scheme and placed me in one of the highest bonus brackets. I received a lump sum on 31 December 2001 and then would receive a major pay rise for 2002. I had more money in my French bank account than I'd ever had before.

My image contract was paid into Luxembourg, so I gave the Cofidis contact in Luxembourg a call and asked if they'd received my 2001 bonus. I was stunned to be told that I had been sent close to €400,000.

Cofidis had first started paying me through their Luxembourg holding company in 2000, but I had not known what to do with it. I repeatedly contacted IMG (who were supposed to be managing my financial affairs), yet IMG repeatedly failed to do anything with the funds. Eventually, I bypassed IMG and then opened a bank account. But because IMG had me sign my image contract as David Millar, it was fairly pointless. In order for it to serve any purpose, a holding company should have been created and been the beneficiary of the image contract.

The image contract, a ploy used a lot in sport, is really a tax avoidance trick. Image contracts escape taxation through canny use of offshore banking. The culture that permeated cycling considered it a schoolboy error for a high-earning professional athlete to be taxed on their full income. That is what you're told – by managers, fellow riders, accountants and agents – so it's hard not to start thinking it's your right as a pro athlete to be taxed minimally.

I had trusted IMG to organise my affairs, just as Marc Biver had told me they would, yet the moment they had finished negotiating my contract I felt they effectively washed their hands of me. Nonetheless, I was contracted to pay them 10 per cent of my principal contract and 20 per cent of all other earnings (before tax) until December 2003. Now I understood why Biver had been encouraging me to win more points. After all, he received a percentage of everything I earned. He was the stereotypical cold-blooded sports agent. It seemed to me that he had completely played me.

Later, I was able to get out of my IMG contract. A London lawyer, Mike Townley, won the case, but IMG fought so hard that the decision was only accepted after they had taken it to the Court of Arbitration for Sport in Lausanne. I think I am one of the only athletes ever to win a case against IMG, and that is thanks to the skills of Mike Townley.

House-hunting in Biarritz was fun. I looked at a few places, including Coco Chanel's first *atelier*, a beautiful old apartment in the centre of town. It wasn't very practical but it appealed deeply to the dreamer in me and I adored the fact that she had started her fashion house within those walls. That was how I imagined things would be – I'd be a former Tour de France cyclist living in Chanel's apartment in Biarritz.

Eventually I saw reason and let go of the Chanel dream. Instead I bought one of the oldest villas in the town, beautiful but derelict.

It still had its original *fin de siècle* electrical fittings. I found a copy of a 1953 *Vogue* in the basement. I loved it.

I was still recovering from my illness, but I caught up with old friends in Biarritz and then made some new ones. Before long we'd created our own little group. There was Sabine, who with her mother owned the Ventilo Caffé; Loïc, a true Marseillaise who loved surfing so much he had moved to Biarritz and taken his flooring business with him, and Olivier, the owner of a restaurant called Le Lodge.

There was also Alain, a true Parisian who managed the Hermès shop in town. Alain had grown up in one of the less salubrious *arondissements* in Paris, but had started working at Hermès as a teenager. He had worked his way up to become head of the made-to-order section in the flagship St Honoré store, before coming down to manage the shop in Biarritz.

We'd sit drinking coffee on the Grand Plage and he'd occasionally say: 'You see that woman . . .? Her bag's worth €40,000.' Neither of us understood why somebody would buy such a bag, yet he'd help create much of the demand.

And there was also a young Australian cyclist called Benny Johnson, who I'd got on with really well during my time in Noosa. He became my protégé and close friend. I wanted him to have somebody to guide him through the shit, even while I was up to my neck in it.

I was still ill, but after a month in Biarritz I decided it was time to get back to cycling. I needed a coach – somebody who could give me a programme to adhere to. I'd been introduced to sports doctor Jesús Losa at the World Championships, although at the time and in subsequent weeks I hadn't really thought much more about him.

Jesús worked for another professional cycling team, Euskaltel. It wasn't difficult to find his number through a carefully chosen Spanish pro that I knew and, after speaking to him, we decided that I would go down to his offices in Valladolid to do physiological testing as well as blood tests.

Jesús was a cool guy, typically Spanish, warm and affable. He was married with two kids and trained athletes from all sports, although his preferred clientele was from cycling. Although he was the official doctor and coach for Euskaltel, he was allowed to keep his personal client base, and this included a certain number of pro cyclists.

At that first meeting in his lab, I underwent the usual physiological tests, to establish a base line of my fitness and 'engine' size. Given that I had been diagnosed with glandular fever, I was concerned, but Jesús seemed absolutely convinced there were no issues. We discussed training at length and it was clear that he had an in-depth knowledge of sports science and pro cycling. Then I brought up the subject of doping.

I wanted to let my body get back to its top level on its own without drugs. More importantly, I wanted to win a road stage at the Tour de France clean. It was a strange attitude to have – after all, I wouldn't have been having a secret meeting with a Spanish sports doctor unless there was a desire to dope (even if, back then, doping athletes wasn't a criminal offence in Spain). Yet that first meeting revolved around me telling him I didn't want to dope – at least not for the time being.

At that time, I didn't consider myself a fully fledged doper. Yes, I had used it to great effect but I didn't yet see myself as one of *them*. I didn't feel like I really needed it – maybe I'd made a mistake the year before. So I told Jesús that I would hold off doping for as long as possible. I had to prove I could win once again at the top level without drugs. I was definitely confused.

The practical side of the relationship was quite simple. I would pay him €12,000 a year for his coaching and expertise; any medical supplies I needed – legal or otherwise – I would pay for separately at the end of the year, in addition to the bonuses that Jesus had earned depending on the number of UCI points I had won.

The bonus system was lucrative for him and, I hoped, would keep him motivated. The downside to the bonus system was that it meant it was in his interest that I dope. I hadn't really thought about that at the time; he seemed like a really good guy who understood my motivations. The thought of him encouraging me to dope seemed ridiculous.

When I got home, I put my head down and, with about six weeks before my first race, the Tour of Romandie, started training. By then, Jesús and I had formed a strong working relationship. His training was advanced and much harder than I was used to. With all of it based around power output and heart rate, I grew used to staring at the computer on my handlebars. Our disregard for my glandular fever had paid off, as I had not suffered once from any more symptoms.

The week after Romandie, I went to a weekend race near Madrid, the Clasica A Alcobendas. The format was similar to the Criterium International race in France in that there was a fairly straightforward road stage and then a mountain stage and time trial. I was surprised to be one of the strongest on the mountain stage, attacking on the final mountain to Navacerrada and dropping some of the best Spanish climbers.

My teammate David Moncoutie took the stage and I advised him so effectively on time-trialling techniques that he managed to hold on to the leader's jersey and beat me into second place overall. I like to think that I remain very generous when it comes to advising my teammates on time trialling.

The result gave Jesús and I confidence in what I could achieve. Although Jesús wanted me to prepare for the Tour de France on EPO, I decided I would only use it for the Vuelta. I felt like everybody only saw me as a time triallist, but, as a rider, I was so much more than that. But I had to prove it by winning a road stage at the Tour clean. If I won doped then it meant nothing, I was very clear on that.

We decided I would go to altitude before the Dauphiné and prepare for the Tour the natural way. So I returned to Navacerrada, close to Jesús and also where many of the Spanish riders trained. It was miserable though, as one of my sporadic bouts of self-doubt settled on me.

Everything caught up with me: the concentrated block of training and racing in the previous months, my lack of Spanish and the isolation I felt being alone. I was cripplingly demoralised and could barely get out of bed. Worse, no matter which way I came back to the hotel, I faced a 12-kilometre climb at the end of each training ride.

One day, a spent force, I simply stopped at the side of the road and waited to hitch my way back up. But no vehicles passed for an hour, as if the gods were playing with me. Eventually, I crawled back up to the hotel, went up to my room and climbed into bed in my cycling gear. I lay there for hours. I texted Jesús and told him I couldn't do it any more, that everything was shutting down.

Without telling me he was coming, he drove up to the hotel that evening and we had dinner together. His gesture meant so much to me. It was wonderful to have company – he explained that he wasn't surprised I was feeling down.

'I work with so many athletes,' he said, 'but it's the guys like you that I like working with the most. You are so intense and I get better feedback from you than anybody else. But you can't be like that all the time – you're going to have times like this, when you burn out. You shouldn't beat yourself up about it – it's just the way you are. You can't hit the highs that you do, and be as intense as you are, without having these lows.'

Nobody had ever said that before – it made a lot of sense to me. He told me to go home the next day and have some rest, and to forget about the altitude training. His visit made our relationship even closer. For the first time, it felt like I had a coach who understood not only my physical strengths but also the psychological characteristics that had always left me in such deep holes.

Even so, I remained erratic. Typically, after resting, I jumped in at the deep end and went on a big ride, hoping to get an understanding of my form. But 70 kilometres from home I simply couldn't go on. I spent half an hour searching for a taxi before I found one that would take me back to Biarritz. It was a little embarrassing explaining to the taxi driver that I was racing in the Tour de France in four weeks time, yet couldn't ride home.

After the Dauphiné Libéré and the British National Road Race Championships, I travelled to Luxembourg for the Tour, head firmly screwed back on. I'd hooked up with Bridget Carter while I'd been back in England. We'd gone to the same primary school and I'd had a crush on her when I'd been at Aylesbury Grammar. She'd become an airline pilot, I was about to ride the Tour de France: we hit it off immediately.

I took fourth in the Tour prologue, which, in hindsight, was a remarkable performance on what was a physically demanding course, yet I was still disappointed. So I set my mind on winning the road stage I so wanted. A few days later, as I sat studying the Tour's road book, after the finish to Plateau de Beille, I realised that the next day's stage, from Lavelanet to Béziers, was my opportunity.

The next morning, at the team meeting, we were asked if any of us were keen on going for the stage. I immediately said that I wanted to win it. Bondue smiled at that. 'Well, that's a done deal – shall we sign on the dotted line now?'

It was the first real transition stage, taking us from the Pyrenees across the Midi. It was also one of my best days on a bike. I led from start to finish, racing in a break with French star Laurent Jalabert, one of my idols and riding his final Tour.

Laurent was wearing the climber's polka-dot jersey and had already been on the attack on his own in the two previous stages, so it was absolute madness that he was attacking again. Yet it was as if he was squeezing the last drops out of his career and the French public loved him for it.

I could see he was tired, so I helped him win those first few mountain sprints of the day, feeling honoured to be able to do what little I could to make sure he rode into Paris with the mountains jersey still on his shoulders.

After we'd exited the Pyrenees, it became a flat race to the finish, with fourteen riders in the breakaway, battling for the win. Tactically, it was going to be a tricky finale. I had no teammates with me and the run-in was not physically challenging: I knew I would have to play my cards right if I wanted to win.

Fifty kilometres from Béziers, Jalabert moved alongside me. 'You need to stop making it look so easy,' he said. 'Everybody is going to be watching you.'

'Really ...?' I said, taken aback by what he'd said. 'And you, Laurent – will you be watching me?'

He smiled and said: 'The opposite, David.' Now I knew that he would repay my help.

On the course profile, there was one tiny climb, about 20 kilometres from the finish. The rest of the run in to Béziers was pan flat. I knew I had to attack on that hill, but I didn't know if it would work or not.

As we began the climb, I drifted to the back of the group and watched. Sure enough, the attacks came and, before long, Jalabert made his move, attacking ferociously hard.

Being the classy rider he was, everybody panicked and chased after him, but he just kept going with the group desperately hanging onto his back wheel. Immediately, I realised what he was doing. I knew that the second he relented, his exhausted pursuers would sit up to catch their breath. That would be my moment.

As he finally eased up and the others breathed a sigh of relief, I launched myself as hard as I possibly could down the left-hand side of the road. I didn't look back over my shoulder until I'd been going for about half a minute, but when I did, I saw there were only four riders left with me.

What I saw told me I was up against it, as three of them – Michael Boogerd, Laurent Brochard and David Exteberria – happened to be among the world's best riders. All were proven winners.

But none of that mattered. I was too good, too collected, too sure of my own strength for any of them. There is a photo of me crossing the line in Béziers that will always be one of my favourites. The photographer had climbed up on to scaffolding adjacent to the finish line and caught the moment of victory. It captures exactly how I felt: invincible.

I'd just killed some of the best riders in the world – and I was clean. I'd taken nothing – no EPO, no cortisone, no testosterone, no painkillers, no caffeine. I had justified to myself that I was a great rider without drugs – yet perversely given myself the green light to dope again.

I'd proved what I could do clean – how much more could I do if I was doped?

*

Cofidis had nothing booked to celebrate the end of the Tour that year, no restaurant or nightclub. So, in my new moneyed manner, I hosted the team at a restaurant in Paris. A lot of my friends were there, including new girlfriend Bridget. By coincidence Team Sky hosted their post-Tour debut dinner at the same restaurant eight years later.

I was scheduled to go to the Tour of Denmark after the Tour, but my mind had turned towards the Vuelta – and renewing my acquaintance with Jesús. That entailed a return to Navacerrada and tackling an epic three-week training camp, fuelled by EPO, testosterone patches and Italian injectable recovery products. The hotel owners, who did everything they could to take care of whichever athletes stayed with them, had it all stored in their fridge in a sealed polystyrene box.

Once again, I returned to a monastic existence. My phone was switched off for most of the time and the distance grew between myself and Bridget. I withdrew from the world as soon as I began to dope, and became a different person, insular and focused. This latest programme was nothing like the first time in Tuscany the year before. Now I was cold and calculating.

I didn't use EPO at first, as I allowed my body to react naturally to altitude before provoking it artificially. I wasn't doing much training beyond riding on the little plateau that was only a few kilometres long.

Jesús had given me training plans with codes on them, according to the drugs I would be taking, when they had to be taken and in what quantities, so my days were very structured.

There was a combination of EPO, testosterone pills and, after a week, one normal dose of cortisone followed by weekly micro-doses. On top of this were the legal injections for vitamins, iron, anti-oxidants and, on occasions, amino acids and glucose. Before long, I was injecting at least once a day. If I hadn't felt like a doper before then, now there was no doubt.

The longer this went on, the more injections and pills I took, the deeper I got into it, the more I felt I had to perform. There was no longer any thought of fun or enjoyment – it was completely

professional now. I had bought into the belief that doping was the only way of being a player in a Grand Tour. That's what the programme was all about: seeing if I could manage it in the Vuelta, and if I could, who knew – then maybe I could also do it at the Tour.

By the time I returned to Biarritz, I was lighter than I'd ever been in my professional career and the same weight I'd been when I was 18. Jesús and I were sure this was the ticket to success – we were following the old Michele Ferrari adage of losing weight, increasing power – and then going faster. The problem was that I'd lost *too much* weight, and with it, the power I needed to go fast. I had become obsessive. I wasn't eating enough and I was stressed. I was trying too hard. I wanted it too much and I had taken it too far.

The Vuelta didn't go as planned. I was still holding on to a top ten place as the race entered the final week, but it was clear that I wasn't at my best. Because of what I'd done to prepare for the race, I kept pushing on and not throwing in the towel. It would have been totally unacceptable for me to have doped and failed. That wasn't an option: mentally, I wouldn't have been able to cope with the consequences of that.

It would mean I'd have to face the fact that it wasn't just my prior refusal to dope that was stopping me from being the most successful rider I could be. I'd have to acknowledge that maybe there were other characteristics preventing me from achieving the success I craved. I didn't want to know what they were.

I started the key stage, climbing the vicious Angliru, in this confused state of mind. The Angliru is in Asturias in north-west Spain and had only been raced on once before. It was reputed to be perhaps the hardest climb that any bike race had ever gone up, a road so steep that cars could barely make it up there. In just a few seasons, it had become the most feared summit finish in the sport.

But the forecast wasn't good and before the start, 'Chechu' Rubiera, who was from Asturias, was telling all the teams that if it rained we should strike. The roads in the region were covered in coal dust from the local mines and could be treacherously slippery in the rain.

There were two approaches to the foot of the Angliru. One took the main valley road, which Chechu said would be quite safe; the other climbed over one mountain then dropped down the other side of the valley to the foot of the Angliru.

This was the route the Vuelta organisers had taken the previous time they had used the mountain. It had rained and there had been crashes everywhere, forcing some of the main contenders out of the race with broken bones. Instead of learning from this, the race organisation had decided, recklessly, to use the same approach. It was clear they wanted crashes and they wanted spectacle. We all agreed we would call a truce to the racing if it rained. They were empty words. When it started to rain, we rode even faster.

The roads were like an ice rink. There was a series of crashes on the descent towards the Angliru and I was involved in the first of these. I got up without serious injury, although my left side had been ripped, but on the false flat leading to the foot of the Angliru my wheels disappeared from under me and I went down again, this time on my right side. It was a farce. I was one of the best riders in the wet and yet I had no control of what was going on. Remarkably my bike was still fine, so I straightened it up and set off again. But it was more dangerous than it had been all day, and we were going uphill.

Soon afterwards, I went down again, sliding along in the middle of the road on my left side. The car that was following me ran right over my bike – and I still had my feet in the pedals. Now I was furious. I dragged myself to the side of the road and just sat there with my wrecked bike, watching as bloodied riders came by. I love competition on an epic scale, but this had nothing to do with sport. We were being exploited. It was incredibly irresponsible of the organisation but they were getting what they wanted – headlines and TV ratings – at the risk of not only our health, but even our lives.

But the peloton had only itself to blame. We, the riders, let them do it to us. We were a bunch of lone-wolves, contracted mercenaries who stabbed each other in the back at every opportunity. We couldn't organise a piss-up in a brewery, I thought to myself as my peers struggled onwards. Then I corrected myself – actually that was probably the one thing we could do.

Eventually, my team car pulled up, with my spare bike on the roof. I got back on, but mentally I had quit the race. Bingen Fernandez, my loyal Basque teammate, finally caught up with me and tried pushing me, but I told him to forget it – we were so far behind that it was over.

It was so dark now that in the pouring rain it felt like dusk. I was covered in blood and had ripped a lot of skin, as coming down on my right side twice had worsened the road rash. I still wanted to finish the stage, even though, at the speed I was capable of, there was still close to an hour of climbing ahead of me.

The last part of the Angliru is the hardest. Over the final 6 kilometres, it averages 13 per cent with some passages at 24 per cent. Bingen didn't leave my side and, as a Basque rider, he was massively supported. Basque fans are among the most devoted in cycling and they were desperate to help him, but every time they tried to push him he would wave them away and tell them to push me.

I was a mess: it was all I could do to keep momentum. With just a few kilometres to go, we had to weave through broken-down cars and the dark misty air stank of burned-out clutches. The fans that were up there had no doubt climbed the mountain on foot and waited all day, but were now trapped behind 2-metre-high riot barriers guarded at intervals by police.

I'd never seen this before at a bike race and I haven't seen it since. Clearly, just to guarantee the spectacle, the organisation had wanted the bloody stragglers to suffer unaided, without any fans interfering in their bloody battle.

Not far from the finish, a fan managed to squeeze between the barriers and came running up to help me on what was one of the steepest parts. It was obvious I was in a lot of pain and although pushing me at this point made no difference to my race, or to the race overall, he wanted to help.

He'd barely started to push me, when a policeman came running over and slammed him against the fence crushing his neck with his forearm. I stopped – which wasn't difficult as I was riding at about 1 kilometre per hour – and went for the policeman. I couldn't believe it was happening. It had nothing to do with cycling.

Somebody had to take a stand against the madness. I decided it had to be me. I hated everything about cycling at that moment. I blamed it for the mess I found myself in, the doping, the loneliness, the craziness, the exploitation.

So just short of the finish line, I stopped. I leaned my bike up against the crowd barrier. Then I ripped my race numbers off and threw them on the floor, leaving my bike where it was. It made perfect sense to me.

The irony was that everybody thought I was protesting because of the difficulty of the Angliru, when it was in fact directed at the race conditions and the irresponsibility of the race organisation. Afterwards, I needed to explain on several occasions why I had done it. My 'strike' started the discussion though, and proved that I had the balls to do it. Funnily, my name is always linked to the Angliru, even though I have posted possibly one of the slowest-ever times for the climb.

*

I was still bandaged after the Vuelta and didn't really have much time to prepare for the World Championships in Zolder, Belgium. But I was committed to racing there, so after ten days off the bike, Rob Hayles was recruited as my temporary head coach. This involved him riding my scooter, while I chased him on my time trial bike. I was in terrible shape, but I rode in the World Championships time trial anyway.

Somehow, I got sixth place, only 35 seconds off the winning time. But the real up-side of making the trip to Belgium was that I met David Brailsford, who was at his first road World Championship in his role as Team GB Performance Director. We were like peas in a pod and instantly became friends.

He was unlike anybody I'd ever met in cycling, especially British cycling. Dave was charismatic, enthusiastic and persuasive. He told me he would do everything he could to help me become World Champion the following year, and that he'd go as far as having one of the Olympic project track bikes converted into a time trial road bike for me.

He gave me confidence and belief, and, most importantly, a desire and a reason to commit to winning the Worlds. My season ended soon after our meeting: meanwhile, I prepared to enter the final season of my contract with Cofidis: 2003 had to be a big year.

All the while, I hid my secret life. In fact, I hid it from everyone close to me until I went back to Hong Kong in the winter of 2002 and spent some time with my dad. But it wasn't an easy visit. Something had shifted in our relationship.

We were both so busy that we didn't see much of each other and, when we did, we were more distant that we had been before. He treated me as if I was somebody special and was almost deferential towards me. I didn't like it. I just wanted us to be the same as we had always been.

One night, we were in a bar in Tsim Sha Tsui with all my old school friends. There was nothing odd in Dad being there with us but, unusually, I was ignoring him. We were all pretty drunk and late in the evening Dad came over to me and said: 'David, let's go outside for a chat.'

We stepped outside, wandered down the street and then found ourselves in one of the narrow alleys so characteristic of Hong Kong.

Dad spoke first. 'What's going on?' he said.

I shrugged. 'What do you mean what's going on?'

'You're acting strangely, David. I'm worried about you, even your friends say you're not yourself.'

It didn't take much to get my anger rising. 'What? Oh *come on*, Dad,' I said. 'You're fucking joking, right? Everything's changed. I'm a different person to what I was.'

He was straining now, trying to reach me. 'But you're not – you're still the same person. That's what I don't understand. Why are you doing this to yourself?'

'. . . if this about my drinking then don't even bother!' Now I was almost shouting.

'Oh, here we go . . .'

Now all the frustration and self-loathing came spilling out. 'You know what, Dad? You know how you think the sun shines out of my arse?' I was shaking with anger.

'. . . Well, it doesn't. I'm not the golden boy. How about you tell your friends that David's a doper? That I take EPO . . .?'

Dad slapped me, hard. I took a step back and we stared at each other. His face crumpled and he broke down.

I went back into the bar. I didn't care.

16

CHAINS AND RAINBOWS

For the first time since signing my contract with Cofidis in 1996, I was facing uncertainty. Whether it was with Cofidis, or with another team, *I had* to succeed in 2003. I was under more pressure to get results than I'd ever been since turning pro; little did I know that the screw would soon be turned even tighter.

My salary for 2003 had reset to its default remuneration, the base level that I had been paid in 2000. This was because I had failed to achieve the necessary points in 2002 to activate the bonus system. This made me resentful. After all, I had missed the first half of the 2002 season because of glandular fever. Yes, I'd then flopped at the Vuelta – yet I'd won a stage at the Tour and been a player at almost every other race I competed in.

Unlike in 2001, when I was unaware of the intricacies of my contract, I now knew exactly what was at stake. I had grown very used to my high income and my spending power. Rob and Vicki Hayles used to say I had a leaf-blower filled with money.

But it didn't make sense to me that there could be such massive fluctuations in what I was paid. Bonuses didn't motivate me – my goals were always to win certain events and become the best rider I could be – it was never about going to a certain race because it was easy to score points, or defending fourth place at another race in order to secure the points. Yet that is what I had to do if I wanted to fulfil my bonus requirement. Effectively, there was no point in going for the big targets because that meant using other lesser races as preparation events and thus scoring fewer points and not making the bonus. It wasn't an ideal situation.

During an interview with the daily sports newspaper *L'Equipe*,

185

I sounded off about it. The next thing I knew I was being called in to explain myself to François Migraine. I apologised to him but insisted that I didn't think it was a good system. Of course, I'd had none of these qualms the year before when I'd been raking in the bonuses and benefiting from them. Money had become a motivation, but only because I'd grown used to it; before having that level of income, it hadn't motivated me at all.

With that realisation came the acknowledgement that I would be doping during the year. Jesús and I had planned that I would *prepare* twice during the season: for the Tour de France and the World Championships. I had become a fully fledged doper, cold and calculating in the manner with which I used drugs. There had been a steady but constant development in my doping use and now I knew what I was. I'd stopped lying to myself: I wasn't a clean athlete any more. I could push it to the back of my mind a lot of the time, but sometimes, usually when I was alone, I was crippled by guilt and self-loathing because of it.

I started 2003 a '*l'eau claire*' or clean. But I was chronically nervous and increasingly fretted about results. My goals were unrealistically high, and as I fell short of them I became even more stressed. By the time I got to Criterium International in late March, I was banging my head against the wall. Fifteen kilometres from the finish of the second stage, a race motorbike put me out of my misery.

Working his way through the peloton, the motorbike driver tried to squeeze through a gap that wasn't there and knocked me off. I was flipped onto my side and pushed along the road until I ended up in a ditch, shocked and seriously ripped up. I was very beaten up in the crash, but the greatest damage was to my right arm. The skin had been ripped off and the team doctor tried to sew it back together in the team bus. But the flap of skin wouldn't stitch, as it had been so badly torn. I was so preoccupied with this mess that I didn't pay much attention to the bruising on my thigh. I flew back to Biarritz wondering if the start to my season could get any worse.

It could. I woke up in the morning with a massively swollen thigh. A few hours later I was under general anaesthetic at the local hospital as the swelling was emptied and a drain fitted. I had to stay in hospital a further five days until they were happy that the drain could be removed. In total, I was off the bike for over three weeks – and then le Boss and I had one of our run-ins.

Although I had only been back on the bike for a few days, le Boss wanted me to race in Trophée des Grimpeurs, one of the most

unforgiving races on the French calendar. I sent him my training programmes from Jesús – including all the codes so that he could see I was being professional – but he was having none of it.

He began lining up the races. Next was the Four Days of Dunkirk (actually a six-day event). I did what he asked and suffered badly throughout, my legs hurting more than they'd ever done before. I could feel the untrained muscles being ripped to pieces by the massive workload and on the last day could barely get on the bike.

Then he entered me for the Tour of Picardie, only four days later, a similarly hard, flat, windy race. At least Picardie was only three days long, with a time trial as the final stage. I could barely walk and wondered how I was to survive. The day before the race I trained for only 10 minutes or so, setting out with the rest of the guys but then turning around because my legs still felt so damaged.

Yet when I woke up on the morning of the first stage at Picardie, the leg pain had vanished. The next day, feeling normal again, I launched an attack, partly to test my form. Before I knew it, I was away with Nico Vogondy, my companion from the Circuit de la Sarthe *echappée* two years earlier.

It seemed a futile move, as we had over 80 kilometres to race, but, before we were caught, there was a time bonus sprint 20 kilometres from the finish that I picked up. I decided it wouldn't be a bad idea to have that little buffer, in the light of the following day's time trial.

My intuition paid off. I took second place in the time trial, just 2 seconds behind the stage winner. What had seemed like a silly escapade the day before had turned into the race-winning move. The 3 seconds I'd won in the bonus sprint enabled me to win the Tour of Picardie by 1 second. Somehow, I had turned things around.

The first phase of my season was over. I returned to Biarritz and then drove down to see Jesús and pick up everything I needed for a two-week training camp in Spain. I'd learned from my mistakes. So, rather than holing up alone on a mountain-top, I had rented a villa on the Costa Blanca, in Calpe, and invited my sister, her fiancé, and our friend James Pope, also Fran's business partner, to come down and join me.

Instead of sending myself on punishing monastic missions, I was trying to be more accepting and pragmatic. I bought a mini-fridge so that I could keep my EPO hidden in my room, away from the rest of the household. At the same time, I made sure Fran and James never knew about my involvement in doping. Maybe they had their suspicions, but I was very good at keeping my secret. They believed in me – they had heard me railing against the doping scene. It would probably have been the last thing they expected, especially as they didn't know the reality of what went on behind the scenes.

But then my career had followed a steady linear progression and everything I'd achieved up to that point was within the realms of possibility as a non-doper. There hadn't been any anomalous results and this was what made it possible for me to keep off the doping radar. In the two previous years I had won races clean, just as I had done by winning Picardie before heading off on my *preparation* camp.

Fran was the chef. She kept my diet on track and, as I steadily lost weight, it felt like doping had become part of my life – simply another part of '*le métier*', the job. But my training was terrible and I never felt less like I was doping than I did those couple of weeks. My body was in revolt after getting thrown into Dunkirk and Picardie. Despite being *prepared*, I was desperate for everything to come together in time for my next big race, the Dauphiné Libéré.

The Classique des Alpes is a one-day race, an aperitif, before the giant climbs of the week-long Dauphiné. I came third and, that evening, on my way down to dinner at the hotel, I bumped into the organisers of the Tour de France at a cocktail reception.

In the spirit of bonhomie, I joined them for a couple of glasses, something that perhaps not many modern riders might do. My sociability met with their approval.

'It's a shame there aren't more riders like you,' they said, 'willing to have a glass or two of champagne, like in the old days.'

Yet I felt deceitful. Shaking hands on a podium was one thing, clinking glasses with the Tour organisers while being toasted was a little harder to swallow.

Over the next week, my preparation paid off and I hit flying form. For the first time, I was racing against Lance in the mountains. I finished third overall in the Dauphiné, behind him and the Basque climber Iban Mayo. Suddenly, riding for the general classification – being a contender – at the Tour itself was a real possibility.

After the race, I flew to Madrid, where I stopped off to pick up the last of the pre-Tour EPO from Jesús. I spent a couple of days in Spain before heading back to Biarritz to fine-tune for the Tour.

The 2003 Tour was the centenary edition, so the race route was designed to pay tribute to all the drama, grandeur and tradition of the previous century. The prologue was on a huge stage, starting under the Eiffel Tower and racing through the heart of Paris. I desperately wanted to win it. If I did, I would then be able to take the rest of the race as I pleased, with no pressure, and hopefully be able to have a proper tilt at the overall classification.

I arrived in Paris in ideal shape. Everything was spot on – Jesús had done his job perfectly. But my prologue bike was a different matter. The team's equipment was laughable and, in desperation, I had sourced my own handlebars and front wheel. I had given up on them ever supplying me with what I needed.

Two days before the prologue, the team mechanics rebuilt my bike. When I popped out to their truck – their mobile workshop –. to check progress, they showed me their latest weight-saving idea, of removing the front derailleur and using only one chain ring. They'd also removed the front derailleur changer, making the bike look very stripped down and more like a racing machine than it ever had done before.

I am passionate about my equipment, but I am no mechanic – it didn't even cross my mind that the front derailleur was a key part of the bike's 'drive train'. It may have served no purpose in changing gears, but it was there to catch the chain if it was thrown off the chain ring. But the mechanics were so convinced it was a good idea, so certain that it would make me faster, that I was sold immediately. I took the bike for a spin and it seemed as if there would be no problem.

But on the morning of the prologue, Bondue took a decision that proved disastrous. All of the chain rings on the team bikes were changed. Bondue had decided that we had to use our sponsor's chain ring for the Tour, rather than the standard chain rings we'd been using for the rest of the year.

As one of the favourites for the prologue, I was the last Cofidis rider to start. I waited for my start time with a sinking feeling, as I watched our riders slip their chains, one by one. One rider actually fell down the start ramp when his chain came off on the first pedal stroke. I began to simmer with anger: I'd been fighting for years to get the time trial bike I wanted, yet nothing ever changed.

It was a typical Cofidis scenario. The chains were derailing because they weren't compatible with the chain rings. At the last minute, as panic spread through the staff, I was asked if they should change my ring back to the standard one. Stubbornly, I refused. I didn't want anybody tinkering with my bike so close to the start, but also I decided if it was going to come off, then so be it. Bondue's head would roll for it.

Once out on the course, I was quicker than I'd expected and came through the first time check significantly faster than anybody else. I couldn't believe it when I saw the intermediate time board giving me a 4-second lead on the next rider. I'd planned to stay within myself the first half of the prologue and then to bring it home with everything I had into the final kilometres. Four seconds was a massive gain considering the course and the conditions. Suddenly, I was filled with the certainty that I was going to win, that there was nothing that could stop me.

As I exited the penultimate corner, I began the final push towards the *flamme rouge*, but the moment I pushed on the pedals all resistance had disappeared. Nothing happened. At first I couldn't figure it out but then I looked down and was horrified to see the chain dangling uselessly off the chain ring.

When I'd stopped pedalling as I cornered, the chain had gone slack and a little vibration from the road had bounced it off the chain ring. In a moment, my chances of winning the prologue of the centenary Tour had gone.

I had no front derailleur to catch the chain and guide it back on to the chain ring, so I had to lean down and delicately pick it up between forefinger and thumb and drop it precisely on the chain ring – while freewheeling down the course. I still don't know how I found the lucidity to do that, as my heart rate was close to 190 and the adrenalin was pumping through me. I managed it, but I was almost at a standstill by the time I had dropped the chain back in place.

I found a final rush of power with the anger that was now raging through me and sprinted as hard as I could. I crossed the line two-hundredths of a second behind Australian Brad McGee. It was divine justice. Brad, one of my closest friends, had managed to stay clean, despite everything. I couldn't help thinking that that was the way it was supposed to be.

Even so, I didn't feel that philosophical in the immediate aftermath. I sat in the team bus fuming, until I spotted Migraine. I homed in on him and led him across to the ONCE team's compound and showed him their bikes.

'François,' I said, '*that* is a time trial bike. I've been fighting for years to get something that is just a little bit like this.'

Then my resentments against everything came spilling out. I demanded Bondue's ceremonial downsizing, making it clear to Migraine that he was at fault and that he should have nothing to do with the sporting side of the team from then on. I got what I wanted. Alain's head rolled and we had a meeting the next morning when the whole team was told this.

It was my payback. I blamed Bondue for a lot of things stretching back over the years; I blamed him for far more than just losing my chain. Deep down, maybe I held him responsible for everything to do with Cofidis – as if he had betrayed me somehow.

The next morning, out of sight of my teammates and the crowds, I sat down in the shadow of the Stade de France and wept. That was when Lance saw me.

Immediately after the prologue, my principal emotion had been anger. The next morning, as we climbed off the bus for the start of the first stage, I was overwhelmed with disappointment.

I thought nobody had seen me at such a low ebb, but there, answering a pre-race call of nature a few yards away, was Lance. He came over, consoled me, and said he'd call that evening. He did, and the conversation helped.

My 2003 Tour didn't really get much better. On the first rest day I woke up with a sore throat that quickly became bronchitis, and suffered through the middle week before rallying a few days prior to the end of the race.

On another day, I would have been excited by the final time trial, but the torrential rain and howling wind dampened my spirits.

I didn't recce the course or look at a course map and my warm-up was laughable, yet as soon as I rolled off the start ramp and realised that I actually felt good I embraced the apocalyptic conditions. It was the first time I enjoyed being on my bike since the pre-chain debâcle of the prologue.

Visibility was terrible and the roads were treacherous – I twice came past guys who were sprawled in the road after crashing. I crashed too, in the last 5 kilometres, yet this didn't stop me winning by 15 seconds and posting one of the fastest ever time trials, with a 54 kilometres per hour average speed. I'm good when I'm relaxed, but I'm even better when it's wet.

After the Tour ended, I signed with Cofidis for two more years. It was the big money contract I had wanted. I had been in protracted negotiations with Bjarne Riis and his team, but now that Bondue was out of the picture, I was sure I'd be able to steer things more myself. In truth, my loyalty towards the team was based more on the longevity of our relationship than anything else.

Brad McGee and I spent some time together in Biarritz after the Tour ended. Brad knew that I had been *prepared* and we both knew that what had happened in the Tour prologue was right – that it was karma – and that he was supposed to win. I had told him this the next day. Brad understood that I had made my decisions, and yet he did his best not to judge. He was one of the few, an untouchable, like Moncoutie.

There was talk of the Vuelta and more *preparation* with Jesús, but I couldn't face it. Instead of heading to altitude and back to doping, I stayed in Biarritz. I had been in regular contact with Dave Brailsford through the year – although he knew nothing of my *preparation* programmes – and now my thoughts were all about racing with Team GB at the World Championships.

I knew I had to ride the Vuelta to find form but I turned up overweight and unfit. I was one of the first riders to be dropped in the first road stage – even I was a little shocked. I got a grip and decided that suffering through the Vuelta would be about getting ready for the Worlds, in just a few weeks time. In the first time trial, I set off expecting very little, yet I finished second. I was baffled;

maybe it was just down to pure talent. However, any illusions I had of sporting genius were stamped out in the next day's mountain stage.

I was on the ropes, last on the road, for most of that day. For a good 80 kilometres, I was with just one other rider, far behind the *gruppetto*. He ended up throwing in the towel, but I knew that I had to finish the Vuelta if I wanted to win the Worlds time trial. Eventually, I caught the *gruppetto* just 4 kilometres from the finish. The toughest day was behind me: from then on I got better and better.

More by luck than judgement – I had come perilously close to not making it through the first week – I finished the race in good shape. Now I had to hook up with Jesús.

On the last day of the Vuelta in Madrid, I picked up a batch of EPO and took the first dose. Jesús had advised me to take the next two doses of EPO directly into the vein. That way, he said, it would work faster and disappear out of my system well before race day. It was the first time I'd taken EPO intravenously.

From Madrid, I flew to Manchester, to spend time with Team GB, testing the new super-bike that had been built for me, before heading out to Canada for the World Championships.

It was a joy being with the British team. Dave was a great leader and an even better manager, and there was focus to everything that they did. Their organisation and expertise made Cofidis look like a small cycling club. Dave had followed through on his promises from the year before and had done everything possible at his end to enable me to win the Worlds. All I had to do was to be physically ready.

After I had finished the doses of EPO, I was left with two empty syringes. I didn't want to put them in the hotel bin, so I slipped them into a side pocket in my suitcase, planning to dispose of them later. By this point, I was so blasé about doping that I didn't really think it was such a big problem to carry around some empty syringes until I found a safe and secure place to deposit them.

By taking EPO I had guaranteed that I would be fulfilling my end of the bargain. Nobody in British cycling had any idea that

I was doping, as they were absolutely ignorant of the world I lived in. They looked up to the European scene, even if, like everybody, they knew there was bad stuff going on. But it never crossed their minds that I was involved in any of it. Because of this it was possible for me to conceal my secret.

Although the bike that Team GB had built for me was a dream – like nothing I'd ever ridden before – I was plagued by doubts. The new bike gave me a clear performance advantage, but that only made me even more nervous as I knew how much time, money and effort had been put into building it for me. I also had EPO, testosterone and cortisone running through my veins – there was surely no way I could lose, yet I was terrified that I might.

But I didn't lose – I achieved a crushing victory. I was so much quicker that I realised that I would win at the halfway point. In fact I spent the last 10 kilometres trying to save energy, so that I'd be good for the road race three days later. After I'd won I stood on the podium, listening to 'God Save the Queen'. I was World Time Trial champion, yet I felt almost nothing. I should have been choked, moved, just as other athletes were at such a moment. I wanted to experience that feeling. Instead, I just thought: 'Job done.'

More than ever, I was fully aware that I needed to rethink what I was doing and where I was going. The time in Canada had allowed me to talk to Dave Brailsford at length. He picked up on my unhappiness and we discussed my future.

The Athens Olympics were less than a year away. There was talk of me becoming part of the ever-improving track team and maybe even riding the individual pursuit. I knew what this would mean and I made the decision that if I was going to work with Dave and the national team then I would do it clean.

I'd become so drained by the professional world. I'd become world champion, but it was a hollow victory. The possibility of working with Dave and Team GB opened up options. He reinforced my self-belief, his was the voice I needed to hear.

I was sick of doping. Team GB offered escape from that world. As we flew out of Canada, I knew it was over, that I'd never dope again. From now on, I told myself, things would be different.

17

GAME OVER

I had thought that I could just stop doping and put it behind me, that ending the cheating would end the lies. I couldn't have been more wrong. Within a few months my life would spiral further out of control than ever before.

Yet I was now a clean athlete, taking that philosophy to an extreme that I hadn't done since my first few months as a pro. Team GB's thinking and professionalism was having a profound impact on me. After long discussions with GB's sports scientists, I decided I would put a stop to *all* needles, which meant no more 'recovery' injections.

They had convinced me that there was no scientific proof of injectable '*récup*' speeding up an athlete's recovery. I simply had to be diligent with the food and drinks I used and my body would recover just as well, if not better.

I was now in a position where I could stand by this and stick to it. I wasn't a wide-eyed, gauche neo-pro who knew no better and was easily manipulated. I was reigning World Champion – and an ex-doper. I didn't care what my fellow pros, team doctors, *soigneurs* or team management at Cofidis thought: if I wanted to do it my way then that was how it would be.

I had realised that the more I doped, the more I hated cycling – and the more it became a job, not my passion. I may have been able to win bigger races but I'd never felt less joy in doing so. That feeling stayed with me, an emptiness, a pointlessness that wouldn't go away.

Dave Brailsford and Team GB gave me another option. They had an anti-doping stance that they truly believed in and they operated in a manner that made you want to be clean. I had in many ways given up on Cofidis and the European pro scene, but the prospect of being part of Team GB for the Athens Olympics inspired me.

I holed up in Manchester and spent increasing amounts of time training on the track. Rod Ellingworth and Simon Jones were coaching me and I spent every afternoon in one-to-one sessions on the boards. Before long, I was in training sessions with the track squad. The level of skill and experience was terrifying, but I loved it.

I hadn't had so much fun on a bike in years and we discussed the realistic possibility that I'd race in the Athens Olympic track team. Soon afterwards, Nicole Cooke and I were announced as the first official members of the Team GB Athens Olympic Squad. The future was looking bright.

My lifestyle in Biarritz was very different from the disciplined environment of Team GB. Work on my house was progressing as it was transformed into the ultimate bachelor pad. From the outside, it looked to be a classic Parisian-style villa, but once inside it was anything but traditional. There was a fingerprint-access front door, 400 square metres of loft space fitted with the most cutting-edge technology available, furniture shipped from Italy, a wine cellar and a cinema in the basement. There were glass panels through each of the four floors, and standing in the basement you were able to look up and out through the atrium, far above.

Tellingly, it had not even crossed my mind to have an area for my bikes. I hadn't wanted the house to have anything to do with cycling. I persuaded myself that it was my ticket to happiness, thinking that when it was finished everything would finally make sense. But the closer the work came to completion, the more I recognised how incredibly wrong I was to have thought that, as I realised that the house was the manifestation of my cheating. I began to dread the day it would be finished and I'd close the door behind me.

I was enjoying a world champion's lifestyle. I had a deal with

Jaguar that meant I had a car waiting for me wherever I went, and an XKR on order. I was an Olympian with medal success almost guaranteed and I was one of the highest-paid cyclists in the world. Yet I was lonelier than ever. I was now seeing a French girl called Katherine de Freycinet but I still struggled to sustain a relationship.

Katherine, a bohemian aristocrat and very French, fitted my new image perfectly. For a few months things between us were good. She would sit in the centre of the velodrome, sketching and writing songs while I was whizzing around the track, learning how to become an Olympian. From the outside it probably looked like a wonderful life.

I began to think that maybe having the fabulous life was what it was all about. Then I'd beat myself up about it, and then tell myself off for that. What right did I have to feel sorry for myself? I had a life people only dreamed of.

But it didn't make me happy. I found it almost impossible to spend time on my own. I had to be with people as much as possible. Before long I couldn't even handle being on my own with Katherine

199

and decided that I wasn't cut out for relationships. I had my house – that was a big enough relationship.

And through it all, my doping past shadowed me. It was always there, hovering. I'd done my best to bury it but it wasn't long before I realised how wrong I'd been to think I could just put it all behind me and move on.

At the first Cofidis get-together for the 2004 season, in Amiens, I found out that Philippe Gaumont had spent a week at l'Équipier's house in Tuscany. I was completely stunned. I'd been able to influence the team to re-sign l'Équipier for one more year. To hear that he was now taking care of Gaumont's needs blew me away.

I stormed through the hotel corridors until I found his room. 'Tell me it isn't true that Gaumont came down to stay with you,' I snapped at him.

He was shocked by my anger. He looked down, eyes averted.

'David, he came down with his family for a week.' He shrugged apologetically. 'He *understands* though – don't worry.'

I was incensed. I couldn't believe how stupid he had been to trust Gaumont.

'You fucking idiot!' I shouted. 'What does he know? Does he know about me staying with you?'

'No, no! Of course not,' he said. There was a pause. 'I don't think so anyway.'

I was panicking, terrified of what could happen. Gaumont knew all about the *omertà*, but he had trouble keeping his mouth shut. There was no doubt in my mind that everybody would soon know that l'Équipier was the team's fixer. If Gaumont got caught, then l'Équipier would be implicated and then, eventually, so would I.

There was a high risk of me being linked to him. The Tuscan trip had been over two years earlier, but that didn't mean it couldn't be traced. I had been so calculating when I'd worked with Jesús. I had reduced the human factor to a bare minimum. Two people were in on the deal – Jesús and me.

My mind was racing: Gaumont, always Gaumont. How was he still on the team? Nobody really knew. There were rumours of him having a series of clauses in his contract that allowed the team to fire him if he went off the rails, while some claimed he blackmailed the team into keeping him on. I think the truth was simpler. Philippe could be a charming man when he chose to be, and no doubt it was this charm that had convinced Migraine to stick with him.

I was in shock, gripped by the awful realisation that word might spread that I was a doper. Finding out about Gaumont spending time with l'Équipier awoke me to the bitter truth: it was never going to go away. I would always have to live with my doping past, no matter how much I cleaned up my act.

Two months later, my worst fears were realised.

An ex-Cofidis rider – Marek Rutkiewicz, a young Polish guy who was mentored by one of Cofidis's *soigneurs* –, was arrested at Paris Charles de Gaulle airport, carrying doping products. The *soigneur*, 'Bob' Boguslaw Madejak, had brought several young Poles across from Poland and secured them contracts, acting as agent, doctor and father figure. Bob was a great *soigneur* and part of the old guard, but from what we could tell, he didn't seem to do anything that was too risky.

As soon as we heard about Marek being arrested we knew Bob would be next. He was in Spain with us at our pre-season training camp, but it was like watching a dead man walking. He was naturalised French and his family lived in France, so he had no choice but to return.

Marek was released after cooperating with the police and telling them what they wanted to know, while Bob, arrested on arrival when he flew home, simply refused to speak. He was of the Eastern bloc old school. In the 1980s, as part of the Polish national cycling team, he had escaped the country and been forced to leave his family behind in Poland for two years until he could get them out. A few months in jail weren't a big deal to Bob.

It seemed obvious to most of us that Gaumont would be the next to be arrested. He had previously been detained by the police and was the obvious target. After the camp ended, when the team returned to France, Philippe and Cedric Vasseur were arrested and held for the maximum 48-hour period.

During their detention, l'Équipier and I were implicated, just as I had feared. People knew I worked with Jesús, but Gaumont wrapped us up in other accusations as well. He claimed that we'd been taking cocaine at the training camp in Calpe. Whatever Gaumont's recollection, I knew this was not true, but he had no choice but to drag others into it all, as he was drug-tested while in custody and knew that he would test positive for cocaine and whatever else he'd been taking.

I knew what I'd done – and I also knew what I hadn't done. I was the golden boy of the team but Philippe made me sound like a monster. I could only surmise that, even in the death throes of his cycling career, he tried to protect himself by implicating me and as many others as he could in order to reduce the impact of his own corruption.

The police were convinced they'd unearthed a massive drugs ring and that Cofidis operated a complex internal doping programme. All of us knew that this was about as far from the truth as was possible, but we also knew they would do everything within their power to prove their theory. Gaumont certainly made it sound as if there was systematic doping, but then he was genuinely convinced that it was impossible to be a successful professional cyclist without doping.

The *L'Equipe* had received leaks of the statements that Gaumont had given to the investigating judge. They had two journalists working on the story and when I saw either of their numbers appear on my phone, my palms would sweat and my heart would race.

I never knew what their latest bit of information would be, so I always assumed the worst. Had l'Équipier talked? Had they found something out that nobody knew?

I was not very good at weathering this storm. For the first time I was being asked, point blank, whether I'd ever doped. Up to that point, I'd never had to lie, simply because I had always been thought of as an innocent. Now I was having to lie, but I didn't live with it well.

The day before I was supposed to compete in Manchester at the Track World Cup, for Team GB, Cofidis withdrew the whole team from racing in order to try to bring an end to the ongoing saga that was the Cofidis affair. We were grounded for a month. During that time, Cofidis planned to put new internal controls and rules in place so that the team could move forward.

The team ran the first of what were planned to be regular hair tests, able to detect drug use over the previous months (depending on the length of the hair and the drugs they were looking for).

We also signed the latest ethical charter, but God knows how many of these we'd signed in the previous years. It was all more of a publicity stunt than anything else, because Cofidis had fundamentally failed when it came to preventing doping. But the last thing they wanted to do was admit it.

The Cofidis affair had also attracted the interest of the French tax authorities. Gaumont had told the police about certain riders in the team receiving income from image contracts paid through a Luxembourg holding company. He had been the recipient of this type of contract when he had first come to the team and was generously paid.

As a result, the police raided the Cofidis headquarters and took all our contracts. It was only a matter of time before I would receive demands from the dreaded '*fiscal Française*'. I got in touch with a UK firm to try and piece together the previous four years of accounts, but it was a gargantuan task and one that had no prospect of a happy outcome. Now I faced the very real threat of losing my house.

It seemed more than likely that I would soon be arrested, so in the spring of 2004 I met with a Parisian lawyer to discuss my rights. As it turned out, I had very few. I had no right to a lawyer and could be held for up to 48 hours. I could be held longer if the judge saw fit, although I would then be allowed access to a lawyer. It was frightening. There seemed to be little I could do; my life was now out of my hands.

Then, as my panic grew, everything went quiet. There were no more heart-stopping phone calls from journalists who had seen the latest leaked reports, there were no more arrests. It seemed that the Cofidis affair had ground to a halt.

I thought that maybe I'd escaped it all, that maybe the investigation had reached a dead end. When it came to doping I had nothing to do with Bob or Gaumont or anybody in the team, except l'Équipier. So, as far as I could tell, they hadn't got anything against me other than Gaumont's allegations.

Ten days before the start of the 2004 Tour de France, I felt that the worst was behind me. Dave Brailsford and Lisa, his pregnant girlfriend, were having a short break in Biarritz before Dave headed off to Athens for the Olympics, so we got together for dinner.

Dave had seen how committed I was to being on his team and living by his standards. He respected me for it. In many ways, the thought of working with Dave and Team GB had saved me from completely losing the plot. They had shown me there was another world beyond the corruption of the European professional scene. I clung on to what they represented: it was what kept me riding my bike when otherwise I simply would have disappeared into a black hole.

We decided to go to one of my favourite restaurants, in Ilbarritz, called Blue Cargo. It's a beautiful converted house, perched on the hillside above the beach. It was the place to be seen. It had an adjacent bar where, late at night, dancing on the tables was considered the norm.

I loved going there. I'd been there before – once on a hot rainy night with Stuey, Matt White and Lance. It had turned into a memorable Blue Cargo evening, Stuey walking around shirtless with a bottle of vodka in each hand serving random people, while Whitey danced on the tables.

The next morning, Lance and Matt flew on a private jet to a race in Germany. Midway through the flight, Lance turned to Matt and said: 'Whitey – what a night. Maybe in my top three best ever.'

Whitey stared back at him, baffled.

'Fuck me, Lance,' he said. 'You should get out more.'

We'd ordered some wine and I'd just finished telling this story, when two frowning strangers walked up to the table and stood over us.

'David Millar . . .?' they snapped at me. They held up their police badges.

'You have to come with us.' We stood up and followed them out into the car park. A third policeman was waiting for us.

They told me to take off my belt and then to remove my shoelaces. It was the first step in dismantling me. Initially, I wasn't scared or nervous, just very angry. One of them was particularly aggressive and seemed to take great pleasure in belittling me. It felt personal, as if they had a vendetta against me.

We were split up and put into different cars. I was on my own and Dave and Lisa were in another car, escorted to Biarritz police station by the angry policeman who spent the journey punching the back of Lisa's seat, scaring her to death. Now Dave unleashed his anger, telling him to calm down and respect his pregnant girlfriend.

They took me back to my apartment. As I unlocked the door one of them restrained me, while the other crept in, gun in hand, to clear the place before we entered. I thought it was contemptible: I was a professional cyclist, not a drug-running murderer.

They switched the lights on and took me into the living room. They pulled one of the dining chairs into the middle of the room, sat me on it and told me to sit still.

'Move and we will take you down,' one of them said to me, with a look that told me that he meant it. I could see that he would not hesitate to use violence.

So I sat there, as still as I could, for the next three hours, as they turned my apartment inside out. At first I felt secure in the knowledge that they'd never find anything, but that smugness steadily dissipated as they started to go through everything I owned, effectively ripping my life apart. I felt violated. It was another step towards breaking me down so that I'd be easier to interrogate.

After over two hours, I could sense their frustration. The last room they took apart was my bedroom and, for some reason, I began to feel a rising panic. There was something there, something hidden, something incriminating.

What was it . . .?

Then I remembered.

The bookshelves.

No – please – you mustn't look through the bookshelves ...

I love books. They're among my most treasured possessions. I take care of them. Even after reading them I try to keep them in perfect condition, the spines undamaged.

A month after I had come back from the World Championships in Canada, I'd finally got around to unpacking. That was when I rediscovered the two used syringes that I'd stowed away after taking my final dose of EPO in Manchester.

By then I'd already made the decision that I'd never dope again. I thought it would be a poignant souvenir to keep the last two syringes that I ever used, so I hid them in the bookshelves in my room. Then I forgot that they were there.

I could hear the jubilation in their voices even before they walked towards me, brandishing the syringes. I felt like I'd been punched. My world came crashing down. Suddenly, I was very scared. Panic gripped me and I denied their existence. They smiled at me.

They took me to the police station and led me to a cell. Later, a friend on the Biarritz police force told me that when they had arrived they had reserved the cell for 48 hours, whether they had found anything or not. They had always intended to detain me for as long as the law would allow.

18

CÔTE DES BASQUES

After 47 hours in custody, I admitted everything.

I was on good terms with the police when I left, the relief of having told them everything putting me in a state of euphoria. I was grateful to them for liberating me from the torment.

I was escorted out through the back door, away from the waiting cameras. Dave Brailsford was there, waiting for me. He didn't look angry, or pissed off, just relieved that I was all right. He gave me a big hug. We got into a car and headed to a hotel. I don't know what I'd have done if Dave hadn't been there, really I don't.

Dave had also had a rough time. They had presumed he knew everything about me and had questioned him for 4 hours. He explained the shock and incomprehension he had felt when they had shown him the two empty EPO syringes. He was only weeks away from leading Team GB's cyclists at the Athens Olympics and had been advised to get out of Biarritz and as far away from David Millar as possible. Despite that advice, he had decided to stay.

Dave speaks fluent French. While I was in custody, he had tried to speak to Cofidis, but they had washed their hands of me. Now he realised how the professional world, my world, operated. He saw that I was now on my own, that the cord had been cut. This was when he decided that somebody had to be there for me when I got out, no matter what I had, or hadn't, done.

He had booked us into the Sofitel, overlooking the beach – one of the most beautiful hotels in Biarritz. We stayed up late drinking. I told him everything, all the dark truths that I'd kept from him. He didn't judge me. He understood what it meant, that my life was now in tatters. But the shit hadn't even begun. In a way, that night was the last before I had to really face the nightmare ahead. When I woke up the next morning, the euphoria had gone.

I spoke to my sister, my mum and my dad. I told them all the same thing: 'It's over.' Dad listened and then said: 'Is it true?'

'Yes,' I said.

'Did you tell them everything?' he asked.

'Everything.'

'David, I'm immensely proud of you,' he said. 'I hope Cofidis will now pay for what they did.'

I hadn't expected that they'd be happy – happy that it was 'over'. But then they had known for a few years that I hadn't been right.

I called Francis Van Londersele, my *directeur sportif* on Cofidis, and told him the same thing: '*C'est fini, Francis.*' That was the last contact I had with Cofidis. They fired me a couple of weeks later.

I needed a little bit of time before going back to my place. My friends, Xavier and Didier, spoke to their neighbour who lived in Paris most of the year, and, very kindly, he let me use his beautiful apartment for a few days. It looked out across the Côte des Basques, the waves crashing in the background, day and night. It would have been hard to find a more beautiful hideaway.

I spent a week there, partly thinking that everybody was being over-protective of me. I was sure I'd be fine back in my apartment. I was wrong. I did go back there to pick up some stuff, but found myself dizzied by the experience. The place was wrecked and reminded me of the state my life was in.

While I'd been in custody, Dave had spoken to Dr Steve Peters, the psychiatrist who had been working as a consultant to the national team. Dave decided to fly Steve down to Biarritz to spend a day with me. A couple of years later, I learned that Dave had funded this out of his own pocket. At the time, it hadn't even crossed my mind who was paying for Steve's time and expenses.

I sat down with Steve just two days after I was released. We met at the Sofitel, just after nine in the morning, and spent the day talking. He told me straight away it wasn't going to be like the therapy sessions I'd seen in TV shows. He spent the morning asking me questions about my life and upbringing, starting at the beginning in Scotland, up until that day. Then we broke for lunch and met again in the afternoon, when he was able to explain to me why I'd made the decisions I had taken.

It was an eye-opening experience.

It became clear that I still had a fairly adolescent mentality, relied heavily on father figures and had created behavioural patterns that were destructive and self-perpetuating. He made me understand that most of the decisions I'd made were unavoidable, considering the personality and upbringing I'd had.

I then understood that my history, combined with the situations I had found myself in, gave a certain inevitability to everything that had happened. There was little emotion involved in the whole process, no floods of tears. It was all very clinical, but I left with the understanding that there was a lot of work to be done.

In the context of my development, I had acted normally. I relied heavily on other people guiding me and had been let down by the people around me, particularly my team. It would have been out of the ordinary, unusual, for me to have not made the mistakes I'd made. So, in conclusion, I was normal . . . and I had always thought I was different.

A few years later Dave told me that when he'd spoken to Steve after our time together, Steve had told him that there was no short-term resolution, that only the passage of time would allow me to sort myself out. In other words, I hadn't quite finished my self-destruction. I still had a little way to go.

Fran had flown over to Biarritz almost immediately and was there, waiting, as I spent the day with Steve Peters. We met at the Côte des Basques after Steve and I had finished talking. I was a bit dazed. I hadn't talked that much about my life to anybody before and I'd certainly never had anybody dissect it in the way he had. It left me feeling very open to the world.

We sat at the top of the steps that led down to the beach. I was in jeans, wearing a T-shirt, leather jacket and some big black sunglasses. I didn't belong there, a brooding presence, on the beach in summer time. Everything felt wrong, as if all the shit that

I protected myself with had been stripped away. I was 27 and I'd thrown my life away. I felt empty.

We sat there in silence for what seemed like an eternity, watching people come up and down the steps to the beach. None of it made sense: how had I done this? I was both angry and sad, filled with incomprehension.

Finally I spoke.

'They said I'd still be able to do the Tour de France.'

Fran looked at me. 'David, I don't know if that's going to be possible.'

There was another long pause.

'Are you still proud of me?'

'Of course I am, you're my big brother.'

I watched some little kids playing in the sand.

'If I ever have kids, I'm never letting this happen to them,' I said, with conviction. A tear escaped from under my big black sunglasses.

France reached across and put her hand on mine.

I looked at her and smiled sadly.

'I wish I had a fast-forward button,' I said.

Biarritz is a small place. It wasn't possible for me to go into town without bumping into people I knew. Those I didn't know probably knew me, and the prospect of walking around daunted me. It was shameful being known as a doper, a cheat. It's one thing doing it in secret, lying to yourself – but there was now no hiding from who I was and from what I'd done. I dreaded living with it.

But my dread was misplaced. I was lucky in that the friends I had made were all great and took particular care of me. Alain and his girlfriend Valerie now had a café-restaurant on the Côte des Basques and I would spend my days between there and Sabine's Ventilo.

They organised mini-football tournaments on the beach and generally it felt like my life was unchanged, even if it was now a life without cycling. Even random people, people I'd seen around but never spoken to before, came up to me and asked if I was okay.

From older members of the Biarritz community to the surfing crowd, there was genuine concern. I had never expected that. One day I was walking through town, down one of the quiet back streets, when a local surfer dude, sitting on his window ledge having a cigarette, called out to me.

'*Daveed! Putain, c'est la merde. Ça va?!*'

I was a bit surprised but mustered a response: '*Ça va, bon, pas trop, mais ca va aller.*'

Then he said the loveliest thing: '*Tu sais on pense a toi, tu n'est pas un mauvais mec – d'accord?*'

'*You know we're thinking of you, you're not a bad guy – okay?*'

I muttered some thanks. It cut deep to realise how lovely people were and how much I'd let them down.

I never met anybody who was critical of me in Biarritz. I think most of them knew me, or knew what had happened, even if they'd never spoken to me. They'd watched me grow and seen my success, yet I'd always been one of the few anglophones who had been totally immersed in French life.

I was fiercely proud of being from Biarritz and in the two previous years I'd become known in the French press as *Un Biarrot*, a local, a part of the town. In my downfall the town took me under its wing more than it had ever done at the height of my success. All of a sudden I was accessible, and people reached out to me. That got me through those first few weeks.

But at some point I had to start dealing with it. I was scheduled to go to Paris to meet with my lawyer, to brief him on what I'd said and for him to educate me on what would happen next. Up to this point, beyond Dave Brailsford and my family, I had not disclosed to anybody what had happened during my 48 hours with the police, but that changed when my entire statement was leaked to *L'Equipe*. This was a legal document that was supposed to remain confidential until the case was presented in court. But there had been leaks about the 'Cofidis affair' from day one, and *L'Equipe* was better informed than the lawyers involved.

Cedric Vasseur, one of my teammates, had been falsely accused of taking cocaine. The urine and hair samples he'd given when arrested with Gaumont at the beginning of the year had tested positive, yet anybody who knew Cedric well knew that he didn't do cocaine.

While Vasseur was fighting this allegation, he also claimed that one of his statements had been forged – which seemed ironic, given that the police were investigating a sporting team for fraud. Cedric was eventually cleared.

I headed back to London and gave two interviews, one to William Fotheringham of the *Guardian*, the other to Jeremy Whittle of *The Times*. I slept through most of the Tour de France. I was effectively running scared and became nocturnal, living in the alternative world that comes to life as the sun goes down. It was good escapism but I was refusing to face the scale of the chaos. I had been paying my house off as the money came in, using every euro I had in Luxembourg. I spent my salary in France on a near monthly basis, and there was money, but nowhere near enough to sustain my lifestyle for more than a few months. Yet I carried on buying the drinks, showing *largesse* – it seemed more important then ever for me to pay now.

It soon became clear that I was going to have to leave France. The French tax office was pursuing me, and it was inevitable they were going to freeze all my assets at some point – not that I had many. My bank accounts were drying up and my house was unfinished and the property of a Luxembourg company. I didn't really have anything else. There were a few watches, lots of books, CDs and DVDs, clothes and shoes.

My house was only a month away from being completed, and yet now I had no money to complete it. I faced the harsh reality that I was going to have to sell it, so I made a big sign with my phone number on it and stuck it in the window. It symbolised, perhaps better than anything else, the scale of my downfall.

My life was like a burning fuse, but there was no bomb connected – it was just going to fizzle out until there'd be nothing left.

19

JUDGE DREAD

No human authority can encroach upon the power of an investigating judge; nothing can stop him; no one can control him.

Honoré de Balzac

My first meeting with the Paris-based judge in charge of the Cofidis affair, Richard Pallain, was on 20 July 2004. Judge Pallain was a fit, health-conscious middle-aged man, who nibbled on big bars of chocolate, while massaging a stress ball.

I had expected robes and wigs, figurines and panelled rooms, yet the courthouses in Nanterre were far from grand. The building housing Judge Pallain was a grey, soulless, shabby tower block. It didn't make me feel like I was being reprimanded by the grandeur of La République Française, defenders of *égalité, fraternité, liberté*. Instead, I felt more like I was being hauled in to pay overdue council tax or cough up for a speeding fine in a local *préfecture*.

Nonetheless, I was terrified and my first meeting with Judge Pallain was a horrible experience. I was scared and physically very nervous. I wasn't in my Biarritz bubble any more, where a round of drinks and a group of friends prevented me from facing up to the bitter truth.

I was grateful that my lawyer was *Batonnier* Paul-Albert Iweins, one of the most respected lawyers in France, with a depth of experience and knowledge of life and the law that I could not even begin to fathom. We hit it off almost immediately.

To walk into the courthouse at Nanterre with Paul-Albert was an honour and a privilege. His serenity and skill helped me enormously during the two years of the investigation. He bubbled with an intellect and curiosity that was matched only by the love he had for the law.

Appreciating the long hours Paul-Albert worked, the time he spent travelling, his juggling of personal and professional, was an eye-opener for me. This wasn't for a finite period of his life, as it might be for an athlete, but for the majority of his working life. I realised how immature I had been ever to have thought I had it harder than other people. It was another reminder of how little I knew about the world.

The first few times we were called to meet Pallain in Nanterre, a handful of photographers, TV crews and journalists turned up. Paul-Albert gave them an appeasing statement while I waited, out of reach, on the other side of the security checks. At that time, there wasn't really anything to say, other than: 'I am sorry.'

Once inside, Paul-Albert told me to spend as much time as possible in the lawyers' private waiting area. This was not normally open to clients, but because of Paul-Albert's standing I was allowed in there. I am sure he knew this would give me confidence and empower me before facing the judge. The only other option was to wait in the corridor outside the numerous *Juges d'Instructions* offices.

I did spend some time out there, watching as, one by one, hollow-eyed, broken men drifted in and out of the judges' offices. Paul-Albert had explained to me that many of those being investigated by the judges were successful, powerful members of French society.

Some of them were in a terrible state as they sat waiting to meet their 'inquisitor'. Once an investigation had got to the point where a meeting with a judge was deemed essential, then the fall from grace was inevitable.

At the first '*confrontation*' with Judge Pallain, we went through statements from the 48 hours I'd spent in police custody in Biarritz. He asked me to respond to any statements or incriminating evidence before deciding whether I was to be a witness or defendant.

It was clear, almost immediately, that I was going to be a defendant, although that hadn't stopped me from believing that, maybe, I just might walk out of his office as a mere witness, free of charges. But the first face-to-face meeting with the judge removed any doubt over that.

In all, the meeting lasted about 5 hours – 5 hours during which he sat and listened attentively as I explained my conversion from idealist to doper. Justifying my mistakes wasn't possible, but I could describe what had happened and try to explain the process that had led me to sit in his dismal office a disgraced man.

Paul-Albert had warned me that I needed to listen to every word and query anything that I wasn't sure about. He also warned me that the judge would manipulate and twist the words of others, but that I was not to be perturbed by this. Instead, I should ask to read the statement of any other witness or defendant he quoted.

Over time, the meetings with Pallain became increasingly surreal. His offices were overheated and shabby, his secretary flirtatious. I was disgraced, exiled from my sport, yet instead of reproaching me, Pallain – the judge seeking to establish my guilt over doping – revealed his credentials as a cyclist by asking me for training tips.

As we met with him more often, he would ask me more detailed questions, about fitness and equipment, even at one remarkable moment comparing Vo2 max levels with me. The judge investigating the Cofidis doping scandal was a 'bike perv' – I couldn't believe it was happening.

Time went on but the case moved painfully slowly. I would receive a *convocation* from Judge Pallain, citing the date and time that I was to be at his office. There was never an agenda, and I would only find out why he wanted to see me shortly before the meeting.

Would it be to go over my statements, or those of others? Would it be a query over phone transcripts? Maybe it would be a confrontation with one of the other Cofidis affair culprits. Or maybe he just wanted some training tips. I would block it out of my mind until Paul-Albert could worm it out of the judge.

The meetings in Nanterre soon established a routine. The night before, I would stay at Harry's place, near the Arc de Triomphe. I'd leave the apartment around 7.30 a.m. and set off on foot down the Champs Elysées towards Paul-Albert's office on Avenue Montaigne.

I would meet Paul-Albert's protégé, Julien, at a little café within spitting distance of their offices, which were above the Chanel store. It was all very Parisian and, like most Parisians, we would start the day with a coffee and croissant.

The café owner and I would often chat about cycling before Julien and I headed off to Paul-Albert's offices to go over statements and discuss the day ahead. Then we'd drive across the city to Nanterre to meet the judge.

Naturally, this being France, we broke for lunch, heading for a little café-restaurant in the building opposite the courthouse, filled with lawyers bolting down a *prix fixe* menu. As the meetings with Pallain came and went, lunch there became a habit and was soon the highlight of every visit to Nanterre.

By the time we'd walked over to the restaurant, Paul-Albert would have said all he wanted to say about the case, so we would chat as if we were simply old friends who'd chosen to have lunch together. We would have a glass or two of wine, I would tell him about bicycle racing and he would tell me about the law. They were some of the best lunches I've ever had, a glimmer of normality in those dark days.

After lunch, we would head back across the road to the hothouse that was Pallain's offices and resume where we'd left off. The statements would be scrutinised and any revisions made. I could imagine how easy it would be to be railroaded into saying something incriminating simply through the judge's chosen wording. But we stuck at it and made endless corrections. At the conclusion of each statement, it would be printed out, we would read it and, if agreed, I would then sign it.

Each statement, printed and signed, was another weight off my shoulders, another little exorcism. It was a painful process, but each piece of paper, detailing my downfall, lightened my mood a little more.

When we finally left Pallain after that first session, I was exhausted. My testimony was clearly going to be an important element in the court proceedings, but by then, I didn't care what he charged me with. I was shattered. I just wanted to get as far away from Nanterre as possible.

After we'd left Nanterre following that first meeting, Paul-Albert drove me back through the rush hour into central Paris. Maybe it was his sense of humour, but he dropped me off outside the Café Drugstore, by the Arc de Triomphe. We shook hands and I got out of the car, turning to look back down the Champs Elysées and beyond, towards the Place de la Concorde.

I stood and stared, remembering when I had raced in the final stage of the Tour de France, and the moment when, after the steady climb towards the Arc, the peloton slows to a near standstill, then turns before haring downhill towards the fountains and the Concorde once more.

I knew from riding slowly through that tight turn that it was possible to see into the eyes of the fans behind the barriers. Now I stood at that spot, as distant from the Tour as anybody. I had built my own barriers and they were bigger and stronger than anything the Tour de France would ever put at the side of the road.

I turned and went into the café. I bought a packet of cigarettes, sat down at a table and ordered a dry Martini. After a little while, Harry turned up. He stared at me across the tables, then strode over and promptly snatched the cigarette out my mouth.

'What are you smoking for?' he snapped. 'You look fucking ridiculous.'

'Harry,' I said. 'If I can't smoke now, then when can I?'

He shrugged and sat down.

I told him about my day, from the broken men in the corridors of the courthouse to the pleasures of our simple lunch, the wonders of Paul-Albert's legal expertise to the weirdness of Judge Pallain. He let me sit, drinking my dry Martini, smoking my cigarette and recounting my woes.

Afterwards, we headed back to his apartment. Harry had asked a couple of people over, as he thought it was best to keep my mind off it all. When we got to his place they were already there waiting. I couldn't switch moods though.

I told Harry I needed a couple of minutes and wandered outside. There was a twilight sky above, but in the courtyard I felt more hemmed in, more overwhelmed, than ever. Most of the time, I coped with what was happening but I would have moments when I couldn't keep the darkness inside. So I would let go and allow it to flow out of me and I would be left sitting there, surveying the world I'd destroyed.

After a while, Harry came out to look for me. He saw me and immediately gave me a hug.

'I need to go for a walk,' I told him.

Paris is a wonderful city to walk around. I found myself wandering through a beguilingly peaceful sixteenth *arrondissement* as the curtain fell on a beautiful summer's day. My black mood slowly dissipated with each step and I realised that perhaps there would be life after all of this, and that it could be a good life, one worth living.

Eventually, I found myself on rue Freycinet. I remember the street name well, because Freycinet was also my ex-girlfriend Katherine's name. Further along the street, there was a beautiful flower shop.

They were closing up for the day, but I wandered in, taking in the colours and the beauty.

And then, standing in that flower shop on rue Freycinet, I knew. I knew I would be okay.

It was going to be hard and I'd still have moments where I'd wobble, yet lost among those flowers, with my senses filling up, wrung out and exhausted though I was, I knew I'd be okay.

Paul-Albert had warned me that the judicial investigation could go on for years. Meanwhile, the fiscal investigation into my tax affairs was rumbling on. Now it was up to my accountants to fight my case and limit the damage as far as was possible.

It was becoming apparent that the French tax authorities were unwavering when it came to retrieving funds that they considered to be theirs. They were draconian when dealing with those who didn't pay their tax in full, and it was all a bit of a shock to the London firm that had taken charge of my file.

Also looming on the horizon was my disciplinary hearing with British Cycling, which would decide the length of my ban. The World Anti-Doping Agency (WADA) code supplies a guideline for the length of ban for doping offenders, but ultimately it is at the discretion of the rider's national federation.

Until then, due to the leniency of some federations, no big-name rider had ever received more than a one-year ban. The hearing was scheduled to take place only ten days before Team GB competed in the Athens Olympics and it was believed this would affect the judgement. Some people wanted them to make an example of me and I had steeled myself for a four-year ban.

I was only 27, but at the time I believed my sporting career was over. I had no hope of coming back to cycling, but I knew I had to go through the process, and had to explain myself as best as I could, for closure, if nothing else.

Compared to the ordeals I'd endured with the French police and Judge Pallain, the hearing in Manchester was surprisingly relaxed. This was a friendlier environment. It also helped that proceedings were held in English.

It was strange sitting in front of the panel and pouring my heart out. They knew me, they knew my story – and they loved cycling. They weren't intent on 'getting' me, or tainting the sport; they were as pained as I was by what had happened. But at the same time, I could see how difficult it was for them to accept how I'd cheated and lied.

But I told them everything and I was able to share my true sentiments about cycling and my team without it being used as ammunition by a judge. I talked of the doping 'system' and explained the 'head-in-the-sand' policy employed by most teams. I hoped they would understand.

Convinced that I would be banned for four years, I waited outside. It didn't take very long before I was asked back in to the hearing.

The panel banned me from competition for two years. It was clear they were shocked by what I told them and understood that there were mitigating circumstances. For professional cycling, it was a landmark decision. Finally a national federation had suspended a 'hitter' according to the WADA code. But having been convicted of doping, I now also had to deal with the pain of a lifetime ban from the British Olympic Association.

When I got back to Biarritz, I couldn't bear to watch the Olympics – apart from one event; the Madison race in the velodrome. That was only because Stuey had told me he was going to win it. He had called my sister in tears when he'd found out that I'd been arrested. Two weeks after that, when he won a stage at the Tour, he didn't hesitate to dedicate it to me, although he knew how controversial it would be to do so. But he's that sort of friend. So when we'd spoken on the phone and he'd told me to watch the Madison, I was forced to confront my absence from the Games.

I got everybody together and we all went down to Alain and Valerie's place on the Côte des Basques. We took over the TV area, turning off the music and cranking up the commentary.

Stuey was as good as his word. A born track rider, he killed it, taking the gold medal emphatically, even though he hadn't been on a track for eight years. He made the rest of the field look like junior racers, but emotionally, his triumph was too much for me.

I thought I'd be able to keep the lid on everything, but the realisation that I'd never return to the Olympic Games swept over me, and, in front of everybody, I broke down. Until then, I'd never shown any of my sadness to my Biarritz friends. Now I sat in a busy seaside bar on a summer afternoon, my head in my hands, crying like a baby.

I knew I had to leave Biarritz. It held too many memories, many good but some bad, from the previous seven years. It was a hard decision to make, but I knew that I wouldn't be able to start afresh as long as I still lived there.

The French were coming down hard on me and it became obvious I would be much better off back in the UK, sheltered by British laws. I had always sworn I'd never return to live permanently in Britain, yet now it was my port in the storm and I was thankful to have it.

The sporting world usually discards an athlete when they are banned for doping. There is no process for helping, or learning from, a sanctioned athlete, whether it's a vulnerable 16-year-old who has been duped by their coach, or a 34-year-old multi-millionaire superstar who has a highly paid medical team. They are all treated the same. Yet Dave Brailsford was already planning my rehabilitation and had talked of me living near Manchester.

So I was lucky to have Dave. He had made it clear to me that, before anything else, he was my friend and that he believed that I should be rehabilitated. Steve Peters supported this view.

The irony was that, in many ways, Dave and British Cycling had already rehabilitated me, prior to my arrest. Thanks to their vision, professionalism and working methods I had stopped both injectable *récup* and doping. Now that Dave knew the full story, he believed even more strongly that I deserved a second chance.

Meanwhile, I was running out of money. It was too expensive for me to pay a removal company to help me get back to Britain, so I decided that I would have to do it myself.

Thankfully, James Pope had offered to help – God knows why –

but then only James would think a road trip involving the packing-up of a convicted drug cheat's apartment would be a fun way to spend your time.

So I rented a truck in London, picked James up and we headed off down to Plymouth to catch the ferry to Santander. We were on a tight budget and the truck was pitifully underpowered. It struggled to go at a decent lick even when empty. Fortunately that wasn't a major worry, as our plan ensured that the ferry would tackle most of the return journey for us.

Back in Biarritz, we got straight to work, loading up the beautiful, lovingly chosen furniture that was still boxed up and standing around in the empty and unfinished dream house. Then we spent the rest of the day clearing out my apartment, as James demonstrated his miraculous packing skills.

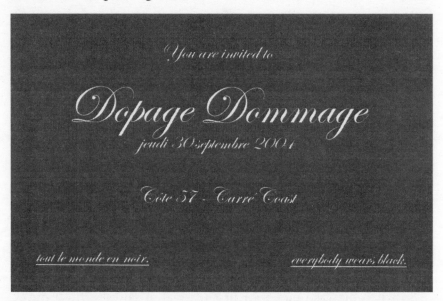

I had decided that if I was leaving Biarritz then I was going to leave in style, with a party. We had designed sombre black invitations reading, '*Dopage Dommage*' – Doping Damage. I wanted it to be a celebration with a hint of mourning. I invited everybody I knew – even the taxi drivers.

One of them, Philippe, an old guy with a limp, had always taken care of me, picking me up from airports after races and scraping me off the street in the early hours of the morning. He was my main man for getting around.

Philippe was the head cabbie and, perhaps because of his limp, a grumpy bastard. Everybody was scared of him, so it was even more special that we got on so well. We had become very attached to each other and I think he took it the hardest that I was leaving.

When I told him that I was going to have a party to celebrate my time in Biarritz, he refused to accept that I was leaving and said he would not be coming to the party. Nobody expected him to show up, particularly as I don't think he'd ever been seen further than 5 metres from his car.

So when he was one of the first to turn up, dressed in black, it made my night. We sat at the bar and chatted – he made me promise that I'd come back, I told him that, yes, I would – yet we both knew I wouldn't. I knew that things would never be the same again. Everybody stayed late, until the end, and the final farewells. For all the loneliness and mistakes, it had been an amazing few years and I had grown to truly love my Biarritz.

James and I had given ourselves one more night in the apartment, to ready ourselves for the drudgery of the return journey. As the rain poured down that evening, I joked that Biarritz was crying because I was leaving.

Perhaps because of the turmoil, or because I'd become increasingly nocturnal, I couldn't sleep. I'd left my longboard out, intending it to be squeezed into the truck at the last. I pulled my clothes on and decided to go out for one last skate.

It was the dead of night, about four in the morning, and as quiet as the winter nights when I'd often had the town to myself. I sat outside the unfinished house that I'd never spend a night in, then rolled down to the corniche of the Côte des Basques, so beautiful in the darkness and the rain, the way only Biarritz can be. I skated all the way down the corniche, memorising every moment. It felt so peaceful.

Finally, I wandered through town and back up to the apartment, remembering all the good times and promising myself that I wouldn't forget them. It was the goodbye I'd never given Hong Kong.

James and I set off early the next morning. It was only about 300 kilometres to Santander, but the route was tortuous, with barely any flat road. The truck was so overloaded that we would slow to an agonising 60 kilometres per hour as soon as we climbed uphill.

Massive lorries would grind their gears angrily behind us, then overtake, horns blaring. It was painful going. Eventually we got to Santander, but as soon as we were in sight of the port we knew something wasn't right. There were no cars lined up waiting, and more worryingly, no sign of a ship.

I started to feel anxious. 'Check the tickets, James,' I said. 'It was today, right? Midday?'

James fumbled in his manbag. 'Yep, all looks good.' Then he scanned the horizon. 'So where the fuck is the boat ...?'

'Oh shit,' I said. 'This isn't good.'

There were storms in Plymouth and the crossing had been cancelled. We'd have to wait for the next scheduled arrival. It was Thursday and the next sailing would be Monday. James was panicking. The chaos of my life had started to get to him.

'Dave – I've got to get home, we've got to get out of here. Seriously, this is too much.'

We had a snack. Over pizza, I faced up to the challenge that lay ahead of us.

'Well, there's no way we can go back to Biarritz,' I said. 'Not after all the farewells.'

James agreed. 'So what do we do?'

'Drive,' I said. 'Head up to northern France and get a crossing there.'

'Yeah, good plan,' he said perkily. 'How far is that?'

'Oh,' I mused, 'it's about the same as going to the fucking moon in that truck.'

Twenty-eight hours later, dazed and confused, we pulled up outside my sister's place in Shepherd's Bush. Then we went to the pub. James somehow made it back to his place in Primrose Hill that evening, although he went a little mad, locking himself out and losing his takeaway curry.

The next day, with help from France and her fiancé Matt, I emptied the contents of the truck into a storage facility in Fulham. I grabbed a holdall of clothes and locked the door. Everything I had from the last nine years of my life in France was padlocked away in that warehouse.

Ten months earlier, I'd celebrated winning the world title by flying to Las Vegas and partying in a suite in the Bellagio. Now home was the floor in my sister's living room.

20

SHAKEN, NOT STIRRED

I could count on one hand the number of days I'd been sober since my arrest.

Drinking had proved to be the best way to cope with everything falling apart. It fuelled indifference. It shut out the world. Nothing seemed that important when I was drunk. I had drinks for certain times, drinks for certain places and drinks according to who I was with. I was becoming an expert. I was becoming a lush.

My old faithful, whenever I found myself in a decent establishment, was the dry Martini, although it had to be *very* dry. I was very particular about that. I was beginning to think that maybe James Bond had been similarly soaked in booze. No wonder he was so cool, so indifferent – he was drunk the whole bloody time.

Back in London, I didn't have anybody to share my constant inebriation with. Even I couldn't face drinking on my own. I also felt bad about hovering, like a black cloud, around the new home of my sister and Matt. Fortunately, they were saved from more Martini-fuelled moping when I was invited to Scotland to stay with the Major.

I'd met the Major the year before, a few weeks after the World Championships, at Harry's insistence, when we both happened to be passing through Paris.

The Major and his better half, Caron, were driving to Mallorca and, on the way down, intended to stay the night *chez* Harry. I was attending a sponsors meeting and was actually booked on a flight to go back to Biarritz, but didn't really have anything better to do, so hung around to meet them.

The Major was in his mid-fifties, while Caron was perhaps ten years younger. She was a wonderfully chic Glaswegian, a quite incongruous mix, brought up in a rather bohemian artistic family, her father a successful architect and her mother a talented artist.

Caron spoke fluent French. Her mother had decided a year in Paris would be good for the kids, although the kids only learned of this when they realised their mother wasn't driving the Citroen 2CV home from school in Glasgow, but on to Paris – and without their father.

The Major is one of the last great eccentrics. Born and bred in Edinburgh, he lived in probably the biggest house in the city, a mansion built for the treasurer of the Bank of Scotland in 1900. Set on the top of a hill and with a winding drive up through the grounds, there was no gate and the gatehouse at the entrance was boarded up. The Major only lived in one wing of the vast residence, having converted the ballroom back to its former glory and the adjacent drawing room into his bedroom.

He was immersed in the motor racing world and owned numerous cars, including some Ferraris, yet his favourite car was a 1990 Mazda 323. He was obsessive about cleanliness, and was almost always the first up, no matter how wild things had been the previous night.

Everybody was known as 'old boy', and he possessed an anecdote, or a solution, that was appropriate to any dilemma you put to him. There was no problem too big or too small that he couldn't fix. He moved with purpose and conviction, never dawdling; there was always departure point A and arrival point B.

'No fucking about old boy,' he'd say.

He and Caron were a breath of fresh air. I didn't know anybody else like them and we became firm friends almost immediately during that first meeting in Paris. They knew how to have fun, were chatty and witty, and seemed to be able to adapt to any situation. I thought they were the epitome of fabulous. They were also perfect company for me during what was becoming a more and more depressing period. I knew if anybody was immune to my black cloud then it was the Major and Caron.

I spent a few weeks up in Edinburgh with them, the longest time

I'd spent in Scotland since I'd left as a child. Surprisingly, given all that had happened, it felt like home. The two of them were fiercely proud and protective of me, and I would never cease to be surprised by how every Scot I met treated me as one of their own. It felt good to be Scottish. I fitted in and felt much less of a nomad.

The Major was in the process of retiring from the business world and was shutting up shop before he left to live in Monaco and Mallorca. This meant he was in a bit of a transitional phase himself, which allowed us to drift around together. He was finally fulfilling everything he'd ever worked towards, but I'm not sure he was really ready to leave Edinburgh.

We were perfect pals for a few months, both at each other's disposal at any time. I got to know Edinburgh, my father's home town, inside and out. After all the places I'd been to, it would be Edinburgh, where it all started, that would help me rediscover myself.

I saw in 2005 with the Major and Caron in Mallorca. My mainly liquid diet was keeping the weight off so I may have still looked like a pro cyclist, but I had become completely removed from my sport.

My body had changed significantly. I was losing that athletic sensation of being in total control of it, a sensation I had always had, except when I'd been injured.

My body and mind were now operating as different entities – I wasn't an athlete any more. That epiphany woke me up to how much time had passed. I hadn't done any exercise in six months, I was smoking sporadically and drinking massively. I'd discarded the one thing I always considered to be wholly mine, to be un-touchable – my athleticism. It was this, more than anything else, that made me break out of the drunken cocoon I'd been calling home.

Soon after the New Year, my appeal against my two-year ban was heard at the Court of Arbitration for Sport (CAS) in Lausanne. A few weeks after my disciplinary hearing the previous August, with hopes of resuming my career hanging by a thread, I had succumbed to Paul-Albert's *sagesse* and the advice of others and given the go-ahead for an appeal to CAS in a bid to reduce the length of my sanction.

CAS transcends all borders and governing bodies and gives all sports-related cases a fair and just hearing. It has the power to overrule any prior decision and to lay down binding rulings on anything from disciplinary sanctions to commercial contracts. In short, whatever CAS decided had to be respected and adhered to.

The hearing took most of the day and was held in a beautiful old house above Lake Geneva. It was a long way from Judge Pallain's shabby hothouse in Nanterre. The British Federation had hired barristers to defend their decision and I was represented by Paul-Albert and his team. But I also had a few supporting testimonies from people in British Cycling, making it all a little confusing for the arbitrators.

We were reasonably confident that I would receive a reduction in my sanction, as the British Federation had dated the start of the ban from the hearing in August – not from the date of my arrest by the police in Biarritz. This was only a difference in time of six weeks, but it meant that my two-year ban made me unavailable for three Tours de France. If it was dated from the time of the arrest, I'd only miss two.

We pushed hard for it to be reduced at least to the date of my arrest. In fact, we hoped to receive a six-month reduction, and I had this in my head as a realistic expectation.

That would mean that I would be banned for 2005 but able to resume my career in time for the 2006 Tour. I had started thinking about my future. After the hearing, I headed back to England and awaited their decision.

I'd listened to Dave Brailsford's recommendation to live near Manchester. The only place I knew near Manchester was Chapel-en-le-Frith, in the Peak District, where Mike and Pat Taylor lived.

So I knocked on the very same door that had welcomed me in a decade before, when I was the 18-year-old kid from Hong Kong, hoping to secure a professional contract.

They were as welcoming as ever.

'David!' Pat said warmly, when she opened their front door. 'Come in, love. Cup of tea? You must be hungry.'

Then came the familiar call down the hallway.

'Mike! David's here.'

Nothing had changed. I stayed with Mike and Pat until I found myself somewhere to live. They were as kind, generous and supportive as when I had first started out.

I rented a little attic apartment called 'The Flat', above a doctor's surgery just a few miles down the road in Hayfield. It just happened to be the same village that Rob and Vicki Hayles had settled in after leaving Biarritz. This was a stroke of good luck that I can only describe as a godsend. I went down to London, hired the cheapest man with a van I could find and helped him unload the contents of the storage unit into the back of his little truck, before trundling up north.

Having a place of my own and all my stuff back was a big step forward. Until then, I had been a hobo, calling in favours. I was very house proud and the first thing I did was unpack all my books and put them in my bedroom, in pride of place, just as they'd been in Biarritz before the police had torn the place apart.

I unpacked the furniture I'd bought for the dream house, finally taking it out of the cardboard boxes that had carried it all safely from Florence to Biarritz to London, squeezing it into the flat in Hayfield. It had cost me more than the equivalent of two years rent for 'The Flat'. Never again would I spend that much money on furniture, I was quite sure of that.

I loved Hayfield. Nick Craig, one of the UK's greatest ever cyclocross and mountain bike riders, lived there with his family. Rob introduced us and we hit it off. Nick and his wife Sarah had lived their whole lives within a 10-mile radius of Hayfield, yet they seemed more open-minded and worldly than most people I knew. They just treated me as the bloke who lived above the surgery. It was exactly what I needed.

In fact, everything about Hayfield and the Peak District was what I needed. More than ever, I understood that much of my life was based on shite. I also began to realise how it was abnormal and unhealthy to be treated as I'd been treated before.

I had a big wake-up call when I went to open a bank account in Buxton. I waited in the queue, then sat down with a trainee, filling in forms and explaining that yes, professional cycling was a paying job – at least, for some anyway. It was a million miles from my visits to the bank in Luxembourg, when Hubert, my banker, would pick me up from the airport, keep the bank open for me and then wine and dine me.

Nor was it like visiting the Crédit Lyonnais in Biarritz, where they had posters of me on the wall and everybody treated me like family. I began to see what a fool I'd been. *How the hell could I have thought any of that was normal?*

A few days later, Paul-Albert called. CAS had made its decision. They'd only reduced the ban by a few weeks, the bare minimum of what we'd hoped. I was distraught. The one bit of hope that I'd allowed myself was now gone. I'd convinced myself that unless the ban was reduced by six months, it would be impossible for me to return to racing. No team in their right mind would take me, after two years without racing, straight to the Tour de France.

Although the ban now expired in June 2006, any decent team would want to see that I'd got some racing miles banked before sending me to the Tour. That meant that I wouldn't be able to return to the Tour until July 2007.

What the fuck was I going to do? All my talk about quitting the sport and doing something else was bullshit. I had to admit that now. Cycling was all I knew. Time out of the professional sporting bubble had shown me that we were blessed to be where we were, doing what we were doing. I was so angry with myself for making life so difficult.

What an idiot I'd been. What a spoilt brat. What a bloody fool.

Over the New Year, I had committed myself to a road trip with the Major. We planned to drive to Mallorca from Edinburgh, via Paris and the Barcelona Grand Prix. I saw it as a final hurrah. I knew that after this trip, I would be leaving that life behind.

I had a video camera and intended to chronicle the trip for

posterity. Unfortunately the batteries died before we'd made it down the driveway in Edinburgh. This may have been just as well. We persevered, caught the ferry from Edinburgh to Zeebrugge, then raced to Paris to meet up with Harry.

We parked, had lunch and set about enjoying ourselves. By the time we got back to Harry's, early the next morning, the car had gone. The Major was appalled. Thankfully, it had been towed, rather than stolen. Perhaps it wasn't the best idea to have parked in front of the Greek embassy.

Later that day, we were off again, en route to Barcelona. Our advance planning hadn't included maps or a satnav. All we had was a compass, as I had convinced the Major this would be a perfectly adequate way of finding our way around Europe. I was asleep after completing one of my driving shifts when he woke me, soon after we'd passed Montpelier.

Inevitably, we were lost.

'Millar ... *Millar*! WAKE UP FOR FUCK'S SAKE!' he bellowed.

I woke with a start. 'What? What's going on?'

'We're lost. There are no more signs for Barcelona.'

'I told you, head south,' I said calmly. 'Look, we're going east. How long have we been going in this direction?'

'Fucking compass,' he snorted. 'We *were* going south. Right, you're in charge, old boy. Use that bike racing knowledge of yours and get us to Barcelona!'

We did everything we could to get there, but we didn't make it in time. After missing the race in Barcelona, we set off for Mallorca, scraping onto the ferry at the eleventh hour, the last car to board. The Major remained cool as a cucumber.

'Only way to travel!' he said rakishly. 'If the road's not bumpy, then where's the fun old-boy . . .?'

Our grand tour culminated at the Monaco Grand Prix. Harry invited me to the race and the Major and Caron joined us there.

The Major's favourite car was the classic yellow Ferrari he kept in Monaco. I went with him to pick it up from storage, principally because I spoke French, but also because it gave us an afternoon to lark about.

It had been stored in a garage in Menton since his last visit. When we arrived, he strode in like he owned the place, but he hadn't been there for such a long time that the car was tucked away in a dark corner.

As soon as he set eyes on the Ferrari, I knew it meant something special to him.

'She's beautiful, isn't she?' he whispered reverentially. 'I love the old girl,' he said, gently running his hand over the bodywork. It was all quite sweet. I left the two of them alone.

Before long, we were rolling back along the coast on our way back to 'The Monte'.

'Have a look in the glove box, old boy,' he said. 'There should be some eight-tracks. Caron got them for me, let's give them a whirl.' I couldn't decide. Frank or Elvis? I went for Ol' Blue Eyes.

So there we were, cruising back along the corniche towards Monte, listening to Sinatra. The Major was in his natural habitat, at one with his car and his surroundings.

Then we came to a tunnel. With a flourish, the Major flicked a switch and two headlights gracefully raised their heads from the tip of the bonnet and lit up the road ahead. It was perfection.

Or it was, until one unexpectedly dipped back down. I decided that ignoring this hiccup was the best policy. Thankfully, it popped up again almost immediately. But then, as it did so, the other one dipped down and disappeared from view.

I didn't dare even turn my eyes towards the Major. He carried on as if nothing had happened and yet the atmosphere in the car had changed completely. I tried not to laugh.

After a while of this, with headlights yo-yoing up and down, he started to mutter expletives and flick the switch in irritation. Finally, he gave up.

The Major sighed. 'Part of the charm, Millar,' he said sagely. 'Ferraris are like beautiful women. Use them sparingly, preferably at weekends.'

'She' hadn't finished with us. As we crawled through the Monaco rush hour, the 'old girl' stopped dead. There was no hope of starting the engine up again, and we sat horrified in the Major's classic bright yellow Ferrari as it snagged up the boulevards of busy Monte Carlo. I sank into my seat in embarrassment.

'Right, old boy,' the Major said decisively. 'You're going to have to get out and push her.'

I stared at him in horror. 'You are joking – aren't you?' Of course, he was right. We had no choice. I got out of the car.

Monaco was the backdrop to my Last Great Bender. After only three days I'd mislaid my passport and was surviving mainly through the hospitality of others. I had become a caricature of myself, the banned cyclist, penniless and barely sober, now just a hanger-on – an embarrassment in hindsight, although I was totally oblivious to it at the time.

On the first night I lost Harry, so I wandered back to the hotel and climbed into bed. Just as I was falling asleep, my phone rang.

'Where the hell did you go?' Harry asked provocatively.

'What d'you mean, where the hell did *I* go? I was looking for you for ages. I'm back at the hotel.'

'Get your arse down to the port,' he snapped. 'I've got a surprise for you.' I could tell he genuinely had something interesting up his sleeve.

Fifteen minutes later, I was stepping onto a very exclusive after party on the yacht of poker player, space tourist and Cirque du Soleil founder Guy Laliberté. He was very welcoming, and spent the whole night DJ-ing in a corner, while wonderfully attired staff served us whatever we wanted. Only a handful of people were there, including Erick Morillo, at the time considered to be the world's number one DJ. I got on well with Erick. Later that morning, the two of us went for a swim around the boat.

I'd lost my passport on the weekend of the Grand Prix, so on Monday I went to the police station. They told me that it was highly unlikely that I would get it back. That wasn't good news. As I pondered my next move, there was only one thing to do: have another drink. I felt sure my passport would turn up.

The Monaco-based Aussie contingent took me under their wing, but, of course, it was Stuey who took care of me the most. He and his wife, Anne-Marie, had moved from Toulouse that winter, and his apartment became home for those last few days.

It was the first time that Stuey and I had seen each other since my arrest. After the Grand Prix, we ended up reminiscing about everything we'd been through. He gave me some money to keep me ticking over, but only once did he put me on the spot.

'Dave – you're going to be okay?' he asked me. 'You're going to sort yourself out? I just need to know.'

Stuey was the only person in the world who could ask me something like that and know he'd get a straight answer.

I paused. I knew how serious he was.

'I'm gonna be fine, Stuey, I promise,' I told him. I meant it.

And that was that. We went back to being a pair of best mates, hanging out together, living the high life. I meant what I'd said to him, and I believed it, even if from the outside it definitely looked like I was at the point of no return.

Harry was anxious about me too. I'd gone to meet him, the Major and David Coulthard at the hotel that Coulthard owned. I turned up drunk, knocked a table of drinks over and was, by all accounts, something of a wanker. Harry was already angry with me for missing the Grand Prix, when he'd secured a very exclusive invitation for me. The shambles at Coulthard's hotel was the last straw.

After that, he distanced himself from me, knowing there was nothing he could do to stop my thoughtless, reckless behaviour. We didn't really speak for months after that evening. We were both angry with each other – me with him for being judgemental, he with me for being an embarrassing shadow of the best friend he loved.

It got worse. A few days later I was down by the beach, having a wine-fuelled lunch with the Aussies. That lunchtime is remembered by those present as much for the record amount of wine consumed as for what happened next.

About halfway through our long lunch, a large group entered the restaurant and headed for a big table not too far from us. This was Eddy Merckx's sixtieth birthday party, and who should be there but Lance Armstrong. Of all the restaurants in all the world, they walked into mine, as I sat, having probably the booziest lunch in the history of my life.

I was in a dilemma. I'd only spoken to Lance once or twice since my ban, and he'd offered me his support both times. I couldn't just ignore his presence and yet I knew I was not in a presentable state.

They spotted me soon enough. I had to go over and say hello. Slowly I gathered myself together, pushed back my chair and plucked up the courage to stroll over in as sober a fashion as I could possibly muster.

I thought it all went swimmingly, that I'd pulled it off effortlessly. I can't remember the detail of what was said, but I went back to the Aussies thinking, 'Well, that went better than expected.'

Unfortunately that wasn't quite how it was seen through the eyes of the Merckx party. Twenty-four hours later, Fran called. Our conversation shook me out of my alcoholic daze.

'David, are you *STILL* in Monaco?' she asked.

'Well, yeah – I've temporarily misplaced my passport.'

Her tone registered disappointment. 'David, for fuck's sake. You know who called me this morning?'

I had a feeling that whoever it was hadn't called her up just to say 'hi'.

She paused. 'Only Lance fucking Armstrong.'

Ah – shit, I thought. 'Yeah? I saw him yesterday,' I said casually.

France was enraged. 'Yeah, no shit you saw him, David,' she spat. 'He reckons you were off your face – out of control. He's worried about you. *Even Lance Armstrong is fucking worried about you!* You know what he said? "You *have* to get your brother out of Monaco ..." You need to pull yourself together and sort yourself out. It's just embarrassing now.'

I was a little confused, given that I actually thought I'd appeared fine to them. 'I thought I'd pulled myself together pretty well,' I said.

Fran sneered. 'I don't think so. He thinks you were coked up or something.'

Now I was angry. 'What!? That's just bullshit. What the fuck does he know anyway? We were just having one of our long lunches. I was drunk, but come on ...'

'Come on yourself, David – just sort it out, will you?'

I could hear the concern and resignation in her voice and that made me take a step back. France was now giving up on me. That was about as deep as the hole could get.

I tried to make peace. 'Listen – I'm sorry, France,' I said. 'This is it, this is the end. I've had enough.'

'Yeah, well, you've said that before. Just remember other people are now looking at you and thinking you're a lost cause. *Just do something,*' she pleaded.

Evidently they all thought I was out of my head on drugs. I wasn't, but maybe my desperation to appear sober came across in a disturbingly manic fashion.

Whatever, I learned a good lesson, one I feel I must pass on to my peers.

Rule of thumb for all professional cyclists: if you think you've drunk too much to go and sit with Lance Armstrong and Eddy Merckx, then you most probably have.

Later, the police called, this time with good news. They'd found my passport.

After I'd picked it up, I sat on the beach in Monaco pondering what had happened. I'd alienated most people and convinced everybody else that I was a wreck. Moving to Hayfield had prepared me for what I was now going back to, the bender in Monaco had reminded of where I'd come from. I'd destroyed as much of the old me as I could. Now it was time to become that new person.

Waiting at the gate for my flight back home that evening, I felt liberated. Then Paul-Albert called.

I needed to be in Paris the very next day. The judge wanted to see me. So, once again wracked by anxiety, off to Paris I went. That meeting in Nanterre turned out to be one of the most farcical episodes even Paul-Albert had experienced as a lawyer.

TERRY ACROSS THE MERSEY

The following is a transcript of an English-language phone call between David Millar and an unknown caller, recorded by the French police three months prior to his arrest.

2 March 2004, 17:11

David Millar: You got it?
Anonymous: Dave – did you really fookin' think I'd let you down?!
DM: How does it look?
Anonymous: Just like you wanted, you're gonna love it.
DM: White . . .?
Anonymous: Yeah – and fookin' shiny. It wasn't easy getting the white we wanted, the guy we use doesn't usually work with that type of powder coating.
DM: No worries – I just need it for the race, the team are useless. I've asked them so many times and they still can't get it sorted on time. It's in their interest, I'm World Champion. Now I'll fly at the weekend!

As part of the investigation into the Cofidis affair, the police had built up a massive dossier that included every telephone conversation I'd had during the four months prior to my arrest. The police had tapped my three phones (yes – I had three phones), which I felt was even more intrusive than the demonstration of power they'd shown in turning my apartment upside down.

I knew that by tapping my phones they'd wasted time, effort and money, because there was nothing to incriminate me from that period. So when they presented a French-language transcription of one of my conversations as highly incriminating, I was baffled. The one thing they didn't know was who the conversation was with.

White had become '*blanche*' in the translation, as good as saying 'blow' or 'charlie' in English. I didn't take cocaine, so as far as I was concerned it was nothing to worry about. Paul-Albert was concerned, however – he didn't want it appearing in court, with me unable to explain it. He had asked if we could hear the tape and get the telephone number so we could clear it up.

When we got to Judge Pallain's office it took three hours for them to find a tape machine and the French transcription of my original conversation. Eventually, they allowed me to read their version of it – a transcription that made me sound like cycling's Bertie Wooster.

DM: You have it..?
Anonymous: David, of course I have it.
DM: How does it appear?
Anonynmous: It is what you wanted, you'll like it.
DM: Blow?
Anonymous: Yes, and smooth. Excuse me for the delay, it's not easy getting the blow you wanted. The chap we know doesn't work with that type of powder normally.
DM: I need it for the race – the team is bad. I've asked them for it and they still can't get it for me in time. They're not interested in me being World Champion now. Oh well, I'm happy you have got it. Now I will be flying like a bird at the weekend!

Still, after reading their rather worrying version of the conversation, I was struggling to think who on earth it could be. The other person's number was on the bottom of the transcript. I asked if I could call it. Judge Pallain agreed.

I punched in the numbers and waited. Terry Dolan, legendary Merseyside bike-builder, a Scouser of Scousers, answered the phone.

'Eh, Dave – all right . . .?' Terry greeted me.

I tried to hide it, but I couldn't help laughing. Everybody, including the judge, stared at me.

'I'll call you back later,' I said to Terry. 'It's a funny story – actually no,

240

it's not a funny story. I'm sitting with the judge at the moment, I'll explain later.'

I put the phone down and turned to Paul-Albert.

'It's my friend Terry – Terry Dolan. In Liverpool. He makes my bike frames. I think I can explain what that conversation is about now.'

Contrary to popular belief, being a professional cyclist doesn't mean you have an endless amount of quality bike frames at your disposal – in fact, the team owns every bike we ride. At the end of every season we return what bikes we may still have at home. Some teams, the good ones, will let you keep one of your bikes, but most won't even allow for that.

So every now and then, Terry helped me out with what I needed. It saved time and hassle. He did this for a lot of the British riders and has been one of the biggest benefactors to British cycling in recent years, generous beyond surely what was economically viable for him.

In 2004, when I started the season as World Time Trial Champion, I was entitled to wear the rainbow jersey of World Champion in all the time trials I rode. I wanted a bike that went well with the jersey – something that most sponsors would be thrilled to provide. But as the season began in February, I still had no time trial bike from the team.

Having battled for so many years with the team, now I didn't even bother. Instead I asked Terry if he could build me an identical replica of the Cofidis time trial frame and give it a paint job in World Champion's colours.

Terry went one better. He'd heard of a new powder coating that gave the bike a shiny, almost reflective white finish. The frame was being delivered to me in early March, in time for the start of Paris–Nice, to my hotel in Paris.

Terry's a brilliant frame builder but it's not always easy to understand him – that's unless you're equally fluent in Scouse. He has become a good friend over the years, and yet even I had trouble understanding him sometimes. I can only begin to imagine Judge Pallain's translator trying to decipher that conversation.

So we started again. There I sat, in Judge Pallain's office in Paris, career hanging by a thread, decoding Scouse, replaying every bit of the conversation, until we finally understood what Terry Dolan had said.

21

LIFE IN THE HIGH PEAK

It was time to get back on the bike.

I'd tried to source equipment from a couple of prominent companies but with no success, so – reluctantly – I went back to Terry Dolan and asked him once again if he could help me out. He had supported me so much in the past that I really did not want to ask him again, when I knew how little exposure he'd get.

Terry being Terry, he said he'd been waiting for the call and had already set aside a bike that was perfect for me. It was a beautiful, no-expense-spared, black – definitely not white – stealthy machine. I picked it up from his warehouse in Liverpool, not far from the docks.

I'd given away all my cycling clothing when I'd left Biarritz, but Dave Brailsford's drive home went right through Hayfield. One day, when he dropped in to see how I was getting on, he gave me a load of kit.

By coincidence, he'd lived in the same village a few years earlier so knew it well. We chatted for a while and then, unexpectedly, he asked if I'd like to come in to the lab and do a Vo2 test.

'But, Dave – I haven't been on a bike for a year,' I said. 'Maybe I should ride for a few weeks first?'

He dismissed my worries. 'Just come on in – get the ball rolling,' he said.

It was a subtle way of motivating me but it worked. I was booked into the English Institute of Sport (EIS) in the following week for a full-blown lab test.

It was almost a year since I'd last ridden a bicycle. I was apprehensive. I'd never enjoyed riding my bike when I wasn't at race fitness – what if I got back on and hated it? What if it brought back too many bad memories?

But I knew I had to do it at some point, to find out what the future might hold. So I set the bike up, pulled on the kit and, finally, stepped outside, locking the door behind me and slipping the keys into the back pocket of my jersey, just like any other cyclist heading out for a quiet spin.

I rolled out through Hayfield into the Peak District. At first, awkward and uncoordinated, I was uncomfortable and felt like I was riding a bike for the first time. How the hell I had ever ridden with my handlebars so low? I could barely even get my hands to sit on the brake hoods, let alone down to the drops.

But all the sensations were fresh and new and it was liberating. I didn't care about where I was going, how long I was going to be out for, what speed, power output or heart rate I was generating. I was riding my bike for no reason other than pleasure and, as the feeling took me over, I realised I hadn't ridden my bike purely for fun since I'd been in my early teens.

There had always been objectives on the horizon, sponsor commitments, schedules and pressure. Now I had no obligations. Now I didn't care that I bore no resemblance to a racing cyclist. It was bliss.

I'd been out on the bike three times when I turned up at the EIS for my test. Because Dave had been so supportive, I had expected the same attitude from others. It hadn't crossed my mind that, as a banned athlete, I perhaps wasn't very welcome there. Carried away by his desire to help me, I don't think this had really crossed Dave's mind either.

As soon as I walked through the door, I sensed it in the air. I wasn't the star any more – I was the pariah. I became very self-conscious – signing in was embarrassing. Writing 'David Millar' and then seeing it there, next to all the other athletes, reminded me that my name was now synonymous with doping. I was out of place.

Despite my unease, the test went well. Even after a year off, I was stronger than many top cyclists after only a month off. The power and fitness would return the more I trained but, most importantly, my pedalling action remained nearly perfectly balanced.

My right and left legs followed almost precisely the same power curves, so at the very least the test showed that I was born to ride a bike. But there were repercussions from my visit.

The next day, Dave got a call reminding him that I was banned from all official facilities – that as a banned British athlete I was banned from *everything*. He listened but then made it clear that he was going to be standing by me and allowing me to use his facilities at the velodrome, even though I was banned from all others. As Performance Director of British Cycling, he had the power to do this. But what was amazing was that he had the strength of character to resist the pressure that was put on him. It meant so much to me.

Dave and I sat down to talk it all through. He told me that he had spoken to his team at the velodrome, asking them how they felt about helping me, and that they'd all offered to support me. This saved me. Many would have been happy to see me eradicated from the history of the sport and banned for life. But if I had been ostracised, as certain people wanted, then I think I would have destroyed myself completely. I didn't have the strength to try and come back on my own.

If it hadn't been for Dave B and British Cycling, I would have ended up a very different man, living a very different life. They knew that what had happened to me was about more than simply my own mistakes – they knew it wasn't black and white. They judged me as a person rather than simply judging my crime. They were strong enough to try and learn from my experience and then to help reconstruct me.

I owe them a massive debt.

I'd realised that I'd be a fool not to go back into cycling. I wanted to try and right the wrongs, to set the record straight – to prove myself without any doubts. To do that, I needed to get back on the road.

It was also the only profession I knew. I was talented and passionate about it, I had the skills and experience – and it paid well, compared to anything else that I might possibly do. This hit home when I went to the Borders bookshop in Stockport to try and get a job.

I barely knew how to fill in the application form. I couldn't remember my GCSE and A-level results, let alone the addresses of my schools. The interview was fine, but what did that matter if I'd been stumped by an application form? I couldn't believe I'd ever even thought that I could do anything apart from professional cycling.

But I also knew that I had to make my comeback mean something, that it had to have some worth beyond my own experience. I knew I could train hard and in time recover my fitness, but I was a doper, a cheat – why did I deserve to come back? I'd thrown away so much, hurt so many people, and taken myself to the very edge. I had to show that it wasn't all for nothing. I had to demonstrate that something had been learned.

One of the points I had made clear to every authority, journalist, friend and family member I'd spoken to was that what had happened to me was preventable.

I had never wanted to dope. I hadn't ridden my bike around Hong Kong and High Wycombe, dreaming of the Tour de France, and thinking, *'I'll do whatever I have to do to win – doping will just be part and parcel of that.'*

I'd spent years resisting doping because I was totally against it. It disgusted me. I knew it was wrong, I knew it was cheating – yet eventually I succumbed.

Yes, I was vulnerable and I was weak and I took the decision to dope myself – but there was nobody offering proactive support to me when I wanted to stay clean. That was due in part to the *omertà* – the law of silence.

The non-dopers were too scared to say they were doing it clean and they would even go as far as defending the guys who doped, in order not to rock the boat. That's how binding the *omertà* was – and sometimes still is.

There was never a voice saying, 'One day you'll be better than all of them, so be patient and be proud.' Instead, clean riders were just looked upon as simple-minded and stubborn.

As I thought more about my comeback, I thought about what I would have wanted to hear. What advice would I have needed to prevent me from throwing in the towel on staying clean? In truth, I knew the answer to this – simply because I'd wanted to hear somebody say it for so many years.

If nothing else, when I came back to racing I could be the older guy, the hitter – the fallen champion who was proactive towards anti-doping and wasn't scared to stand on a soapbox and talk about doing it clean. That was my prerogative now, my obligation. My arrest, admission and ban meant that the *omertà* no longer applied to me.

I wanted to help younger riders, to prevent them from going through everything I'd gone through. I recognised that this would mean taking on new responsibilities.

Every interview I gave would have to confront doping, and I accepted that was going to be integral to my return to cycling. I no longer had the right to avoid the subject. I was in a very rare position to make a difference, to tell people what I'd been through and also to explain that the world of sport wasn't as black and white as some would like to think. It gave everything I did a *raison d'être*. I believed I could make a difference.

I had a year until the 2006 Tour de France. The first thing

I needed to do was to speak to Jean-Marie Leblanc, director of the Tour. Jean-Marie had watched me win the prologue at the Tour de l'Avenir in 1997 and also followed me when I'd won the first stage of the Tour in 2000. I felt like I'd particularly let him down. I needed to apologise to him, face to face.

I also wanted to ask him if he'd allow me back into the Tour de France. I called the offices of the Tour in Paris and left my name and number. Thirty minutes later, he called me back.

'*Daveed? C'est Jean-Marie Leblanc.*' He sounded jovial, which I definitely wasn't expecting.

'Jean-Marie, thank you for calling me back.' I spoke my most formal French, trying to be as polite as possible.

'David, it's good to hear from you,' he said. 'Where are you?'

I was surprised by how friendly he was.

'I'm near Manchester, that's where I live now,' I told him, as I stood in Mike and Pat's garden.

'That's different to Biarritz – *non*?! Well, you would not believe where I am ... *PLOUDANIEL*!' he exclaimed excitedly.

'Sounds familiar – but where is it?' I had absolutely no idea where it was.

'*Daveeed* – it's where you won the Tour de l'Avenir prologue in '97.'

'Of course it is!' I did remember now.

The small talk carried on for quite a while. His manner was so relaxed and friendly that it put me completely at ease.

Eventually, I found the courage to ask him.

'Jean-Marie, I was wondering if it would be possible to meet with you. I'd like to explain everything that happened.'

He was receptive to the idea, and said that I should come to Paris a few days after the Tour ended on 27 July.

Jean-Marie's positive response enthused me. I didn't even know who the World Champion was, who'd won Milan–San Remo, the Tour of Flanders or Paris–Roubaix, but as the Tour gathered pace, I began to get sucked back into it all again. I didn't have satellite TV, so instead relied on the internet and occasional dashes to Nick Craig's house to watch Eurosport as my way of keeping up with events. Now I was following the Tour as a fan – not a jaded, embittered professional – and I loved it.

Towards the end of that July, I stayed with my sister in London. Sunday was a beautiful summer's day, perfect for lunch by the Thames, so we headed over to Putney. We found a riverside restaurant with seating on the water.

As we walked through the restaurant to our table, France gave me a nudge. 'Oooh, you're in luck today,' she said. 'Look – a table full of blondes!'

'Very funny,' I said dismissively. Romance hadn't been on my agenda for quite a while.

'Hang on – you *are* in luck – I know one of them.' She sounded genuinely shocked.

'Who?' I said. 'Which one?'

'Nicole.' I had no idea who Nicole was.

'That trip with the Major?' France said. 'Mallorca at New Year? Remember Desirée? You met her there – well, Nicole's her daughter.' But the moment had gone and I still hadn't been able to spot Nicole. We sat down and ordered lunch.

In hindsight, Nicole was very brave because later on she came over and said hello. Knowing how shy she can be, that's actually quite remarkable. But thank God she did because it changed my life. I was smitten immediately. She was lovely and there was something quite magical about her.

We chatted and then, by coincidence, we ended up in the same pub after lunch. We all sat down together and Nicole and I hit it off. She knew nothing about cycling, or my life, which made it all the better. The next night, more bravely, she had dinner with the Millar siblings at France's club.

I then disappeared back up north. There was no contact for over a week, until I finally cracked and called her. That was it – we became an item.

My life had turned a corner. The future was opening up for me. Good things seemed possible. I had followed the 2005 Tour de France avidly, falling in love with it all over again. I didn't care about what went on behind the scenes or feel resentment about not being there. I relished the fact that it existed, and with that came the final and most radical awakening: I was lucky.

I rediscovered my childhood dreams watching the 2005 Tour. I had fulfilled that dream once, but I'd let it slip through my fingers. Now I'd been given a second chance. This time I'd do it properly and I'd treasure every moment.

The Amaury Sports Organisation – ASO – owns a host of French sporting events, as well as the Tour de France. ASO also owns *L'Equipe*, the renowned sports newspaper that published my statement to Judge Pallain. The Paris offices of *L'Equipe* and ASO sit side by side on the same site at Issy-les-Moulineaux, on the banks of the Seine.

I did my best to be invisible as I sat in reception at ASO, waiting to see Jean-Marie Leblanc. I really did not want to be spotted by any journalists from *L'Equipe*. I hid behind a newspaper, trying my best to get past the second sentence of the article I was reading, but incapable of focusing beyond what I was going to say to Jean-Marie.

Finally his secretary emerged and took me through to his office. Jean-Marie was on the phone but he looked up and smiled as I sat down. The room was filled with an overpowering – an overwhelming – stench of cheese.

I studied the room. It was a big office, with views over the river. There were all sorts of bits and bobs scattered around the shelves, and boxes stacked up, yet nothing stood out apart from a photo of the Pope. He was sitting with another man in what looked to be a prison cell.

Jean-Marie put the phone down and we shook hands. He was immediately warm and friendly. The boxes, he explained, were the accumulated booty of three weeks on Tour, of being the guest of honour in town after town around France.

Similarly, he said, the cheese had been a gift and he'd left it in the fridge but underestimated its aroma. He opened the fridge door. Cheeses, *charcuterie* and bottles of champagne were crammed into it. Well, what else would you expect of the director of the Tour de France?

Then we sat down again. I was far from the first rider to let him down – he had been director of the Tour during perhaps its darkest hour, when the Festina affair had almost brought it to a standstill. But I didn't waste any time and immediately apologised to him for having cheated at his race.

He accepted my apology, but also wanted me to explain how and why. So we sat there for about half an hour, while he asked me questions and I gave him answers.

Then I told him I wanted to come back and make a difference, to race clean and with pride. I told him I'd like to make the following year's Tour de France my first race back, but that I didn't want to make his life difficult.

'You will have served your time,' he said. 'That is punishment enough.'

As I listened to his voice, a weight lifted from my shoulders.

'*Mais alors, Daveed,*' he said, 'you cannot ride the Tour if you do not have a team . . .'

This was a valid point.

'At the moment I'm trying to rebuild my life,' I said. 'Once I feel like I am in the right direction, I will start talking to teams. In all honesty, I haven't really thought about that bit yet.'

Jean-Marie listened.

'Well, look – maybe I can help you,' he said. 'There are not many teams that are suited to your new attitude, so we will have to think carefully. Let me call up Roger now and speak to him first, see what he thinks.'

'Roger' was Roger Legeay, his close friend and boss of Credit Agricole, one of the biggest and oldest of the French teams. Jean-Marie called him and they chatted for 5 minutes.

Although nothing concrete came out of the conversation, Jean-Marie said he would do his best to help me. I knew how influential he was. His support was more, much more, than I had ever expected.

Then he stood up.

'Now, let's go for lunch!'

As we left the room, he pointed to the photograph of the Pope.

'You see this photo, David?' he asked. 'This is the Pope forgiving the man who shot him. I like to have it here. It's a good reminder of how we should live our lives ... showing forgiveness.'

Jean-Marie's chauffeur-driven car took us to a restaurant attached to a small sports stadium. He was clearly a regular. All the staff welcomed us with a '*Bonjour*, Monsieur Leblanc, Monsieur Millar.'

There were photos of many sportsmen and women on the walls. I paused and studied some of them as we walked to our table. Then I saw a big photo of me in a kilt with my bike, and below it one of my actual bikes on show. I was humbled. I didn't know whether Jean-Marie had chosen that restaurant specially – in hindsight he must have done – but it was the first time that I had felt proud of being a professional cyclist for a very long time.

We had a wonderful lunch. Jean-Marie ordered a bottle of champagne and we had a wide-ranging conversation. Then, as we were leaving, the staff wished him happy birthday.

He had given so much to me, on his birthday of all days, and demonstrated his generosity of spirit. As we said our goodbyes, he reiterated his support. It was another step forward. In those few hours, he had made me see so many good things about professional cycling that I'd been blind to before.

My financial circumstances however were dire. I was ruined. I had debts totalling over £800,000 and no prospect of any income for probably another year. The only asset I had was my house in Biarritz, which was up for sale. But, not surprisingly, it was proving difficult to find a buyer for an unfinished, state-of-the-art, bachelor pad.

I was going to have to take it on the chin and lose an awful lot of money on it. It was clear that I'd be very lucky to clear half the debt through the sale of it.

The majority of the money owed was to the French tax authorities. They had taxed everything I'd earned during the previous four years at 50 cents per euro – and then added a 40 per cent penalty on top of that. The remaining debts were legal and accountancy bills. It was an unfathomable amount of money really.

The French were non-negotiable. Forfeiting the debt through bankruptcy was an option – I'd be protected under UK law, but not French law, and this was no use as I wanted to return to France. I was in debt to the French Republic until I paid back every cent.

There was also something about declaring bankruptcy that I didn't like. Aside from the stigma, it didn't feel right – it didn't offer any closure. I decided that I would pay back my debts. I agreed with all my creditors to pay them back in full through an Individual Voluntary Agreement (IVA). This was formalised when I submitted the IVA to the Stockport courthouse on 12 August 2005.

I submitted my monthly living expenses to an insolvency lawyer. Once this was accepted I received an allowance while the rest of my income went towards repayment of the debts. At the time, I only had enough for my month-to-month living. But I finally paid off the debts in April 2009. It was one of my proudest achievements.

The financial limitations taught me to curb the out-of-control spending that was part of my lifestyle. I had no concept of managing money; it came in, it went out. I learned how valuable it really is, and I also learned that it wasn't my God-given right as a professional sportsman to avoid tax.

Beyond that, I had one goal: to be on the start line of the 2006 Tour de France. I had a little over ten months to turn my body back into that of a professional cyclist. I knew I could do that – the difficult bit would be finding a team.

I didn't know where to start when it came to finding a team. I hadn't been 'on the market' since 1996 when I was an amateur looking for that first pro contract. I had given a couple of interviews in which I talked about my plans for a comeback and after that I heard that a small Spanish team, Saunier Duval – a team I would have never even considered in my pre-ban days – were interested in me.

They had probably the smallest budget and one of the more eclectic rosters in the peloton. They were an opportunistic team – they had to be with such a small budget – and it was clear in their eyes that I was an opportunity: a big-name rider going cheap.

Former pro Max Sciandri had contacted me to ask how I was

getting on and what my plans were. Max is about as Italian as they come – except that he's English. He was born in Derby and his mother is English, and in truth that's where his Englishness begins and ends. He grew up in Tuscany until his early teens, and then his family emigrated to California, when his father went into the restaurant business.

Max recounts with pride his tale of driving a 1967 Mustang around the West Coast, as a 17-year-old toyboy to a successful woman in the movie business. But he missed Italy and cycling, and so left his family in America and went back to his beloved Tuscany to chase his dream of being a professional cyclist.

He became one of the best one-day riders of his generation and also proved his Englishness, winning two of the World Cup races that used to be held in England and taking a bronze medal in the Atlanta Olympics in the road race, in British colours.

When I told him that I was training again he asked if I'd like to come and stay with him in Tuscany for a while. I loved Hayfield but the training wasn't ideal, so I made the first of what became bi-monthly visits to Max in September 2005. Steadily, my strength and fitness was reawakened.

Max loves cycling. He also loves cars, watches, motorbikes, furniture, clothes, snakes, wine, food and women. But he loves cycling most of all. It was great spending time with him, and his excitement about my comeback was palpable.

Max had a beautiful Tuscan villa on the side of a valley, not far from Pistoia. He'd spent years renovating it, but had recently divorced. His wife and three kids had moved out, leaving him skulking around what was now a cold and dark empty house. I could see why he'd wanted me to come over. I nicknamed him Edward Scissorhands.

Max knew everybody in cycling and he said that he'd speak to a couple of teams for me. At first they were interested, but each time it would fall through. My last chance appeared to be with CSC, the team run by the Danish former Tour winner, Bjarne Riis.

Jean-Marie had asked Riis to consider me so I met with him in Lucca. Bjarne was very straightforward and as we chatted he asked me about my life before the ban. I told him, candidly, about life in Biarritz, living in the apartment.

He was shocked to hear this, stunned that I'd always lived on my own.

'Who did your washing and cooking?' he said. 'That's no way for a professional to live.' I found his attitude – that marriage was a career move – amusing and very old school.

Then I told him that my dream was to make the Tour de France my comeback race.

'That's not possible on our team,' he told me.

I understood. CSC had many good riders who wanted to be on the Tour team; it wouldn't have been right to have me, fresh from a doping ban, walk straight into the team and take somebody's place.

He also believed I'd be better building up to the Vuelta a España, which started two months after my ban ended. He was probably right about this too, but it didn't fill me with the same motivation. I needed the grandeur of the Tour to make sense of it all.

My options had narrowed. If I wanted to start the Tour, the only choice I had was Saunier Duval. So we agreed to meet. I flew to Madrid and arrived at their hotel on the evening of the last day of the 2005 Vuelta. It was the first time I'd been to a bike race in fourteen months and it felt like home.

I'd been wrong to think I'd have teams chasing me. I was in absolutely no position to be looking down my nose at others. My life was now very different, but I still hadn't fully understood that I no longer had the same status within professional cycling. Now I felt lucky to have just one team wanting me. I didn't care who or what it was – I needed them more than they needed me.

The Saunier Duval team was run by Mauro Gianetti and Matxin Fernandez. Mauro, the manager, was a Swiss-Italian ex-pro who lived near Lugano, while Matxin, a Cantabrian Spaniard, was the head *directeur sportif*. Matxin had been an amateur cyclist but had started directing young and then worked his way up through the ranks.

In 2005, he was the youngest head *directeur* amongst the top-ranked teams of professional cycling, an impressive achievement for a man who had not earned his stripes racing with the pros. The two of them were entrepreneurs – their team was able to gain results in some of the biggest races and maintain a full complement of riders and a complete race programme on what was a shoestring budget. It was remarkable really.

There was another side to this success though. The majority of their riders were paid very little. These were the riders who didn't quite make the cut with other teams, for one reason or another. In some ways, it was the perfect comeback team, because if a rider had lost ground, due to injury, illness or a doping ban, then the one team sure to take them was Saunier Duval. But such an environment was best suited to the desperado mentality, and many in the team – perhaps too many – had nothing to lose.

I knew this was the environment I'd be going into, but convinced that the sport had surely changed in my absence, I was confident that it couldn't be that bad.

I told myself that I was worrying for nothing, that my anxiety came out of my past bad experiences. Anyway, everybody at Saunier Duval was incredibly friendly, much more so than Cofidis had ever been. Perhaps it had a lot to do with the natural warmth of the Spaniards but it was an unexpectedly welcoming team.

As I sat with Matxin and a translator in the hotel in Madrid, we agreed that the Tour de France would be my first race back. Then I'd tackle a couple of the big August one-day races before going to the Vuelta a España. This was more like it.

We agreed there and then that, in principle, I would sign with them. The money was less than I'd hoped for, but I was in no position to negotiate. I was tied to a two-year contract, which expired on New Year's Eve, 2007. It wasn't ideal, but I'd get to fulfil my plan of making my comeback at the Tour.

A couple of months later, Mauro and Matxin came to London. We signed the contract in the conference room of my law firm in central London. We had a drink to celebrate and then, with a hug and a handshake, I clambered into a black cab with the bike and clothing they'd brought for me.

It was a typically dark but cheery winter evening in London, with commuters and evening shoppers teeming through the West End. As the black cab began its stop-start journey back to my sister's place in west London, I sat there with my head against the window, watching it all go by.

I felt no excitement or joy, just weariness. I stared at the bulging bike bag, with SAUNIER DUVAL emblazoned across it, crammed in alongside me.

It hit home. My comeback was really happening.

22

LA ROUE TOURNE

In January 2006, I left for my first training camp in two years and my first with a team other than Cofidis. I arrived at the hotel later than everybody else, so I hadn't met any of my new teammates when I went downstairs for dinner. Walking into that dining room was nerve-wracking. I didn't speak Spanish and I only knew a couple of the twenty-six riders. I had no idea what sort of welcome I was going to get.

But I needn't have been nervous as everybody was enormously friendly. It was a very different environment from that of a French team, in which there was a clear hierarchy between both the riders and the staff. Everything seemed much more egalitarian among the Spanish.

I had grown so used to the permanent moaning within Cofidis that I believed it to be normal. It was refreshing to meet people who were happy with their lot and who worked above and beyond the call of duty, without resentment or complaint.

Despite my lack of Spanish, we managed to communicate well enough. Another of those in the 'Last Chance Saloon' was one of my old Cofidis teammates, Christophe Rinero. He'd won the polka-dot King of the Mountains jersey in the 1998 Tour but his career had spiralled downhill ever since.

I'd always got on well with Christophe. I could remember sitting on the balcony of an anonymous post-race hotel in 1999, chatting away with him. He was smoking his pre-bed cigarette (an old school habit amongst some of the Frenchies), telling me how much he'd just like to pack it all in and open a flower shop. It was pretty clear even then that he wasn't cut out for it, yet he had kept plugging away.

Years later, while training in the Pyrenees, I bumped into him on the road. We ended up sticking together and tackled the Col du Tourmalet near the end of the ride. Once a strong climber, he was a shadow of his former self.

At one point, as we worked our way up the mountainside, he said: 'Do you know who has the record for this climb?'

'I have no idea, Christophe,' I replied.

'Monsieur Rinero!' he announced proudly.

I was stunned. '*You* have the record for the Tourmalet? Shit, Christophe – that's crazy!'

'*Oui*, I know! I was on my own, I attacked at the bottom, the 1998 Tour. Phewf! So long ago, huh ...?' That's right, I thought to myself as we rode through the hairpin bends. Times have changed.

Christophe's presence at Saunier Duval made things a bit easier. We could speak French together and we had a shared history. The other person who really helped me feel at home was Txema Gonzalez, a *soigneur* I'd known for ages. Txema was one of those rare friends in pro cycling who transcends team loyalty.

We'd never actually worked on the same team but had always hung out together. He spoke English and was a breath of fresh air. He loved his job but he didn't live for it and had interests that went way beyond cycling and that he kept separate. He took particular care of me, knowing that I was perhaps a little more fragile than I appeared.

Heartbreakingly, Txema died suddenly in 2010 at the Vuelta a España while working for Team Sky. It was devastating news for everybody who knew him.

'You're only as good as your last race,' they say. My last win had been the world title in 2003 – and that had been stripped from me for doping. I may have once been a Tour de France stage winner, but in a sense I was starting from zero.

But I'd promised myself that the comeback would mean something, so before Mauro did his first team talk, I took him aside and told him he should be vocal about the team's position on doping. I'd learned that no matter how many ethical charters were signed, or how many doping controls were in place, or how extreme the punishments threatened, they meant nothing if the employers didn't take a proactive anti-doping stance. It is also the responsibility of the team to prevent their riders from doping, yet this was something that people still didn't really understand – especially team bosses.

I had seen it at Cofidis, where the team management had their heads firmly buried in the sand, considering their responsibility fulfilled if we signed a meaningless piece of paper promising we wouldn't dope. Yet they allowed us to use whatever doctor we wanted and to race with incredibly suspicious blood values. If the rider was caught then it was his responsibility and the team would claim it had done everything possible to prevent it. In fact, all the team had done was protect itself. That was how the system worked.

I wanted to help the guys who were clean, I wanted them to feel that they were being supported. I wanted to hear Mauro say convincingly to his team that he believed in clean sport, that he expected his riders to be dope-free and that he would help and support them in the process. But it became clear that stating this hadn't even crossed Mauro's mind. It was a taboo – doping and anti-doping were bracketed together. If you didn't talk about one, then you didn't have to talk about the other.

Mauro did say a few words, but it lacked conviction. As I listened to him speak, it was clear the majority of those in the room didn't really care or even find it valuable to hear what he said. I had hoped there would at least be a feeling of support towards Mauro and respect for him taking the stance, but there was nothing. It was an awkward and embarrassing moment that everybody wished hadn't happened.

I'd thought that the majority would have been fervently anti-doping and vocal about it too, but this was definitely not the case. So I decided my best policy was to lead by example and be vocal myself. I made it clear that I would not be using any injected *récup* and shared my views and experience with anybody who would listen – especially the younger riders.

Once I got back home, after the camp had finished, I got in contact with the anti-doping arm of UK Sport. If I was going to make a difference then I needed to share my experiences with the agencies responsible for anti-doping. I'd realised that if I stood little chance of having any influence on my own team then I would stand little chance in the big pool of professional cycling. Maybe it was time to take a slightly different approach.

I was an open book when it came to talking about my experiences in doping but I hadn't been contacted by any anti-doping agencies following my ban, which surprised me. Nobody had tried to tap into my knowledge and experience.

This seemed a wasted opportunity – having been through it, I knew more about the realities of how a culture of doping operated than most. Now that I was back on the comeback trail, I thought it was time for me to be the instigator.

I wrote a letter to UK Sport explaining who I was and why I was contacting them. Soon afterwards, they replied and I met with Andy Parkinson, who had recently become their head of operations. Andy was very receptive, and much more open-minded that I'd expected. We spoke at length and I was able to tell him both about the lessons I'd learned and that I was available to help them.

Andy told me he would give serious thought to how my experiences could be of benefit, but he was sure that I could help them. It was a first step in feeling that everything I had been through had some worth – that it hadn't all been for nothing.

On my next visit to Tuscany, Max suggested that I should meet a good friend of his – Luigi Cecchini.

The Italian was one of the most famous coaches in professional cycling, but also one of the most controversial. His clientele was a who's who of famous cyclists. Some, like Bjarne Riis, Tyler Hamilton and Jan Ullrich, are probably better described as infamous.

I was hesitant, so I asked Max if he would understand my new outlook on cycling. Max said that, before anything else, Luigi was a lover of cycling and that he'd be a good person for advice on how to train for my deep-end comeback at the Tour de France.

Having a coach who could tell me what I needed to be doing in training would make a world of difference. As for Luigi's reputation,

I didn't think that I, of all people, was in any position to judge somebody on their reputation.

'He's a good man,' Max said. 'Judge him for yourself.'

So I did. At the time, I was training blind – I didn't have a coach who was working with practising professionals and so had no comparison or performance objectives. I didn't know how to quantify my training and gauge whether I was even capable of starting the Tour.

In terms of profile, both Cecchini and Michele Ferrari were at their peak in the mid-1990s, coincidentally the period when cycling was at its most EPO-addled (EPO was not fully outlawed until later). Back then, it was considered prestigious to be a client of either of these doctors but, post-Festina, modern cycling dictated that a relationship with either had to be kept quiet. This didn't stop me wanting to meet Cecchini. In hindsight, despite everything, I was still naive.

I knew nothing about him, apart from his 1990s 'reputation'. I'd read an article in a cycling magazine, back in the day, when he and Ferrari were feted for their God-like ability to create champions. But I felt that Max's opinion of him was enough reason for me to give him the benefit of the doubt. In a way, I was treating him with the same open mind that I hoped people would have when they met me.

He was different from what I had expected, genteel and kind, and bore more resemblance to an upper-class gentleman than a sports doctor. He lived a few kilometres from Lucca in a gargantuan old villa. His son drove a Porsche and his wife owned the most expensive clothes shop in town.

His office was in converted stables, opposite the imposing main gates, and was crammed with cycling memorabilia. It felt like a sporting man cave, full of everything that the owner loved. There was everything he needed for running physiological tests and also a small TV, beside the desk, on which he watched all the races. A little later on, when the season was in full flight, I returned to find him sitting there, glued to the TV screen like a super-fan, looking out for his protégés.

Max introduced me in Italian. He and Cecchini chatted for a bit then I told him, briefly, what I'd been through and why I was coming back in the manner I was. I told him that I believed it was possible to win clean at the highest level because I had already done it. I told him that this was the most important thing about my return to cycling, that I wanted to do it without injections and without doping, and I wanted my first race back to be the Tour de France.

He listened intently. Once I'd finished, he sat there in silence for a bit, thinking about what I had said, before responding in near-perfect English.

'Well, David,' he began, 'I know you have a big "engine". I have seen you race and Max tells me that you are different. I believe you can do what you want to do, and I think you are right to think you can win clean.

'The sport is changing – I know, I see the blood levels. The Tour de France as your first race back . . .? This will be a big challenge, a *very big* challenge. You will have to train very hard and very well. It is possible, though. Yes, I believe it is possible.'

This was not an impulsive response – what he said had an air of authority. It was what I wanted and, more importantly, needed to hear. It was important too that he backed my clean stance. If we weren't on the same page regarding that, then there was no way I could have even considered mentioning his name again – let alone working with him.

I did some tests out on the road, one hill climb, one simulated time trial, then Luigi started training me. There was never ever money involved and it was never even discussed. I'm sure I'm probably the only professional rider he has ever trained for free. We got on extremely well, and I never even got a hint of him being involved in anything to do with doping.

That was until the Spanish doping investigation, *Operación Puerto*, which implicated some of Cecchini's clients, exploded in the build-up to my comeback race, the 2006 Tour de France.

I rode my first Tour in 2000 in the aftermath of the Festina affair;

I made my comeback as the fallout from *Operación Puerto* spread through the peloton.

Puerto was the biggest scandal to hit cycling since Festina. It put to shame any claims of the sport cleaning itself up. A Spanish police investigation into Eufemiano Fuentes, a prominent sports doctor based near Madrid, had revealed a doping ring that reached far beyond the borders of Spain. Although there were over a hundred clients listed in Fuentes's files and he admitted that other sports were involved, only cyclists were ever investigated or sanctioned.

One of the four arrested in the initial police operation was Manolo Saiz, at the time the most famous team boss in cycling and the president of the Professional Cycling Teams Association. When Saiz was arrested he was scheduled to be meeting Fuentes and was carrying €50,000 in cash. His arrest signalled his downfall and that of his team, the all-powerful Spanish Liberty Seguros team.

The pivotal evidence in the investigation was the cache of code-named blood bags found in Fuentes's offices. *Puerto* revealed that the increased efficiency of the latest EPO test had sent the doctors back to basics. Blood transfusions, once considered outdated, had come back into vogue.

Blood would be extracted during a training phase, allowing the body to replenish itself naturally (or with help from EPO micro-dosing while at altitude). It would then be reintroduced just before a big objective or during a stage race. Blood transfusions markedly boosted performance, especially in Grand Tours.

Being away from the sport for almost two years had allowed me to distance myself from the harsh realities. I had tried my best to defend cycling, convinced that during my enforced absence there had been a change in attitude.

At first, *Operación Puerto* shocked me. Then it worried me, especially when I began to notice that some of the cyclists implicated had connections to Luigi Cecchini. I had realised, given my history and the media cynicism towards cycling, how my contact with him would be seen.

I was sure Cecchini wasn't mixed up in any doping practices himself, yet it appeared some of his clients might have had their doping requirements taken care of in Spain by Fuentes. I was in a tight spot. A couple of weeks before the Tour started I thanked him for all his help and stopped working with him.

It was a rude awakening. I had to be very careful about who I worked with. I couldn't claim to be naive any longer. I might have changed, but that did not mean the sport had. Generally, I am not a cynic, but it was clear that it was maybe a safer policy than any other when dealing with professional cycling. I would have to strike a balance between my belief in the future of professional cycling and my cynical understanding of the harsh realities.

The 2006 Tour, bookended by two huge scandals, was another blighted edition of the old race. As *Puerto* took its toll on the peloton, I became the go-to guy, the repentant ex-doper willing to actually discuss what nobody else wanted to.

The role fitted me well, perhaps because in some ways it was what I had prepared for. Within hours of being back on the world stage, I was in the limelight and convinced that I was helping by giving a balanced and educated opinion on what was going on. I was assuming the responsibility I knew I would be burdened with on my return to the sport. It didn't frustrate me – I knew it was my place.

On the eve of the prologue, I dropped off a letter to Jean-Marie Leblanc's hotel thanking him for supporting me and promising him that I wouldn't let him down. I had also enclosed blood test results from the previous six months. The doctor in Hayfield had taken samples monthly so that I could demonstrate to whoever asked that my blood values were normal and that I was not doping. I knew that it was up to me to prove my innocence from now on.

In theory, I had a chance of winning the Strasbourg prologue. Training had gone amazingly well but it had been impossible to replicate the intense demands of 'real' racing. We'd attempted to replicate race situations by using motor-pacing. This was the only option we had but we were convinced that it would do the job. It didn't.

Cecchini had been able to compare my training data with those of practising professionals, current and old. My numbers were through the roof and I was beating records held by some of the most successful cyclists. This gave us a false impression: instead of being one of the strongest racing cyclists in the world, I had become the best-trained cyclist in the world. There is a massive difference between the two. I was in fantastic condition to train, not to race.

Even so, I was enjoying every moment, finding it simply wonderful to be back at the race I loved, despite everything else that was going on. I just wanted to soak it all up, appreciate where I was and to remember where I'd come from. It wasn't the mindset of somebody who was going to rip the course to pieces.

I knew within a kilometre of the prologue starting that I didn't have the form for it. I simply didn't have the top-end power to explode my way through 7 kilometres. I finished fourteenth, while Brad Wiggins, riding his first Tour, placed fifteenth. It wasn't an auspicious start but I didn't really care. I was back doing what I loved.

As for the reaction from my fellow pros, they were welcoming, understanding that I'd admitted to my mistakes and taken my punishment. They knew I was a talented cyclist who had made mistakes, that I had taken it on the chin and that I was trying to come back in a positive manner and without any bitterness. So many others embroiled in a doping scandal have chosen to deny, deny and deny, before eventually reaching an endgame that forces them to admit their guilt.

Over that first week of the Tour, I discovered a love for different aspects of racing that I hadn't had in the years building up to my ban. I wanted to be everywhere, doing everything, involved all the time. During the Cofidis years, I would have avoided the chaotic front of the bunch during those final dangerous kilometres, but now I was up there, getting stuck in, trying to help our team sprinter. I found it exhilarating, and every day when I crossed the line I had a big grin on my face.

Those rose-tinted glasses were lost on the roadside somewhere in the Pyrenees. As soon as we hit the mountains I was reminded of just how horribly hard the Tour de France could be. Not even my biggest, hardest training sessions had come close to stretching me as far as that first day in the mountains. Even though I'd done a five-day reconnaissance mission in the very same mountains with John Herety, an English ex-pro cyclist, in May, the Pyrenees were excruciating. I finished just in front of the *gruppetto* that first day and in a similar position on every other day in the mountains. It hurt so much: I had completely forgotten how much suffering was involved.

By the end of the Tour, I was on my knees. I got in a couple of breakaways and one succeeded in making it to the finish, but I had no chance of being a contender for the win. I'd been the instigator of the break and the first to attack in the finale, having decided that if I was going to fail, then at least I'd fail with panache.

Yet standing on the start line on the final day of the Tour, I couldn't help but feel empty. I had not been a player over the whole three weeks; instead, it felt like I'd been chasing my tail the whole time.

I'd never considered myself to be that ambitious or driven before, yet I stood there waiting for us to roll out through the start line knowing that taking part wasn't enough. I wanted to be a racer, not just a finisher. I also knew that nothing I said or claimed about my sport or myself mattered if I didn't show myself to be a winner once again; a clean winner.

Later that afternoon, Floyd Landis stood on the Champs Elysées podium wearing the yellow jersey after one of the most incredible comebacks in Tour de France history. But it was bullshit. Floyd tested positive for testosterone and then spent the next four years denying it, fundraising for a 'fairness' campaign, before finally admitting to doping in 2010.

As I write this, over four years later, Landis has announced his retirement from cycling. When I heard about his positive control, I tried to contact him more than once to tell him to admit to whatever it was he had done, that it was the only thing to do for himself and for his sport. He never responded. He has yet to explain his positive doping control in the Tour and remains adamant that cycling will always be riddled with doping.

As he retired, Floyd said: 'I'm relatively sure this sport cannot be fixed, that's not my job, that's not my fight.'

I don't agree. I think it is the obligation of every athlete who admits to doping to try and repair their sport, whether they think it's futile or not. Athletes must understand that admitting to their mistakes is not the end of the road – in many ways it can be the beginning of something much better.

I was exhausted when I got back to Hayfield. In fact, I'd never been so tired after a Grand Tour. I moved slothfully between sofa and bed for five days before being flown out to Hamburg for a one-day race. But my ambition to race and to win clean had been replenished.

Unlike Floyd, the Tour hadn't broken me – it had fixed me.

23

TIME TRIALS AND TRIBULATIONS

The epiphany I'd experienced on the start line of the Tour's final stage had left its mark on me. I was 29 but I still had plenty of ambition – if anything I was more driven than I'd ever been, having realised how much I loved racing and also that my career wouldn't go on for ever.

It was becoming clear that if I wanted to be truly professional I had to live somewhere near fellow professionals in a suitable climate with the perfect roads and terrain. From my experience, there are only two places in Europe that tick all these boxes: Tuscany and Catalunya.

Before I headed off to the Vuelta a España, a race I loved, Nicole and I spent some time in Girona, about an hour's drive north of Barcelona. Neither of us had ever been there before, but I had heard good things about it from other riders.

We'd tried Tuscany – Nicole had come out to visit me when I was training at Max's house – but it didn't feel right, so after speaking to fellow pro and Girona stalwart Christian Vande Velde during the Tour de France, we homed in on the Catalan city.

Christian and his wife Leah welcomed us with open arms and we stayed with them for a few days before I headed off to Malaga for the Vuelta. Girona was perfect; the weather was fabulous, the roads quiet and varied, and there were half a dozen English-speaking professionals living there, ensuring that there would always be training partners. This was key because my attitude had changed – I no longer wanted to isolate myself from my profession.

Although we were only there for a few days, we decided to make Girona our new home. Nicole was absolutely fearless in her commitment to living abroad, which made the decision to move to Spain all the easier.

I arrived at the 2006 Vuelta relaxed and fresh – the opposite of my state at the start of the Tour. But I was already starting to feel a little isolated from the team. During the last week of the Tour, when I had been exhausted but had maintained my stance against injected *récup*, I think they genuinely thought I was simply stupid, a fanatic regarding my cause. They had no real understanding of my reasoning or beliefs.

In my races with them I had taken to working as hard as I could. I hadn't regained the confidence to race for myself, so it was easier to win respect by being a *super-domestique*. It helped me fit in and be accepted, something which, despite the ethical divide, was important to me.

When our young sprinter Francisco Ventoso won a stage in the Vuelta, he surprisingly dedicated it to me. I had become his lead-out man, something I had never even tried while at Cofidis. In another stage, a couple of days later, I put myself on the line to help another teammate. He didn't win and I realised that I was sacrificing myself too much, just to try and fit in. It was time to rediscover my old self-belief, even if it meant risking failure.

There was an individual time trial stage looming and I was convinced I could win it. My form was picking up and my physical condition was light years away from where it had been at the end of the Tour. I could feel myself becoming one of the strongest and fastest in the peloton once again.

I may have lost my edge in the road stages but a time trial was far simpler. I just had to get from point A to point B faster than everybody else. But there was an obstacle – Swiss rider Fabian Cancellara. In my absence from the sport, he'd developed into a monster of a rider and the undisputed king against the clock.

The time trial was in Cuenca, one of the classic Vuelta finishes. There's a cobbled climb up through the old town before it levels off, loops out through a valley, and then descends back into the new town.

We'd ridden this finale in the previous day's road stage and

Fabian and I were clearly on the same wavelength because, with no commitments to the overall standings, we both sat up at the bottom of the cobbled climb and relaxed a little, in order to save our strength for the next day.

But there was one big difference. Fabian was chatting, joking about and not really paying much attention. Meanwhile, I stayed at the back of the group, studying the road, memorising as much of it as I could and gauging how long I would be able to remain on the time trial bars. Watching Fabian laughing and chatting as we rode over the course made it all the easier for me to focus – I knew I was gaining an advantage.

In the Saunier Duval team, nobody got up before nine on a time trial stage – they considered it a virtual rest day. Despite that, at seven the next morning I was out on my time trial bike, riding the course. My weary mechanic, David Fernandez, who looked at me as if I was madder than ever, had to get out of bed and open the team truck to give me my bike.

As I studied the course once more, I knew what I had to do, and that was to limit my deficit as much as I could to the top of the cobbled climb, then take time along the plateau section before attacking the descent to the finish.

I threw myself into the descent in my time-trialling position. It was possible, but it was going to be a big risk and scary as hell. I told Matxin and David, who would be in the following car during the race itself, that I would be taking a lot of risks in the final kilometres but that I knew what I was doing. If I crashed, then so be it.

Later that day, towards the end of a hot afternoon, I came over the top of the climb 11 seconds behind Cancellara. But I didn't panic. Keeping to my plan, I chipped away just over a second on every kilometre to the finish line and narrowly beat him. My victory margin was less than a second but I only came close to crashing once. I think that was the last time anybody ever went faster than Fabian downhill.

It was the moment I'd been waiting for, certainly since my ban and perhaps since the butterfly *récup* needle had first dropped into my vein all those years before. I had proven my point.

In the post-race press conference, I said what I now believed in and had proven through winning, and I said it because I knew I owed it to my younger self. It was what he had always needed to hear.

'I want everybody to understand something, even my fellow professional cyclists and the fans who love cycling: I am doing this on nothing, only on bread and water. I do not believe in any injections of any sort for recuperation. We can perform at the highest level in cycling without medical help.

'Today was a purely physical test. I won, and I am 100 per cent clean. Some people may not believe me, but if you know me, you will believe me after what I have been through. I love my sport and I want everyone to know that you can win the biggest races on bread and water.'

Because I'd beaten Cancellara in the Vuelta time trial, great things were expected of me in the World Championships later that autumn, my first appearance in Team GB colours since winning the world title in Canada.

I flopped completely in the time trial, suffering from exhaustion and a very badly timed puncture. But I redeemed myself in the road race, ending up in the defining move of the last lap. It was the first time a Team GB jersey had been seen in the finale of the professional men's Worlds for a long time.

A couple of weeks later, I entered the National Track Championships. I won the 4-kilometre individual pursuit, and – as I didn't defend my title – have since kept a 100 per cent undefeated track racing record. But then beginner's luck probably played a bigger part in that win than was acknowledged at the time.

Bit by bit, I was being accepted back into the fold. That autumn, I was invited to the Tour de France presentation, in Paris, unveiling the details of the 2007 race, scheduled to start in London. The presentation is a grand affair, held in the Palais des Congrès, just off the *périphérique*, and always followed by champagne and canapés.

As I mingled with the crowds in the foyer of the auditorium, I saw 'JV' – former pro Jonathan Vaughters. Jonathan had dropped out of the world of pro cycling a few years earlier, reappearing every now and then writing for magazines. He was now managing a small start-up cycling team in the States.

I was surprised to see him. Jonathan had endured a hard time as a pro and eventually decided that enough was enough, returning to his Colorado home and turning his back on professional cycling. I didn't know his full story, but it had always been clear that he was an outsider, separated from others in cycling by his intelligence as much as anything. I'd never known him well enough to notice that he was something of an outsider in all walks of life, and that the older he got the more eccentric he became.

An intellectual athlete is considered to be an oxymoron, or at least a rare bird in the menagerie that is professional sport. But there are intelligent athletes – it's just that they sometimes lack higher education, because they have devoted so much of their youth to reaching the top in sport. The most successful athletes have an intelligence that is more like that of a very successful businessman. They are able to manage, motivate and inspire in equal measure.

They may be out of their depth in many situations but in their world they are extremely well educated and accomplished. Jonathan has more of an education-based intellect, making him very different from most in the sporting sphere, and this sets him apart.

He has a scientific brain but is also a loner – in fact he's almost antisocial – and that is not the sort of personality that makes the pack-like existence of professional sport very easy.

Yet he can be, and often is, very funny. He has a natural desire to provoke, like the naughty boy who lives and breathes to annoy adults. Much of this aspect of his personality is clear from his dandyish dress sense, as his sartorial taste definitely complements his quirky nature. But I have always really liked Jonathan. He's an interesting man, and when I met him again he was in the process of building a professional cycling team.

I'd put Benny Johnson – my young protégé who'd briefly lived with me in Biarritz – in contact with JV. Benny was now based in Nice and, although back in Australia for the winter, was in search of a team for the next year. On my recommendation, Jonathan took

Benny on board, but also asked, cryptically, what I'd be doing in 2008 and said that he'd like to talk to me at a later date.

This had all seemed a bit strange – I didn't give it much more thought. After all, I was hoping to be signing for one of the bigger teams in cycling when my Saunier Duval contract ended – not a small, slightly kooky, argyle-clad outfit, filled with American kids and managed by a man who had nothing to do with the European establishment.

But there was JV, alone in the crowd, a little out of place, hanging around at the Tour de France presentation.

'Hey, Jonathan – I didn't know you were going to be here.'

'Ah, Dave – how are you? Well, y'know. It wasn't really *planned*.'

Typically, it felt like we were meeting for the first time, even though we'd known each other for ten years.

We carried on making small talk.

'Thanks for sorting Benny out,' I said. 'He's a real talent, but he's just not had the right break. I think your team will be perfect for him.'

'Yeah, he seems real smart, I think he'll fit in,' JV nodded.

'Sooo, *uhhh* – listen,' Jonathan said, 'come with me. I want you to meet somebody. His name is Doug Ellis – he wants to start a Tour de France team. Let's just say he has the means.'

I followed JV across the foyer and there, standing on his own, equally out of place, was Doug, a lean, tall, personable and friendly American, yet with nothing about him to indicate wealth or power.

We got chatting and, as it turned out, Doug didn't have an invitation for the presentation. I had a spare ticket, so I gave him one. Our meeting that morning was very brief, yet it fuelled a curiosity in me about what JV was planning. But it would be months before I learned that JV and Doug were deadly serious in their aspirations.

When I'd started out on the road towards a cycling career, I'd never ever imagined that the Tour would one day start in London. So it was an emotional moment when the London start was fully unveiled in the Palais des Congrès that morning. The presentation also marked the end of Jean-Marie Leblanc's reign as director of the

Tour. Jean-Marie was honoured on stage as he handed the reins to the incoming director Christian Prudhomme.

As Jean-Marie left the stage and walked back to his seat in the front row of the auditorium, he stopped and shook my hand. Afterwards, he told me he did it so that everybody could see that he supported me.

But not everybody felt so forgiving.

Afterwards, while mingling with officials from the Tour organisation over canapés and champagne, I needed to pop to the men's room. But in the warren of corridors, I got a little lost and then stumbled across a separate reception for representatives of the London start and their guests, including some British riders.

At first I was pleased to see so many familiar faces, but I quickly sensed that I wasn't welcome there. I was still the pariah – in fact, the event had never been mentioned to me. As that realisation sank in, I felt a flush of embarrassment and left. It was a harsh reminder that I had a long way to go before I would be forgiven.

The case that Judge Pallain had put together with the police over the previous two and half years had finally been handed to the Nanterre prosecutor. The hearings began in November 2006 and took five days.

There was no jury, but three judges, presided over by Judge Ghislaine Polge. We were in the number one court of Nanterre, one of the most important courtrooms in France. There were ten defendants, seven of them cyclists from the Cofidis team, charged with 'acquiring and possessing banned substances'. We all sat at the front of the court facing the judges, our lawyers seated behind us.

Over the course of the five days we were called up one by one to stand in front of the judges and answer their questions. All witnesses that were involved in the Cofidis affair were questioned. It was very drawn out; on one day we were in court for over twelve hours.

I told the hearing about the culture at Cofidis. 'Get results and do what you have to do,' was how I described it. I detailed my stay with l'Équipier in Tuscany, and explained how I had learned to inject EPO. 'Everybody pushed me on the Cofidis team,' I said. 'It was torture.'

On the final day, the prosecutor presented his recommendations for sentencing and said: 'When initially reviewing the case I questioned whether David Millar *should even be here.* Fortunately for the court, he has been present, as he's given us an articulate point of view that has been valuable to the case as a whole.'

After all the stress, time, and money that the affair had cost me, I had in the end simply been seen as a 'point of view'. It was the icing on the *gâteau* of *justice française.*

Paul-Albert had asked to give his closing argument first as he needed to leave. He had never interrupted the progress within the court, considering the best policy was to simply stay quiet and let everybody else make a show of themselves. He had told me that much of the effect of the closing argument was down to presentation.

Instead of standing up at the lectern, he had a table moved out and put at the front of the court so he was almost on the same level as the judges. He then gave an eloquent and mostly improvised discourse to the whole court. It was, to use a word he'd introduced me to, '*brilliantisme*'.

And that was that. Later that day I left the court in Nanterre for the last time. Shortly after the New Year, three years after the first arrests in Paris in January 2004, the sentences were announced.

I was acquitted, while many of the others were given suspended sentences of three to six months. The *soigneur*, Boguslaw 'Bob' Madejak, from whom the whole case originated, was sentenced to a year in prison, nine months suspended.

The court was damning about the team itself, and also found Cofidis SA and Cofidis Competition guilty, saying the proceedings had demonstrated that the riders 'must absolutely obtain a result or risk seeing their contract not renewed and losing all hope in cycling'.

Finally, it was over. At last, I could move on.

We loved life in Girona. Waking up to blue skies was invigorating and refreshing and the Catalans were friendly and welcoming. But as the season loomed, training, first because of the court case and then because of a crash, was not going well.

Christian Vande Velde and I were becoming firm friends, although I began to doubt his fondness for me on our first training ride of 2007, when we suffered a miscommunication exiting a roundabout and I came tumbling down very heavily on my right leg.

The muscle was badly damaged and there was nothing for me to do but rest for three weeks. It was also the last time I didn't wear a helmet in training. Ironically, Nicole had given me a hard time over not wearing a helmet just as I was leaving the apartment.

Ten minutes later, I was lying on the tarmac wincing, with Christian standing over me.

'Damn, that's some strong voodoo Nicole has,' he said.

Meanwhile, JV and I had started to correspond more as it became clear that his team was going to happen. Yet it seemed like such a gigantic leap. I couldn't quite grasp what their vision was and it took me a good couple of months before I could finally put into words what they wanted to do. Without that, I couldn't commit to it, let alone convince others.

They wanted to create a Tour de France team that was clean and that would offer a vehicle for riders to reach the top in cycling without ever encountering doping. It would be a team that riders, fans and the media could believe in. It would aim to give back to the sport what it was missing: trust.

The most important way of achieving this was to create an internal, yet independent, anti-dope-testing programme. This would offer an insurance policy for the team, allowing its riders to be tested even more rigorously than the authorities whose responsibility it was to test professional cyclists.

This internal programme would not only test for banned substances, it would also create a blood profile for each cyclist. This profile would allow those responsible for the independent testing programme to monitor for the effects that the undetectable banned substances would have on the cyclist's blood values. In other words, if it was still impossible to find the cause, then they would find the effect. It was a first generation 'blood passport'.

This worked as a deterrent in that it would be extremely difficult to dope and not be caught. If you signed a contract with the team you would be fully aware that you were committing to being more controlled than your competition, so immediately the contracted rider would be buying into what the team was about.

This was a strong psychological tool. In doing this we were taking a proactive stance in preventing doping. There would be no 'ostrich politics' – the management and sponsors were making it clear that they did not want doping to take place and that they'd do everything in their power to stop it.

I had explained to the anti-doping agencies that, as a young athlete, I had given up on the sport's authorities. It was so easy for us to dope if we wanted to, and it was so prevalent around us. In fact, I'd never had an 'out of competition' anti-doping control before 2006. At the time I was doping, there wasn't even an athlete's whereabouts system, so even if the anti-doping controllers wanted to test me away from a race they'd have very little hope of finding me (and none if I didn't want them to). There were no repercussions to face if they couldn't find me. This bred contempt for the system, such as it was.

Contempt for the system and resentment of its inadequacies were often the first step towards doping. Knowing that others were getting away with it – and knowing how they were getting away with it – fuelled cynicism. Faced with doping all around you, it became increasingly difficult, and then impossible, to respect those charged with prevention, detection and punishment.

And then what – who or what were you left to rely on? A good apple in a bad barrel will more often than not be ruined. The people of influence in professional cycling were too often bad apples.

It was the hypocrisy that was the hardest thing to live with. To hear the biggest, most influential names in the sport say, '*Doping? In cycling? But everything is fine!*' was laughable. For a while, I had been one of those people – this is what's easy to confuse with the oft-cited '*omertà*'. Instead of saying nothing they would simply lie about the gravity of the situation.

There's no doubt that, after a few years of the blood tests that were introduced after the Festina affair of 1998, there was enough knowledge and data to understand *exactly* what was going on. If a team boss wanted to, he could analyse his riders' blood test results, his TUE (Theraputic Use Exemption) certificates, or could find out who his private coach or doctor was and whether he was acting suspiciously.

Yet few ever did and most would claim complete shock and incomprehension when one of their riders failed an anti-doping control or found themselves implicated in a doping scandal. Team bosses didn't want to know what was going on; worse, they refused to admit they had the power to prevent what was going on under their very noses.

What Jonathan and Doug wanted to do was to change this mentality. They wanted to demonstrate that a team manager and his sponsor could assume responsibility for their actions. They implemented their internal anti-doping programme as soon as the team entered the professional ranks, only three years after JV had created the original junior team in his hometown, back in 2004.

The goal was now to take this attitude to the Tour de France and in doing so change cycling for the better.

The Slipstream dream excited me so much. It gave me an opportunity to implement everything I had learned from my own mistakes and use it to help and develop others.

It was Jonathan's less than orthodox thinking that made it possible for me to be a part of it. I was the first big-name professional he approached, which – considering that I was an ex-doper – seemed like madness, in the light of what he was trying to achieve.

Only JV could have the chutzpah to think that signing an ex-doper as the flagship leader of a 'Clean Team' could work. But he was right – he knew the world of professional cycling, he had been as its mercy and had left the pro scene a disenchanted young man.

Jonathan had made his own mistakes, he'd been in the wrong place at the wrong time with the wrong people and had made decisions that he will always regret. More than anything, it was this sense of regret that drove him to make his team different from any team that had gone before. In many ways, I was to become his muse.

As I became more enthused about the Slipstream project, I contributed my own ideas. One of the things I'd learned from my time with British Cycling was how valuable a central hub is. Until recently, almost all professional cycling teams had a 'virtual' existence. The main office and team HQ, where all the equipment is stored – bikes, wheels, spare parts, clothing, food, bottles and vehicles – will be in one location.

Sometimes that will be close to a sponsor, as with Cofidis, whose team HQ was near Lille. If the team is run by one person, who has guided it through several different guises, then it will usually be found near that person's home. For Roger Legeay, that means Paris and for Jonathan Vaughters, Boulder, Colorado.

Yet the riders and racing staff have no ties with this hub. Maybe they'll pass through once or twice a year, sometimes not at all.

Supplies for the riders are simply dispatched from the hub to each race, wherever that may be.

This works well on a logistical level, but it creates detachment on a psychological level and the riders – left for too long to their own devices – feel all the more like hired mercenaries. They may meet once or twice a year as a semi-complete team of riders and support staff for training camps, but the rest of the season just wait for the email with the travel info that will take them to the pick-up point for their next race.

When most riders are on one- or two-year contracts it is easy to see how there is no sense of loyalty or understanding of the responsibility each rider has towards the team as a whole. The biggest teams on the pro circuit are made up of a hundred people, something that most riders are unaware of. When a rider dopes they put all those hundred jobs at risk because in modern cycling many teams will not survive a doping scandal.

That detachment from the team's beating heart only fuels the possibility of doping, which was why I recommended to JV that our team should have a central hub in Europe, where we obliged as many personnel as possible – staff and riders – to live.

This would also serve as a massive advantage when it came to managing the riders. The team would be able to assume responsibility for their performance, providing coaching and training sessions, nutritional and medical support, and the latest in technological and scientific advances. It was one thing to prevent them from doping, but we also had an obligation to offer them the resources to make them the best athletes they could be.

For our European programme of racing, the logical location for this central hub was Girona, where the majority of American cyclists already based themselves during the February–October racing season. The team would remain registered to its Boulder office in order to keep its American licence and origins, and a core team of staff would live and work there, but the majority would be based in and around Girona.

The logistics were complicated and it took a few months to map it all out. But we needed to move forward and sell the idea to others – riders, race organisers and eventually sponsors. Until it could stand on its own two feet, Doug was underwriting the team's financial requirements and, in doing so, giving Jonathan and I the freedom to create our dream team.

I was juggling excitement about the future with my disillusion about the present. Away from Slipstream, other relationships were causing me stress.

I'd had a difficult time at the early season Saunier Duval training camp and had become increasingly isolated from the team. By the time I got to the first races, I was desperate to show myself. Starting 2007 badly was the worst-case scenario for me because I was hoping to garner some good results to boost my value when it came to contract negotiations for 2008, in the hope of paying off my debts.

I had barely made a dent into my gargantuan IVA with the salary I was on from Saunier Duval. My first races of the year were a joke, but then I started to feel better before Paris–Nice, the biggest stage race of the early season. Apart from a couple of stress-relieving drinking sessions, I'd taken very good care of myself.

Because of the leg injury, I'd been put on a different programme, but this separation was symbolic of my situation within the team. I had come to see how helpless I was in making any difference in the anti-doping battle if I didn't have the complete support of those in power.

Away from racing, I was coming out as an anti-doping activist. Since our first meeting, Andy Parkinson from UK Sport had thought of a good use for me – as the keynote speaker at the UK Sport anti-doping conference in London, which took place the week before Paris–Nice began.

I'd given interviews and held press conferences, but I'd never spoken publicly in this way before. I was very nervous but decided that the best thing I could do was simply to tell my story, and to try and get across what I'd learned, in the hope that my experience could be used to support anti-doping.

Thankfully, it was a big success. It was a full house and everybody seemed genuinely interested to hear what I had to say. My performance was far from polished but I managed to get my message across. Afterwards, as we mingled over drinks, I spoke to a lot of delegates.

Many said that, before, they had always seen the problem of doping as a black and white issue, but by the time I'd finished speaking they understood it was in fact grey. What surprised me was that almost nobody there had ever heard a doper's story, let alone met one.

One of the biggest sources of knowledge on doping is a doper. But the majority of guilty athletes never admit to doping, even when convicted, preferring to deny and then lodge appeal after appeal, rather than risk the career ruin that admission of guilt might lead to. Often, if they do finally accept their fate, they remain bitter and resentful, unwilling to help.

I was an exception to that rule of thumb. At the lowest point, I had hated my sport so much that I was happy to be out of it, so in that sense the consequences of admitting to doping, while devastating, had offered liberation of a sort.

Mine was a rare path, but one that fortuitously led to my total reform and a new-found passion in educating people on what, up to that point, had always been a hidden dark world.

As relations with Saunier Duval grew trickier, I was kept going by my increasing passion for Slipstream. JV and I were talking more regularly and in greater detail, and we both knew that I would be joining the team. Even so, we still hadn't discussed contracts, let alone money.

The Friday before Paris–Nice began, JV invited me to dinner. I didn't know at the time but he is something of a gourmand, so when I arrived at a beautiful little Michelin-starred restaurant in a back street in Paris, lugging my bike and bags with me, I was unprepared. The only saving grace, as I bumped into the furniture under the withering gaze of the mâitre d', was that I was impeccably attired in the Paul Smith three-piece suit I'd worn for the conference.

During the evening, we agreed that I would ride for Slipstream Sports the following year. We still didn't discuss money or contracts. It was an old-fashioned gentleman's agreement, sealed with a good bottle of wine and a handshake, which, considering what we were setting out to try and do, was quite appropriate.

I won the Paris–Nice prologue, celebrating my victory only metres away from where I'd had lunch with Jean-Marie Leblanc on that summer day in 2005.

Mum was at the race and Paul-Albert had watched on TV. Afterwards, he called to say how proud he was of me, of the comments I'd made in the post-race interview and of the high opinion the commentators had of me.

Technically, I'd ridden the course perfectly, taking the hill easier than most, but then finishing really strongly. Even when my saddle broke, 3 kilometres from the finish line, I didn't panic and came flying through the last corner, clipping the kerbs and barriers.

I had the best Paris–Nice of my career, something that impressed Jonathan no end, as he knew that my winter training had been compromised and that I'd been somewhat occupied with other duties in the preceding week. He was doubly relieved as he'd feared that decadently wining and dining me less than 48 hours before the race had perhaps not been his smartest move.

My last flash of form that spring came in the Three Days of De Panne in Belgium. I'd won the time trial there, nine years earlier, but this time I was well and truly beaten into second place by local hero Stijn Devolder. The up-side was that, after the race, I met up with Matt White as we were both staying in Kortijk until the Tour of Flanders, three days later.

I'd known Whitey for years. He'd been on small fringe teams for the majority of his career, finally getting his big break with US Postal in 2001. Later, he joined me at Cofidis in 2004.

He was one of those rare riders, a fully committed *domestique*, with no aspirations for victory or achieving results for himself. Matt knew exactly what he was paid for and that was to work for his leaders until his job was done. Once he'd done everything he could to support their ambitions, he'd save as much energy as possible, so that he'd be able to repeat the performance the next day.

He was probably one of the best *domestiques* in the world. One moment his turn of speed would be ripping the peloton to pieces, as he set up his team leader, then 10 minutes later he'd be in the *gruppetto*, asking around to find out how his leaders were doing at the front of the race.

But it is his charismatic personality that really sets Matt apart. He is a force of nature. Just having him in the vicinity raises your energy levels. Blessed with the classic Aussie dry wit that often reduces people to hysterics, he was also perceptive enough to notice if there was something wrong. He's a good listener who always finds the right moment to come and chat; that ensured that everybody wanted to talk to Whitey.

His love for sport – all sport – was almost comical. Able to hold an educated conversation with a fan of any sport, he also acted as coach and mentor to his wife, Jane Saville, an Olympic walker.

This always perplexed me.

'Whitey,' I'd ask, 'how can you coach Jane? You know nothing about walking . . .'

'Dave, mate,' he'd reply with a shrug of the shoulders. 'It's easy. Athletes are all the same – cyclists, walkers – whatever. They're all insecure. You just gotta make 'em feel good; tell 'em to train when they need to train, and make 'em rest when they need to rest.'

Then with finality, he'd say: 'Yep – psychology, mate!'

But God – he loved his cycling. It was his grand passion and he had expert opinions on everything and everyone. When it came to racing, he was a deadly serious, focused, elite athlete.

The Slipstream project needed a *directeur sportif* who was fresh and would buy into the ethos of the team. But we simply didn't know where to begin. Then it hit me – Whitey would be perfect. He was only 32 at the time and planned to continue racing for a few more years, but, with Jonathan's consent, I set out to persuade him.

I knew how important the *directeur sportif*'s role was because, in my experience, there are very few good ones in professional cycling. The role has become somewhat diluted over the years. In the old days, the DS would also be the boss of the team, and would double as employer/coach/manager/father, much as *soigneurs* would have been doctor/confidant/mother – as well as a masseur.

These days the *directeur* is less of a boss than in the past. There are so many roles within a team that the *directeur* has little personal contact with the riders. There are coaches, psychologists, PRs, scientists, doctors – in many ways, the only time riders will actually interact with their *directeur* is in the pre-race meeting and over the short-wave radio earpieces that we use during the race. It means that one of the most important relationships within a professional cycling team has been lost.

I wanted to try and bring that back and JV welcomed the idea. I knew that Whitey was perfect for it – I just had to persuade him. That night in Kortrijk, we had a few beers, got a little tipsy and I planted the seed in his brain. It would take me another few months of relentless persuasion before he came on board.

Things were going from bad to worse with Saunier Duval. On the morning of the Tour of Flanders, I saw one of our riders clearly delay his appearance for a random UCI blood test, vanishing for almost 30 minutes before reappearing to have his blood drawn.

His behaviour was very suspicious. I had registered the look of fear and noted his body language when he initially found out we had been selected for blood tests. That, combined with his inexplicable non-appearance at a race two weeks earlier, pointed to his use of EPO.

His 30-minute disappearing act led me to an inevitable conclusion. If his hematocrit had been beyond the 50 per cent level, he would have been able to drop it back down below by hastily introducing plasma into his bloodstream, which takes at least 30 minutes. The whole scenario confirmed what I was finding impossible to ignore: some of my teammates were doping.

A few weeks earlier, our a young Italian climber, Riccardo Ricco, had run amok in Tirreno–Adriatico. He then swaggeringly announced he would be attacking on the Poggio, the final climb in the marathon one-day Milan–San Remo race a few days later. Ricco was as good as his word and did not let the expectant media or fans down with his 'panache' that day.

This was extraordinary behaviour for such a young pro and was particularly suspicious as Ricco – who had failed hematocrit tests as an amateur – was renowned for constantly grazing the upper limits of the blood controls.

Ricco was about as suspect as any rider I had seen since I first turned pro. He regarded me, the repentant doper, with such complete incomprehension that when I had tried to speak to him it was like talking to a brick wall.

Although only 22, he was so adept with needles that, before big races, he would sit and inject himself in the team bus. 'Just some painkillers,' I was told. I'd tried to put a stop to this, but with no success.

I had told Matxin and Mauro that he was highly suspicious, yet they said there was nothing they could prove, and that anyway, they'd heard he was a freak – maybe he was just 'special'. In reality I felt that they didn't care, so they turned a blind eye. The media saw him as the biggest, most exciting talent in cycling in years, the sponsors loved the exposure – why should Mauro and Matxin be concerned?

Ricco's arrogance and the episode at Flanders had tipped me over the edge. I contacted the UCI saying that I had suspicions about doping practices within my team, and that I wanted them to be aware of this. They told me they were looking into it.

But there were issues. Mario Zorzoli, the UCI's chief medical officer, is a good friend of Mauro Gianetti. I am not suggesting that this affected Zorzoli's work, but it was indicative of a wider conflict of interests. The UCI's positioning, as both promoters of cycling and guardians of its ethics, has always been controversial.

Even though it was obvious that the team was teetering on the edge of systematic doping, and even though I had also made it clear to Mauro what I thought, nothing happened.

Any suspicions I had became evident to the wider world at the Tour of the Basque Country a couple of weeks later. The Saunier Duval riders sent to the Basque race dominated the event in a manner reminiscent of the notorious EPO-fuelled performances of the 1990s.

It pissed the peloton off. My peers were confronting me, asking me what was going on, saying it was ridiculously obvious that the team were doped up to their eyeballs. I looked like a fool and I was embarrassed that I could do nothing to stop it.

Because they did nothing, I'd given up on speaking to Mauro or Matxin. Instead, I wrote a long letter to UCI president Pat McQuaid, following up conversations we'd had and telling him that something needed to be done.

> ... I agree with what you said about sanctioning team management – I do think they are changing now but only because their livelihood relies on it, not for any real ethical reason. They HAVE to be more proactive, they have to sit down face to face on an individual basis with their riders and tell them not to dope – this is something that doesn't happen.
>
> Teams need to be held responsible for the actions of their riders. I know the directors and management say this is not possible, I beg to differ. For the moment riders have consequences for their actions, teams do not. Whether this means short-term suspensions of teams from racing or big fines I don't know, but consequences are necessary.
>
> Remove injections of any sort and half the battle is won, in my opinion. We do not need to inject ourselves with vitamins and sugar and amino acids to finish a three-week stage race, that is bullshit. I am proving it and am happy to be an example. I finished the Tour tired, but my health was fine. It should be considered a bad thing to inject oneself, not a necessity.

Around the same time, Christian Prudhomme, director of the Tour de France, called me, asking me what the hell the team was up to. I told him what I knew and explained there was very little I could do, that I'd tried everything I could.

Then I wrote another long letter, this time to both Prudhomme and McQuaid, asking that they get together and speak to Gianetti, saying that their combined forces would surely stop what was going on.

... the current anti-doping system is being cheated by the riders with the will to do so, and, without a vast amount of money, resources and cooperation from teams, this will not be changing in the near future.

I had no problems telling both of you what I knew [about Saunier Duval] but it also makes me realise how hard it is for somebody within a team to make a difference. I don't think there is anybody else in the peloton with my background trying to make change happen as much as I am – yet I cannot do anything in my own team! That is very scary and should be a lesson to all of us. I cannot do anything without you ... all of us working independently will not do much but make noise. Working together we can make a difference, and force change.

The sport is changing for the better, but not enough and not definitively. I fear that there is simply a calm before the storm for the moment. If fundamental cultural changes do not take place, I see it all flaring up again in two to three years, and then we're all at the end of the road ...

But in 2007, the UCI and ASO, the Tour's parent company, were arch-enemies. They were locked in a bitter feud, fuelled by a power struggle over who controlled the sport. Lost in the midst of all this was the struggle to combat doping.

ASO was only prevented from forming a splinter group, thus removing the Tour de France and all its other events from UCI jurisdiction, because of a Brussels Directive and intervention from the French government. My gripes with Saunier Duval were an irritant in the middle of all this. But by flagging up my concerns about the team, I was walking on thin ice.

Even though the team's attitude frustrated me, I was desperate to be selected for the London Tour start and I knew I had to be discreet. At the same time, my good relations with the UCI and ASO, and an ever-improving profile within the media, meant that, in truth, the team couldn't simply bench me. But I didn't want to risk not being at the Tour so decided that, in the short term at least, I should keep my head down, ride out the remainder of my contract and put all my energies into Slipstream.

But on my return from racing in the Tour of Georgia in America, Mauro called me telling me that I had to ride the Tour of Romandie. The Swiss race had never been on my programme and was, I felt sure, going to derail my build-up to the Tour. He also wanted to speak to me, he said. I feared the worst, thinking that I was going to be fired or told that I wouldn't be selected for the Tour.

In fact, Mauro was very sympathetic and I saw another side of him. He understood what was going on, he said, but there was so little he could do. The riders were pushing the limits but he couldn't just suspend them from racing for that, because there would be legal repercussions from the suspended riders and the team would be thrown into disarray.

When he told me that he'd heard I'd spoken to the UCI and ASO, I didn't really know what to do or say. I just sat there, understanding that nothing would really change and that I was being appeased. I realised too that I was powerless.

I crashed badly in Romandie, almost replicating my injury from the start of the year. From then on, my Tour de France performance was up in the air. I knew my form would be a long way short of what I'd hoped for.

I tried to disengage myself from Saunier Duval. I knew that I'd done everything I could. I was completely open with Mauro about Slipstream, thanking him for believing in me and for giving me the opportunity to make my comeback, while explaining that Jonathan had made me an offer that I couldn't possibly refuse.

I think Mauro was happy for me, I genuinely do. He completely understood my reasoning and wished me every success. From that moment on, our relationship was much better. I gave Saunier Duval everything of myself when it came to racing, but my head – and heart – were elsewhere and I think this suited them just fine.

JULY 2007

As I type this I am travelling towards France, through a tunnel under the English Channel. I am leaving my homeland, a man at peace, a state of mind I feared I would not be experiencing this evening.

It had all started to get to me, the whole Tour de France in England thing. I was overwhelmed by the whole experience. I'm not used to being so in demand. It was not something I was very comfortable with.

As soon as stage one – from London to Canterbury – started, I felt relaxed. The amount of people watching matched – maybe even surpassed – the numbers watching the prologue in London. It was wonderful, and seeing them all made me realise what I had to do.

The first time I ever saw the Tour de France was in 1994 when it last visited England. I travelled down to Brighton with a friend to watch the race. We arrived over four hours before it was due to pass and got our position on the barriers down on the seafront, where we'd be able to see the race go past twice.

There were so many people out that day, and so much waiting around, but it was all good fun. Late that afternoon, the race came past. Three riders were off the front with a big advantage as they arrived on the finishing circuit to compete for the win.

The breakaway came flying by, then we waited nervously, clock watching, for the bunch to come into sight. Finally the motorbikes came into view, but there was no bunch, only a lone rider. It was Chris Boardman.

He'd counter-attacked on the climb when the peloton had entered the finishing circuit and came by on his own. Seeing a Brit out there, ahead of the peloton, sent everybody wild. He ended up finishing ahead of the bunch and taking fourth place, even jubilantly punching the air as he crossed the finish line, all very un-Boardman like. But I remember how much it had made everybody's day, seeing a home rider putting on a show. It's something I've never forgotten.

As the peloton left London in front of huge crowds, those memories made me realise that I needed to put on a show too. I was driven by pure emotion, but I was also very calculating about when and where I made my initial move. I only attacked once, so that goes to show that I got it right.

I waited until a group had escaped from the front of the peloton and the bunch was giving chase. When we were completely strung out, and one rider had decided to try and bridge across, I jumped onto his wheel and sat there waiting for him to tire. I knew that he'd expect us to work together – we were brothers in arms until we reached the safety of the break ahead. I didn't want any brothers though. I waited patiently for him to swing over, expecting me to set the pace, and then launched one huge effort that left him far behind and took me up to the group ahead.

But the peloton wasn't giving up. I looked over my shoulder and saw an approaching mass of riders, spread menacingly across the width of the road. At the bottom of a steep hill, I decided to make my move, leaving behind the group I was with, and distancing the peloton in the process, I felt so strong, completely within myself, adrenalin flowing, as the emotion took over.

Now I was where I wanted to be. I was leading the Tour de France, on my own, through England.

I didn't care that it was a futile move. I felt like I owed it to the crowds who had come out to cheer the Brits on. I'd never seen so many people at the roadside. They were perched on lamp-posts, standing on walls, leaning out of windows – and endless kids hauled up on their dads' shoulders. The crowds parted ahead of me as I climbed up the hills and the villages and towns welcomed me with a deafening roar. Goose bumps rippled over me.

Four riders were chasing me, but I ignored the time checks. I was only interested in the gap I had to the peloton and once that reached 5 minutes, I regretfully eased off the pedals and slowed to await my four pursuers.

During that lull, I was able to pay more attention to what was going on around me. There were banners and Union flags bearing my name and in places *ALLEZ MILLAR!* was painted on the road. I was popular, people were cheering for me. I'd hoped Brits still supported me, but I hadn't expected it, and I was so thankful and so proud. But that happiness was tinged with sadness. I wanted to stop, shake hands, and say sorry to everybody for my past mistakes.

By the time the group of four caught me, I had already claimed one sprint bonus. I took the next one too. I'd also taken the first King of the Mountains points, but had opted out of the next one. As we closed on Canterbury, I was leading the Mountains classification with only one more climb to tackle.

Now I had real hopes of taking the King of the Mountains jersey at the end of the day, but I was tiring. Inevitably the breakaway would be caught, so I radioed behind and got my team to start chasing. Meanwhile, I dropped out of the breakaway group and awaited the peloton's arrival. The tactic was simple: my team would shut down the break while I rested in the peloton. When we hit the last climb I would be replenished enough to score the King of the Mountains points I needed. It was a calculated gamble.

The peloton reeled in every rider from the break apart from Stephen Augé of Cofidis. He'd stayed away and was going to score maximum points on the last climb, which meant I had to secure second place to have any hope of taking the Mountains jersey. Fortunately, I still had the legs and took second with a teammate sneaking into third behind me.

During the final 20 kilometres, I was filled with cramp. I couldn't get out of the saddle, but the finale was fast and mainly downhill – if it hadn't been, I don't know what I'd have done. I finished the day third overall in the race classification with the polka-dot King of the Mountains jersey on my back. It had been an amazing day.

But I still want to say thank you – thank you to everybody who shouted for me, made banners and painted my name on the road. You carried me along and gave me a polka-dot jersey that I had never imagined wearing. And maybe there was a teenager out there who will be racing in the Tour one day, who'll remember seeing me pass by and who will do the same thing if he ever gets the chance.

I'll do my best to make sure he never has to experience what I went through to get there.

24

THE PERSUADER

Whenever I gave interviews and spoke about how long it would take for cycling to heal itself, I would usually say ten years. Sometimes, people would be shocked or depressed by this answer, but then another scandal would come along to prove my point – just as it did in July 2007.

For the Festina affair read *Operación Puerto*, for David Millar read Alexandre Vinokourov.

Once the race had left England, things got worse at the 2007 Tour. The British tabloid press – not for the first time – called it the Tour de Farce. After tying himself in knots over whether he had lied to the UCI, his team and the media over missed doping controls, the race leader, Michael Rasmussen, quit the race in shame under cover of darkness. Hot on his heels, Kazakh Alexandre Vinokourov, lauded for his coverage and gutsy riding, tested positive.

Vinokourov – 'Vino' – and his Astana team had arrived at the Tour with the intention of total domination, but a crash in the first week had effectively killed off his overall chances. But in a startling return to form, he recovered to win a time trial in dominant fashion and then one of that year's hardest mountain stages in the Pyrenees. *L'Equipe* hailed it as *Le Courage de Vino* – within 48 hours, *courage* had turned to *dopage*.

On the Tour's second rest day in Pau, Saunier Duval had organised a press conference, publicising the sponsor's involvement in conservation. Knowing that not many from the media would come to us, we took it to them, holding court in the press centre at the Palais des Congrès.

There were three Saunier Duval riders: Spanish climber Iban

Mayo – the day after the 2007 Tour finished it was announced that he had been random controlled that very day and had tested positive for EPO – Christophe Rinero, my old Cofidis teammate, and myself.

It was a lacklustre affair. Almost all the questions were directed towards me and there was little interest in Saunier Duval's good deeds. The few journalists there were trying their best just to find things to ask, hoping perhaps to give the whole affair some heart. It was a little desperate really and in truth a bit embarrassing.

So we were all easily distracted by a buzz that suddenly started to wash over the press room. Watching from the platform, as people started running, phones rang off the hook and shouts erupted across the desks, it felt like a tsunami. I could feel something malevolent in the distance heading my way. Then it hit us, full force – a tidal wave of shit.

British journalist, Daniel Friebe told me what had happened. Vinokourov had tested positive after his two stage wins. I was in total shock.

I collapsed inside. Vino had been one of my heroes. I loved his attacking style and truly believed if anybody could do it clean, then he could. Admittedly, I'd been a little disturbed when it had been disclosed pre-Tour that he was trained by Michele Ferrari, and his total avoidance of tackling the subject of doping disappointed me too, but, at the same time, if I was clean and never doped, I'd be pissed off about being asked about it over and over again. And, after all, I'd worked with Luigi Cecchini and been clean – I wasn't exactly in a position to jump to conclusions about Vino working with Ferrari.

Daniel asked me for my reaction. My response was simple, off the cuff. 'We may as well pack our bags and go home,' I said. Mayo and Rinero, sitting alongside, sensing my mood, shifted uncomfortably in their seats.

As soon as I said it, I knew I couldn't throw in the towel like that. I wasn't allowed to believe that. I'd promised myself that when coming back to the sport I would take responsibility. So I tried to gather myself, to defend the progress being made in anti-doping, saying that the very fact that Vino had been caught was a massive step forward. I remember giving my heartfelt opinion on it all and there being a ripple of applause when I'd finished. But the shock was deep, and it was all such a blur.

We stood up to leave. A huddle of journalists quickly surrounded me and Paul Kimmage began to berate me. I can't even remember what Kimmage was saying, but I felt woozy with it all, desperate for some fresh air. Eventually the huddle broke up. Jeremy Whittle from *The Times*, who'd seen me go through a lot, always there as a witness and often as a friend, sensed my unease.

'David,' he said. 'Are you all right?'

I began to well up.

'I just feel like crying,' I said and then sat down on the nearest chair.

He put his arm around my shoulder and allowed the mask to fall. I just sat there, head in my hands, in tears. Meanwhile, Kimmage watched from across the room.

In the *Sunday Times* that weekend, Kimmage skewered me, accusing me of crying for Vinokourov, talking of my 'tears for a cheat'.

He was wrong. They were not tears for a cheat, nor were they tears of self-pity, desperation or fatigue.

I wept because suddenly, definitively, I fully understood the gravity of what I'd done to my sport and to everybody who had believed in me, cheered for me, defended me and trusted in me. I'd broken their hearts the way that Vino had broken mine.

The Tour de France always ends with a party and 2007 was no different. I didn't linger at the Saunier Duval function as I wasn't really hanging out with the riders by this point. We weren't enemies – we just didn't really have much reason to spend time together away from racing.

Afterwards, Nicole and our photographer friend, Camille McMillan, popped into the CSC team's bash, hooked up with Christian Vande Velde and then headed off to the private party that the Discovery Channel team – who'd just won the Tour with Alberto Contador – was hosting in the Hotel Crillon.

We wandered into the penthouse of the Crillon and, to our surprise, stumbled on one of the cooler post-Tour parties that I've been to. Given how corporate Discovery could be, this was a surprise.

Discovery had the best after party?

Although Contador had won the Tour, the team's management figureheads – recently retired Lance Armstrong and his long-standing colleagues Johan Bruyneel and Bill Stapleton – couldn't find a new sponsor. Yet – after winning eight Tours and also earning significant wealth – instead of thanking the sport and bowing out graciously, they were critical.

'It's not an environment right now that's conducive to a lot of investment,' Stapleton said, as a way of explaining their inability to find a sponsor.

'Clearly things need to improve on many levels, with a more unified front, before you would see us venture back into cycling,' Lance stated.

Bruyneel, Stapleton and Armstrong, in particular, owed everything to cycling, and yet now they treated it with what I felt was disdain.

I'd written to Lance criticising his disregard for the state of cycling, and attacking the way that the Discovery team had signed Ivan Basso, despite the allegations of doping against him. Basso was still at the centre of the *Operación Puerto* storm and, due to the tacit agreement between most teams not to sign or race those under investigation, their pursuit of Basso had seemed deliberately provocative. I believed that to be particularly irresponsible and of no help to the state of cycling at that time.

The thought of them walking away from cycling like that was on my mind when I saw Lance at the Crillon and wandered over to say hello.

Earlier that day, I'd been among the only guys in the peloton not wearing Livestrong-branded sunglasses on the final stage, something I was sure he knew. Oakley – a company that sponsored dozens of cyclists and that I'd had a long relationship with – had sent people round the team buses the day before the Paris stage, handing out black-and-yellow Livestrong sunglasses for the riders to wear on the Champs Elysées.

I'd always liked Lance, but I didn't feel like representing him or his brand. I could have justified wearing the glasses and supporting the cancer charity, but at the same time Livestrong, especially at the Tour de France, was much more representative of Lance Armstrong, the brand, than it was of a cancer charity. So I took the decision not to wear the sunglasses. I didn't think it had been fair of Oakley. It seemed to me that the company was almost forcing them on us, and I really didn't like that.

Lance is a charismatic but controversial man. All the good he's done has been tarnished by the never-ending accusations. His wins in the Tour de France came during what was one of the most doped periods of professional cycling. Almost every single one of his ex-teammates who attempted to come out of his shadow was caught for doping and some have also made allegations against him. Tyler Hamilton, Roberto Heras, Floyd Landis – they were all Lance's lieutenants who changed teams and tried to beat him. Yet, once on other teams, all of them ended up failing doping controls.

I can't say definitively if Lance doped or not. Yes, there are all the stories and rumours, but I never saw him dope with my own eyes. If he did dope, then, after all that he has said and done, it would be unforgivable. Certainly, his performances in the Tour were extraordinary, unprecedented, but then he's unlike anybody I have ever met, a force of nature. But I felt he could have done more and he should have done more against doping; he was in a position to make a difference and to help his sport, but I never saw any evidence of that.

He is a phenomenal human being – I would never argue against that. He lives life on a different level, controlling his world in a omnipotent manner, leading by example but also by fear. His ability to motivate, based on his absolute self-belief and complete fear-lessness of failure, is legendary. His own lack of fear brainwashes those around him to believe in everything he does.

But you don't fuck with Lance because he will not forgive you – in his mind, in cycling at least, forgiveness equates to weakness.

What also sets him apart is his ability *always* to be switched on, to not make mistakes. Every detail is thought of and taken care of. Yet there's no doubt he's an odd fish, and sometimes unpredictable. After we started chatting at the Crillon, I quickly got on to the subject of the Livestrong sunglasses.

'Of course I noticed you didn't wear them, Dave,' he said, calmly, 'but it's your choice.'

I explained that I didn't agree with Oakley forcing them on us, that they didn't have the right. So what did Lance say in response?

'You want me to speak to Oakley and get them to sort you out a new contract?'

That threw me, although not for long. So then I asked him if he'd received the emails I'd sent him the year before, taking him and Discovery to task for signing Basso, emails that he'd not responded to.

'Yeah, I saw them,' he said.

By now, drink in hand, I was warming to my theme.

'Look, Lance – I know how much you love the Tour,' I said, 'but you're alienating yourself from it more and more. What are you going to do twenty years from now if you're not welcome back?

How can they invite you back as a past champion if you treat the sport like shit and are clouded in controversy . . .?'

Lance stared at me. So did a wide-eyed Christian and an increasingly unnerved Nicole, standing alongside me. I continued, undeterred.

'You didn't win seven Tours without loving the sport – I know that. Give something back, help us clean up the sport, it doesn't matter what happened when you raced, it's what happens now and in the future . . .'

I awaited his response.

'Dave,' he said, 'of course I love the sport, but I can't help it if it won't help itself. I've got bigger things to do now, Dave, and shit – life is amazing away from cycling. I could tell you stories you wouldn't believe. I'm moving on.'

I shook my head. 'Lance, that's bullshit. You will *always* come back to cycling . . .'

We talked a little more and I told him about what Jonathan and I were doing. I knew Jonathan and Lance had history and I didn't want that affecting Slipstream's future, so I suggested that we should be allies, not enemies. We parted on good terms, I think – but I'd perhaps lectured him for a little too long – 10 minutes too long . . .

Camille took a photo of our encounter. Lance is staring at me, stony-faced, as I lecture him. Alongside me is an edgy Christian, who had been on one of Lance's Tour-winning teams and knew better than to say what I was saying.

Sadly, I think it was the beginning of the end of my friendship with Lance. He'd always stood by me and supported me, but I was now a different person from the person I had been when we'd first met. And I could no longer pretend otherwise – even with Lance.

Saunier Duval dropped me from their team for that autumn's Vuelta. I was pissed off but I knew that I was paying the price for my conflicts with the team earlier that year. It wasn't the end of the world, but it was the end of the Worlds, because, without racing in the Vuelta before the World Championships, I stood little chance of competing against those who had.

So I focused on other things and was very proud to win both the British road and time trial titles. As I had won the individual pursuit title earlier in the year, this meant that I held three of the most prestigious national championships.

It was very important to me, and it meant that I'd race all road events in the following year in the white jersey of British national champion. It felt fitting that I'd be launching my dream team wearing my country's colours.

My standing as a reformed athlete was growing and UK Sport had put me forward as the British nomination for the World Anti-Doping Agency's Athlete Committee. This was a complete surprise and a great honour. It gave my anti-doping role within sport an official title.

Each stakeholder country in WADA can put forward a rec-ommended nominee for the committee. It's then up to the WADA executive committee to select who it believes is an appropriate addition and matches the cross-section they are looking for.

The majority of the committee is made up of former athletes, but there are a few who are still active. But there wasn't – nor had there ever been – an ex-doper or a professional cyclist.

Suggesting my name was a forward-thinking move by UK Sport, but one that we thought might not be supported by WADA, which had long been critical of cycling's record on doping. But my nomination was approved and I was elected to a three-year term on the Athlete Committee. I was now officially part of WADA, the global agency promoting anti-doping – something that would have seemed preposterous a few years earlier.

Meanwhile, Slipstream had signed almost all its riders, securing three of the biggest names in American cycling – Christian Vande Velde, Dave Zabriskie and Tyler Farrar. I'd played a big part in securing their signatures. In fact, I'd spent hours persuading all our bigger names to come to the team.

It was a labour of love for JV, Doug and I. We didn't follow the usual route of bouncing numbers back and forth to agents. We wanted whoever came to the team to understand what we were about. I loved this and became our chief persuader.

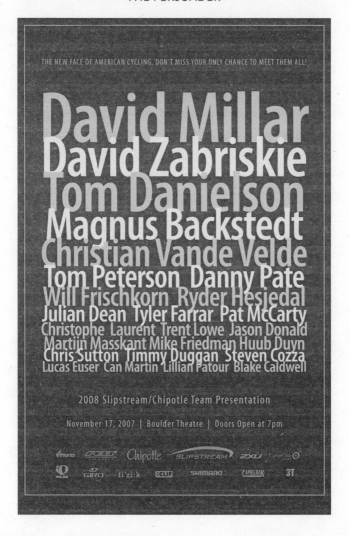

Our first get-together was in Boulder, Colorado, in November 2007. There was immediately a different vibe from any cycling environment I'd known before. Everybody was excited, from the young bloods getting their big break to the seasoned campaigners like myself. We all felt that we were part of something different.

I finally signed my contract during the camp. We'd agreed financial terms months before, but, more importantly, I also became a part owner of the team. This was rare in cycling, and demonstrated how the relationship between Doug, JV and myself had grown over the previous year. It also meant that my money was where my mouth was, and we thought this to be very important, given how much of myself I was putting into it all.

We had a blast in Boulder. Our recruitment strategy had worked well and we were all slightly different from the usual professional cyclist and, paradoxically, our individualist maverick personalities knitted together well. As most of us came from the English-speaking world, we had a cycling culture that was different from the traditional one. This was new-world cycling – there was to be no more old-world mentality.

It was an attitude that carried us through that first year. From our garish orange and blue argyle kit to our complete transparency with the media, we stood out. At one of our first races, the Tour of California, I even shared my room for two nights with a journalist. Fortunately, he was a cool guy and we talked as much about music and books as we did about cycling, but it wasn't exactly conducive to resting during a stage race. Visiting the restaurants of one of our sponsors, Chipotle, for appearances and signings in each of the towns the race visited wasn't the best move for post-race recovery either, but we were on a steep learning curve.

The Tour of California was our first major outing as a team and we were dominant. Christian and I both finished in the top three, Tyler spent a day in the race leader's jersey, and we won the teams' classification. As the year went on, we proved to be good at hitting our objectives.

Young Dutch signing Martijn Maaskant rode to a superb fourth place in Paris–Roubaix, we won the team time trial stage on the first day of the Giro d'Italia and Christian took the coveted Giro leader's pink jersey. It was a massive result for Slipstream – our first Grand Tour and we won the first stage and put an American into the lead. The result was the perfect example of the mixture we had created of science and spirit.

But on the day, what made it possible for us all to implement that blend was Matt White. He had been on the steepest learning curve of all, having been thrown in at the deep end from the beginning of the year. By the start of the Giro, Matt had learned an unfathomable amount and was already capable of doing his job better than 90 per cent of the *directeurs sportifs* already in cycling.

The rousing speech he gave us before the Giro's team time trial remains one of my most memorable sporting moments. We were inspired, and I'll never forget us congregating after the finish and congratulating each other on the perfect ride. We all knew that we couldn't have gone any faster and, even though we had to wait another 45 minutes before we were confirmed as the winners, we didn't care what the result was as we had nothing to reproach ourselves for. It was an amazing feeling.

It was my first experience of the Giro and it was easily the most physically demanding Grand Tour I'd ever done. I wasn't exactly on top form having peaked for the very start of the year, yet on the sixth stage I found myself in contention for the win. I had nothing planned that day and, in fact, was so relaxed that I'd missed the peloton rolling out from the start, because I'd been chatting to Max Sciandri in the start village.

I tagged on to the very back of the bunch and was perfectly

happy to just sit where I was and make my way to the finish, with as little exertion as possible.

But that day my legs felt magical. I was so fluid that I couldn't feel the pedals, so I decided I'd make my way to the front of the peloton. When I got there, the attacks had already started, and the next thing I knew, I had broken clear with four others. In total, we rode in the break for 180 kilometres.

I felt in control the whole day. When it became clear that we wouldn't be caught before the finish line, I weighed up my options and assessed the other riders. I planned to control any attacks in the group and win in a sprint.

But the others in the breakaway knew that, if we finished the stage sprinting, I was the most likely to win, so one by one they attacked. Each time, I chased them down, and reeled them in, but the acceleration to shut down the penultimate attack caused something to go wrong with my chain.

As we were inside the last 2 kilometres, there was no time to change bikes, so I couldn't do anything about it. The final attack came under the '1-kilometre-to-go' *flamme rouge*. As I sprinted after the move to close it down, my chain snapped. I ground to a halt, while the others rode on to contest the stage.

I knew what had happened instantly. Anger coursed through me. In one furious movement, I was off the bike, standing in the road and, in a red mist, hurling the bike powerfully over the crowd barriers.

The bike went arching through the air into the Italian countryside, while I was left standing like a lemon in the middle of the road, live on TV. I was so angry. I knew how rarely the stars align like that and I was furious that victory had been taken away from me because of the rarest of mechanicals.

People may love Italy but I hated the rest of that Giro. Every day my loathing grew, particularly as we travelled more kilometres in the bus, transferring to and from stage starts and finishes, than we did racing on the bike. The Giro made the Tour seem a civilised affair and the Vuelta feel like a holiday camp.

After the race ended, our grand plan was to go straight to altitude in St Moritz and then to the Pyrenees, first to recover and then to train. JV was a big fan of altitude training and he was convinced it would give us a significant advantage at the Tour. He was right.

I was flying in the Tour's first few days, finishing second in the time trial by only a second (on the day, I was actually a distant third, but the winner was Stefan Schumacher who tested positive and was later wiped from the results).

My form only really lasted for the first week, but meanwhile Christian developed into a Tour contender, finishing fourth in Paris with little support from the team. It was a strange experience for me. I'd gone from the team's big name and hope to an also-ran, while watching Christian race against the best and finally take control of his fate. I wasn't jealous, but I wished I could have been him. I would have loved to have experienced that.

Christian had come to Slipstream after a spell as a *deluxe dome-stique* on the CSC team. His father had been a pro rider and he'd grown up among the biggest names in American cycling. He was freakishly talented, and had turned pro in 1998 on Lance Armstrong's US Postal Service team. For a while he was touted as 'the next Lance', but he suffered from high expectations and repeated injuries, not to mention the somewhat unhealthy environment of pro cycling during his first years as a professional.

The US Postal team wasn't known for nurturing riders and it wasn't long before Christian was jettisoned from the team. His battle back to the top had been a long and painful one and his attitude had become that of a worker. He didn't see himself as a winner any more so to see him rediscover himself at the Tour was emotional, and I was very proud of him.

There was a real togetherness about Slipstream. Everything was so different from how it had been for me in the past. We all got on so well and had so much fun, and, most importantly, we shared a mother tongue. Since turning pro at 19, I'd never been on a team where we spoke English, yet it had never occurred to me how important this was.

Sharing a common first language felt like such a luxury. Communication was so much better. It didn't matter that we were

American, Australian, Canadian, Scottish and Kiwi – we were English-speakers in a foreign world, and it proved to be a very powerful bond between us.

I think we were respected for bringing a breath of fresh air to a stagnant arena. We never took ourselves too seriously and demonstrated that being clean didn't mean bring boring or worthy; in fact, quite the contrary, we were fun and interesting.

As I relished racing with Slipstream, Saunier Duval finally fell into the abyss. Predictably enough, it was the precocious Ricco who led the way. This time he didn't get away with it and both he and Leonardo Piepoli tested positive after winning Tour stages in the Pyrenees. There was little joy in watching their downfall, only satisfaction in knowing they'd been caught.

On the morning that the police turned up at the start village to arrest Ricco, our team bus was parked alongside theirs. As we watched the mêlée, all of us had something to say about him, except Christian who just stayed quiet. At first I didn't understand him, but then I realised why. Christian was angry.

Ricco represented a lot more than just another doper to Christian. He represented every doper, every cheat that had ever ridden past him and crushed his own hopes.

When he was younger, Christian had been discarded, written off for not living up to expectations, without anybody truly understanding the reasons why he couldn't compete. Things were now changing but Christian would never get back the lost years of his professional career.

The more she learned about my old life, the more Nicole was thankful that we'd met when we did. Often, when I was in my cups, re-telling some anecdote from the past for the umpteenth time, she'd shake her head in disbelief.

'Oh my God,' she would say, 'I'm so glad I didn't know you then.'

Nicole much preferred the Hayfield-living, clapped-out Mazda-driving, penniless me to the Biarritz-based, Jaguar-wielding, fashion-victim playboy. She found even the thought of it ridiculous.

'You were such a dick, David!'

My feet are always on the ground with Nicole.

It was down to her support and belief that I'd made my comeback so quickly and to such a high level. She was strength personified when it came to supporting me. But being a professional athlete's partner or relative is not easy because we live very selfish, goal-oriented lives.

Although we're often at home, we are rarely actually *there*, our heads being wrapped up in whatever our next sporting objective may be. At times the self-absorption is taken to the point of obsession. Life boils down to the cycle of racing, training, eating, resting, dieting.

And if one of those functions isn't going well, the subsequent neurosis leads to misery. The smallest issues can become the most important things in life and reality slips away. Nicole is good at keeping me in the real world. I can have my bubble, but it's not quite as small as it once was.

In the old days, I had always yo-yoed between the obsessive and the cracked. I never found balance. I even convinced myself that's how I was programmed to be and that in order to get the best out of myself, I had to live that way.

But when I met Nicole and saw how hard she worked every day in London, I realised that balance was possible. She worked like a maniac when I met her, but she knew what the real world was about and she couldn't believe how easy we had it as professional cyclists.

We get paid to compete in sport, we get paid well, we often enjoy public acclaim and we live in beautiful places. Competition is tough and there are sacrifices, but in many ways we don't have to work that hard.

Nicole loves sport. She dreams of being a successful athlete, and possesses the work ethic and competitive spirit to have reached the top, if she'd had the raw physical talent. She never lets me forget how lucky I am and the good fortune I have had to live my dream.

I spent three years telling Nicole we'd never get married. I couldn't understand why we needed to. We loved each other and would always be together – why ruin it by getting married? Marriage made no sense to me and I was passionately against it.

I wondered if that anxiety was rooted in my parents' divorce. But Nicole's parents are divorced too and yet she is a strong advocate of marriage. In the autumn of 2008, I realised that I was making no sense. If I knew we were made for each other then I should stop being, as Nicole would say, 'a dick'.

Whitey accompanied me as no-nonsense moral support when I went to the jewellers to pick up the ring. A week later Nicole and I travelled back to England to visit her family in Henley-on-Thames. I planned to ask her when we were there.

It was ironic that on the way to Henley, the ring tucked safely away in my jacket, Nicole told me that she was no longer bothered about marriage. Later on that evening, after I'd asked her dad's permission, we went for a walk.

I finally plucked up the courage to ask the question and then to offer her the ring.

Nicole looked puzzled.

'David – *really* . . . ?' she said.

Jonathan Vaughters and I had long wanted to sign Bradley Wiggins to Slipstream, but he hadn't wanted to change his professional team in an Olympic year. So we had to wait until after the Beijing Games in 2008.

I didn't know Brad that well at the time, but we had always had conversations and I felt that we were closer than most in the peloton. In truth, this had only ever been due to our shared nationality. We didn't have a relationship outside of cycling, but this wasn't unusual. There were many riders that I got on with well in the peloton, yet had never hung out with off the bike.

Our bond had been formed in 2007, on three memorable occasions. The first came when we'd found ourselves climbing the Ventoux, side by side, and had both removed our helmets, as a mark of respect, as we rode past the Tom Simpson memorial. Later that summer, at the Tour de France, our teams had been staying in the same hotel when the police had taken his Cofidis team into custody after one of its riders, Cristian Moreni, tested positive.

Brad was mortified by the Moreni affair. That evening, we had chatted for a while, and the next morning I gave him one of my Saunier Duval T-shirts, so that he didn't have to wear Cofidis-branded clothing on the way home. Then, over a beer, as the season ended, we had one of our deepest conversations about my past and our futures. I was looking forward to having him as a teammate.

That November, Brad and I flew out to Boulder to join the team for our annual 'bonding' week. We began to spend a lot more time together, and got on even better than I'd expected.

He was good company, very funny to be around, but I felt he had something of a chameleon-like personality: a strong desire to blend in and tell people what he thought they wanted to hear.

His ability to observe and assimilate was best displayed in his phenomenal ability as a mimic. He had us in complete hysterics most of the time. He is a born entertainer. When he's had a few drinks, Brad morphs into his Liam Gallagher persona, an act that bears little resemblance to his real self. It's funny watching him trying to be edgy and cool, when he's one of the straightest people I know.

Brad is a very dedicated, driven, self-obsessed and ultimately, sensible man – he wouldn't have achieved the success he has achieved if he wasn't. On form, he is a superb rider, but the talk in his own book of nearly becoming alcoholic during his post-Beijing Olympic comedown doesn't add up for me. He is too controlled for that.

Brad looks after number one and that's one of the traits that makes him so successful. But I think he sometimes takes advantage of the admiring and respectful reaction to him.

When we signed him, he was one of the world's best prologue riders and a possible future contender for the Classics. Contrary to what JV would have people think, we had absolutely no idea he would become a Grand Tour contender or challenger in anything but the flattest and most simple of stage races. We never expected that he would one day finish fourth in the Tour – as he did in 2009.

Brad's quirky personality was perfect for our team, and his approach fitted the way we operated, because he is very professional and dedicated. His ability to nail objectives is remarkable and comes from years of controlling variables and targeting one-off events – such as the Olympics – on the track. After many years of under-achieving in road racing, he was finally beginning to show signs of development. We planned to bring it to fruition.

Just as we were getting ready to move on with the Slipstream project, my sister started calling me more often, asking hypothetical questions about setting up a professional team. By 2009, she was working closely with Dave Brailsford, acting as his right hand as he worked towards his dream of putting together an elite European team.

Prior to the Beijing Olympics in 2008, SKY had sponsored what was to become one of the most successful British teams in history. The Brailsford-led track team took over the Olympic velodrome in Beijing, winning the majority of gold medals on offer, as Brad, Chris Hoy and Vicki Pendleton became household names.

Sponsoring Team GB was a masterstroke by SKY and, buoyed by Olympic success, they were quickly infatuated with cycling. It offered the perfect marketing tool for them, a mass participation sport that reached a massive audience. As SKY's interest grew, Dave used his influence and the track team's success to lever the sponsorship he needed in order to create his Tour de France team. Fran was now effectively drafting the blueprint for this and I offered her and Dave as much advice as I could.

Dave's vision was more Formula 1 than professional cycling, but they had to learn an awful lot very quickly, and had to grasp the fundamentals of what was effectively a completely foreign sport. Track cycling and road racing are completely different beasts.

I was fascinated by their plan. In many ways, much of what we'd created with Slipstream had been based on what I'd learned from Dave. His methodology and management style, militaristic in its precision and planning, was like nothing else that existed in cycling.

Initially, it was out of the question that I might leave Slipstream, but the prospect of working with Dave and my sister captured my imagination. Before long, the subject had been broached and I met with Dave and France.

The thought of joining SKY was exciting, but neither Dave nor I could fully commit; I felt great loyalty and love for where I was and Dave had a more surprising reason – that I wasn't to discover for a few more months.

JV, Christian and most of the Slipstream team seemed resigned to the prospect of me leaving for SKY. They knew how close I was to Dave and were aware of the admiration I had for him. The fact that my sister was the other key player made it seem all the more inevitable. Yet I didn't want to leave; every time I went to a race I was reminded of what an amazing team Slipstream was. I was totally confused.

Then I broke my collarbone in Paris–Nice and found myself on the sidelines, with too much time to think. Eventually I decided I would definitely stay with Slipstream. Then I decided I'd absolutely definitely go to SKY.

In the end, the decision was made for me. Dave told me that SKY couldn't take me because of my doping past and that he would be enforcing a zero tolerance policy towards any members of the SKY professional cycling team having any prior doping history.

I understood their position and didn't hold any bad feelings, certainly not towards Dave. After all, he'd stood by me through the most horrible of times when everyone else had fled. Dave didn't owe me anything. In fact, it was the reverse, because he'd contributed hugely to my renaissance.

But it brought home how little Dave and SKY knew or understood the world the team would soon be entering. In the current climate, it is nigh on impossible to construct a professional cycling team without people involved who have encountered doping in one form or another. Doping had been so prevalent on the European scene that the whole team would have to be under 25 to come close to guaranteeing no doping history. Even then, you couldn't be sure.

This was where JV and Slipstream had been so smart. He had accepted the pragmatic truth that, in order to create a clean modern team, you had to acknowledge the past. He knew that the past couldn't be swept under the carpet; it had to be understood and accepted, not ignored and forgotten.

Part of Slipstream's bid to be as transparent as possible meant confronting our demons. One of mine came in the form of Irish sportswriter and former pro cyclist Paul Kimmage, a winner of sportswriter of the year and also author of the ground-breaking, *Rough Ride*.

Kimmage and I had history. When I'd been embroiled in the opening cross-fire of the Cofidis affair and mired in denial, Paul had wanted to interview me. Paranoid and scared, not to mention knowing that he was fervently anti-doping, and – so I thought at the time – anti-cycling, I declined.

That made him angry. Typically, he wrote about me anyway and published an article, in which it became clear that I had threatened to sue him and the *Sunday Times*. It became a bit of a mess, although not one that I was particularly concerned with as a far bigger judicial problem was heading my way.

The conflict left its mark on Paul though, and was probably one of the reasons why he held me in such incredibly low esteem. That said, I think there are many people on Paul's radar that are held in low esteem, so it wasn't as if I was getting his undivided attention.

His 'tears for a cheat' article on me after the Vinokourov doping scandal simply reinforced the sentiments we shared for each other. I saw him as bitter, small-minded and unforgiving. He didn't believe I had reformed – he saw me as lying scum.

That was how things stood when JV called me to ask if I'd be open to being interviewed by him. He also asked if I'd mind if he followed the team through our first Tour de France. Initially, I wasn't keen and expressed my doubts to JV, but then, after some thought, accepted that it would be the ultimate display of transparency. Showing a renowned and sceptical journalist who hated my guts and didn't trust me or believe that we were sincere and trustworthy would surely silence the majority of doubters. There was no option really.

Paul came to our training camp in the Pyrenees about two weeks before the Tour started. This seemed like a good idea as we had a fair bit of ice to break through. I had already decided that I had no problem wiping the slate clean and in fact felt I had become quite accustomed to it.

But I was interested to see how Kimmage would be with me. Paul seems on edge the whole time and finds it very hard to make eye contact unless he's The Interviewer. There is no spontaneity in his style; it is not a conversation. Instead, it is a formal interview that has been scrupulously researched and structured. He is a professional through and through. First though, we had to bury the hatchet.

I was very welcoming to Paul, which I don't think he expected. We shook hands, went up to the apartment I was staying in and sat down at the dining table.

'I want to show you something,' he said.

This was classic Kimmage, no messing around, straight to the point. He handed me a pile of faxed pages, with key sections highlighted.

Jeremy Whittle's book, *Bad Blood*, had come out that very day. In one chapter, Jeremy met with Paul to talk about doping. Kimmage had been unflinching in his criticism of me and of my comeback to the sport.

One strike and you're out [he'd said]. I find it hard to accept that he is now being heralded as a whistle-blower. He didn't blow any whistles, didn't do any favours to cycling.

When I see Millar welcomed back like a hero ... I mean – I tried to do the sport a service. But he hasn't shat on any of his pals, he's still playing the game, still respecting the omertà.

Millar should not have been let back into the sport. He should have been banned for life. Until the sport does that, there's no chance.

I read through the pages slowly, enjoying how uncomfortable Paul was. I knew what he thought of me and in some ways it was actually liberating to have him sit and watch me while I read it. I put my hand in the fire and held it there.

I didn't think Paul was objective about cycling.

Confronting doping – confronting me – was so personal for Paul. Sometimes I couldn't believe that he even covered cycling, given his bitterness and the emotionally charged hold that it had on him.

I'd been amazed to read an article he'd authored about the *Etape du Tour*, the mass-participation event, organised by ASO, that recreates a mountain stage of the Tour de France. In the piece, he had belittled all those who took part, making them sound like complete imbeciles for wanting to emulate professional cyclists.

I thought it was a very misjudged piece, but it allowed me to look at him differently. He had never forgiven cycling for what he perceived it had done to him. He was an embittered fanatic, but as my mum always told me: 'There's a very fine line between love and hate.'

And I think this was the problem. He still wanted to love cycling, but he couldn't reconcile the grey world in which it existed with the black and white world he longed for.

I put the pages down.

'Well, I think we've both said things about each other,' I said. 'If we're going to do this then we need to start at zero.'

He nodded and we shook hands.

I genuinely meant what I said. After all, I was the ex-doper, the enemy. If he was willing to give me a second chance then I was sure I could win him over; I was just as sure that he wanted to be won over.

He wanted to believe in cycling again and I wanted to help him rediscover his faith.

25

KEEPING THE FAITH

Bradley Wiggins shone at the 2009 Tour de France. He reached a new level, performing as Christian Vande Velde had done the year before. But, unlike Christian, Brad was supported through the race by a brilliant team.

Brad's performance a few weeks earlier at the Giro d'Italia had hinted that he might perform well in the mountain stages of the Tour, but we didn't expect him to be one of the best. He was definitely the star of the show, but he couldn't have done it without Christian and the team.

As Brad blossomed and the Tour went on, Christian reverted back to his old role of the loyal lieutenant. Christian shared his years of experience with Brad, telling him everything he'd learned the previous year, when he'd found himself in exactly the same position.

In fact, it was amazing Christian was even riding in the Tour that year. He'd crashed badly in the Giro, breaking bones in his back and ribs and had only been on his bike for three weeks before the Tour started. Under those circumstances, Christian's seventh place finish overall, with little training and despite being still injured, was even more impressive than Brad's fourth place.

My job at the Tour was to work for Christian and Brad and to protect their place in the classification. I made sure that they were always in the best positions for the most critical moments in the race. As a team, our collective performance was phenomenal. We almost won the coveted team time trial, which, considering that the majority of the team had been struggling after only 8 of the 38 kilometres, was remarkable.

Brad, Christian, Dave Zabriskie and I rode the last 30 kilometres on our own with Ryder Hesjedal clinging on for dear life as our fifth man. That was all-important as the collective time is taken on the fifth member of the team to cross the finish line.

It was a close thing and we narrowly missed out. The Astana team of Lance Armstrong and Alberto Contador only beat us by 18 seconds – and that was with their nine-man team intact for the whole stage.

On the stage to Verbier, we again demonstrated collective discipline and power, leading the peloton to the bottom of the climb and supporting Brad with a fantastic lead-out on the lower slopes, so that when the inevitable Contador acceleration came, he was in the best possible position.

But then I'd never been on a team that rode with the same discipline and motivation as we did in that Tour. Every day we rode our hearts out and we were finally rewarded with second place in the overall team classification. In only our second year in existence, we were one of the strongest and most organised teams in the world. It was incongruous, given our happy-go-lucky, relaxed, 'whatever' reputation.

On the Tour's final stage, we had planned to set up our sprinter Tyler Farrar, by leading out the sprint on the Champs Elysées. To ensure that we were as quick as possible, Tyler, Brad, Zab – Dave Zabriskie – and I wore our time trial speedsuits and brought out our fastest, lightest wheels, even though we had ride the cobblestones of the Champs. Wearing speedsuits, designed to be skintight and aerodynamic, in a normal road stage wasn't the done thing, but then we were so keen to support Tyler that we didn't care if the other riders laughed at us.

We wore our normal race jerseys over the top, thinking that would hide our plan. Zab had even gone so far as to wear two sets of race numbers, one set on the *faux* jersey he was wearing over the top of the speedsuit, the other on the speedsuit itself. But, unwittingly, he blew our cover, pinning the race numbers so low on his speedsuit that, once he was on the bike, all four numbers were perfectly visible.

Then, rather than concealing our cunning plan, Zab only drew attention to himself. As the race rolled away from the start area, he announced that he needed to do a number two – while wearing a speedsuit in the peloton.

Zab takes a keen interest in bodily functions. He even owns his own colonic irrigation machine back in the States. When his house was broken into, perhaps unsurprisingly, it was one of the few items that the thieves left behind. He's also got an eccentric sense of humour. Sometimes I think his deadpan, desert-dry wit would suit a Coen brothers film.

This, after all, is the man who has his own lubrication company, DZnuts, pronounced Deez Nuts. He even had 'Official Applicator' T-shirts made ('For the ladies,' he said). He's also a little OCD when it comes to cleanliness, so there was little chance of him pooing 'wild'. And, as he didn't have his habitual baby wipes, I couldn't foresee a happy ending.

Taking a dump is not the easiest thing to do while racing in the Tour de France, but it's particularly inconvenient when wearing a race jersey over a full-body, super-tight, aerodynamic speedsuit. Thankfully, his need arose during the promenade section of the stage, as the peloton rolled gently through little villages in the countryside outside Paris.

As I watched his anxiety grow, I couldn't contain myself.

'Zab, you're screwed,' I guffawed. 'You'll lose minutes just undressing . . .'

'I know, Goddammit,' he snapped. 'I gotta make a plan.' He was clearly using all his mental energy to restrain the turtle's head.

I was in hysterics as I rejoined the bunch. Then, out of the corner of my eye, I caught a glimpse of him skidding to a halt outside an Indian restaurant and running through the door, shouting in alarm, much to the complete bafflement of those standing around on the pavement, who'd come to applaud the heroes of the Tour.

About 20 minutes later, he was back in the bunch, riding alongside me, filling me in on the grisly details. He'd run into the restaurant shouting, 'TOILET?! *EMERGENCY!*' while simultaneously struggling out of his speedsuit.

Moments later, he'd strolled back through the dining room to his bike, bidding onlookers a cheery goodbye, while thanking them – '*Mercyyy, Mercyyyy*' – in his deep, Utah drawl.

Our sprint lead-out for Tyler on the Champs Elysées went almost perfectly, as the whole team did their job – except Brad.

One by one, we took a huge turn at the front, keeping the pace as high as we could to prevent attacks, so preparing the way for Tyler's sprint. Christian and I led the peloton into the final kilometre, and when I peeled off, expecting Brad to be in his designated position to set up Tyler's finishing sprint, he was nowhere to be seen. Instead, Ty's final lead-out man, Julian Dean, had to make double the effort. But without Brad taking his turn, Julian was faced with too far to go, effectively ruining Tyler's chances in the sprint.

I was furious. It was the one day that Brad was asked to give something back to the team, after we'd given him everything for three weeks. Yet I felt he hadn't even tried and had remained about 80 places back in the middle of the bunch, without even telling us he wasn't going to help.

We felt let down by him. We'd done so much to help him, yet he couldn't even make this final gesture of camaraderie on the last day. He was the polar opposite to Christian, who was always part of the team, whether leading or helping. To me it was thoughtless of Brad that he did not see the symbolic nature of what he'd been asked to do. It was an omen of things to come over the next few months.

For the first time in my career, I had ridden all three Grand Tours – the Giro, the Tour and the Vuelta. After I won the final time trial in the Vuelta – my fifty-sixth Grand Tour stage of that year – I headed back to Girona.

Brad had made Girona a second home, spending periods training and living there. In the two months since the Tour had ended, we'd had no contact, but as we'd roomed together for most of the Tour and I'd captained the team that had taken him to his Tour success, I'd been looking forward to meeting up, for lunch or dinner, and celebrating his success.

But I didn't hear from him. It seemed he had already forgotten the team. All we heard were rumours of him leaving Slipstream and moving to SKY, who were desperate to sign him after his Tour performance. In fact, Brad had another year on his contract, but this didn't seem to be an obstacle to Brad, Dave Brailsford or to the people at SKY.

I knew the rumours about Brad and SKY were well founded. During the first rest day of that summer's Tour, we were sharing a room and Brad had disappeared for a few hours. When he got back, I asked him where he'd been. He told me the truth – that he'd been meeting with Dave Brailsford, who wanted to break his contract and sign him to SKY for the following year.

What he told me didn't affect our state of mind because we had a professional job to do and we did it. But I also expected that, whatever the final outcome of his negotiations, Brad would still respect us as teammates and friends.

During that year's World Road Championships, the speculation continued. In an interview with the BBC, Brad fuelled the intrigue even further when he used a football analogy to explain his perception of the difference between Slipstream and SKY.

'It's a bit like trying to win the Champion's League,' he said. 'You need to be at Manchester United and I'm playing for Wigan.' Brad subsequently said it was a wrench for him to leave Garmin, and too good an opportunity to turn down to work with David Brailsford. It seemed to me, though, that he had no feeling for what we'd achieved as a team. It also ensured that Jonathan and I hardened our hearts towards him.

After he'd made that hurtful comment, we looked forward to watching him fail. We knew what he was capable of as a rider and we also knew that, in the 2009 Tour, the stars had aligned perfectly for him.

I actually found what he said quite funny. He was digging himself a hole. We were certain that he'd never be on the podium at the Tour, which made it a little easier to hear all his big talk. As we listened to him, Christian and I just shook our heads in amazement.

Nonetheless, I took the whole affair badly. JV and I had wanted to keep Brad – I had agreed to a large pay cut on my 2010 contract so that we could offer a new deal to Brad that came closer to matching what SKY had offered him – and this meant that I became more personally invested in the whole saga. Inevitably, Brad eventually left. He didn't thank us, nor did we feel we were given the respect we were due. I have found it hard to forgive him.

I finished paying off my debts in 2009. Nicole and I had been living off my IVA allowance for long enough to have developed a sensible attitude towards money. I'd broken free from the status-based attitude within the professional sporting world – our lifestyle didn't match what I earned or my position within cycling – and no longer suffering from 'status anxiety' was liberating.

Nicole and I got married that autumn. It was a magical day that exceeded our hopes and expectations. The service was in the church in the village where Nicole had grown up, and friends and family came from all over the world. Stuey, Whitey, Ruggero and Nicole's brother Dom were my ushers and Harry was my best man.

Nicole looked stunning and was so wonderfully happy. I would live that day over and over again simply to see everybody I love so happy. In my speech, I thanked everybody for coming and then talked of 'a life less ordinary'.

Then I spoke about my parents. 'I've not been the easiest son. I know I've brought you as much heartache as I have joy, but you've been wonderful and I thank you, Mum, Pater-san, for making me who I am.'

I thanked Nicole's mum and dad, Nigel and Desirée – Desirée who had met me in Mallorca when I had been there with the Major and who, with premonitory powers, promptly telephoned Nicole to tell her she'd found the right man for her – and then spoke about Frances.

'I hope that if Nicole and I are lucky enough to have children that they will have the good fortune to love each other as much as we do, because a life without my sister would have been so bloody dull,' I said.

Nicole had abstained from having bridesmaids, so I had been unable to resist the opportunity to dress some of cycling's best known names in skirts, with the ushers all sporting kilts.

'It has been an ongoing debate between Stuey and Whitey whether they would be going *full Scottish* today,' I said, while crediting Nicole for allowing such a lethal combination of gentlemen to have such important roles. 'No doubt we will find out before the night is over.'

Now that my debts were paid off, Nicole and I could finally start thinking of getting a mortgage and moving forward. We'd done our research over the previous two years; we knew the market and what we wanted, and we had found a house near Girona, close to where we were already living, that fitted the bill. We had a concrete future plan and life was sweet.

One lunchtime, after I'd got back from training, I was making something for us both to eat when the doorbell rang. There were a

couple of letters for me to sign for, one of which was from the Spanish tax office. I presumed it was the receipt for my second payment of 2008 tax, but it was a bill, which puzzled me. I opened it, glanced down and saw an unfathomable, terrifying number. It didn't make sense.

I felt physically sick. I'd paid everything back. I looked again. I had a week to pay it all or everything would be seized. In an instant, everything had changed and I was back in my nightmare of paranoia and hopelessness.

'Calm down,' I told myself. 'This is a mistake.'

Then I looked closer. The French tax office had taken advantage of a very new EU law that allowed them to make fresh demands through the Spanish tax authorities.

I was catapulted back in time, reminded of something long forgotten, of very dark places and even darker feelings. The amount they were demanding was within €500 of the asking price for the house we'd found.

The next week was horrible. It was both heartbreaking and terrifying telling Nicole. There were sleepless nights and tearful days. Only three months after concluding five years of paying for my earlier mistakes, our future had been torn from us. We deserved far more. I felt sad for Nicole and fearful that, after living in blissful ignorance, dreaming of a house, kids and a secure future, I had let her down.

I had to deal with the problems quickly though and so went to work with seven different accountants in three different countries. I had already spent £200,000 on accountancy fees.

I transferred our money out of Spain and came to terms with the fact that buying a house and building a life there was no longer an option, as long as the French were still after me. I knew that the tax authorities in France would happily battle for years and that the only place I was protected legally was the UK, due to the IVA that had been agreed in 2005. My Spanish accountant managed to stop the seizure, at the death, but the French clerk in charge of my dossier was on holiday during the whole manic week.

I needed perspective though and it came from Fran. She sent me a text message, a week after the arrival of the letter, that reminded me of where I'd come from. I'd been in a much worse place – being reminded of how sad I'd been in Biarritz allowed me to put things in perspective.

> We sat on those steps, on that beach, and we promised we'd never be there again.
>
> We spoke about a fast-forward button, and how, in that horrible time, being able to press it and see what the future held would be both scary and comforting.
>
> Well, imagine if we'd had one and pressed it.
>
> You'd have seen that in five years you'd have met and married a beautiful woman, had your bike racing back, and would be held in higher esteem by your peers and the wider world than you ever were.
>
> You wouldn't have believed it.
>
> Breathe deep. Hang on. And rage, rage, rage, against those who try to break you.
>
> You beat them once. YOU WILL BEAT THEM AGAIN.

I'd felt like giving up when I'd received that letter from the tax authorities. France's message reminded me who I was, what I'd been through, and it helped me to stop feeling sorry for myself.

I had lived a short time without a future, completely lost – never alone, but very lost. We say in bad times that it's happening for a reason, perhaps – because it makes us feel better – to give times of strife a higher purpose, even if we find it hard to believe.

Nicole and I were awoken to what we had and where we'd come from. We stopped living in the future. We already lived a wonderful life – we didn't need anything else. It was time to slow everything down and live in the moment. France was right, I thought – '*fuck 'em . . .*'

I knew I had paid my debts, that it was unjustified to demand more of me. I could beat them, and I didn't care how long it took.

I wasn't going to give up or run away. The past is as important as the future, but we only live in the here and now. I hadn't appreciated that until I'd had my dreams almost wrenched away from me once again.

Eventually, we did win. The claim for further tax payments was dropped.

During the off-season, all that remains of Girona's multinational pro-cycling fraternity are Canadian rider Michael Barry, and I. We're the seasoned campaigners, the veterans.

In the past, this period, leading up to Christmas, had always been the most trying part of the year for me. Unfit, battling bad weather and loneliness, the major races seeming a world away, I never enjoyed riding in winter, putting up with it only because I had to. But Michael and I had spent the previous two winters training together, 'getting the miles in', as they say.

As we rode, we got to know each other even better. I'd never considered myself anything other than a racing cyclist; I was a thoroughbred, baffled by how or why people rode for fun, for relaxation or simply to escape. Riding with Michael was different. He introduced me to an ideal that I'd never previously grasped: cycling for the sake of cycling – which, in fact, I'd experienced briefly when I'd first got back on the bike after being banned.

We spent hundreds of hours riding around Catalunya, Michael regaling me with anecdote after anecdote. After thousands of kilometres together, he'd got in the habit of starting each story with: 'If I've told you this before, stop me.' But the stories are just as entertaining the third, fourth or fifth time, and he spends 90 per cent of the time talking, so it seems fair to allow for some repetition.

The Catalunyan landscape is sublime at times and, on our long winter rides, Michael and I experienced this more than most. Now I'm older, there's no longer a direct correlation between my fitness and enjoyment on the bike. I didn't really care any more if we had to go slow because we couldn't go fast. We'd stop at times and take photos, we had tried and tested enough cafés to whittle them down to particularly trusted regulars, we had mountains we'd climb simply to get to the top, and routes to complement the accompanying weather. Out on the road, we'd talk and talk. It was fun.

Michael comes from a cycling background. His father, Mike, is originally from London, where he was immersed in the post-war cycling club scene – a scene that was social, not competitive, with tea and toast stops de rigueur. Mike Barry migrated to Toronto in the 1960s and eventually became a frame builder, developing his own Mariposa-branded bikes. A traditionalist through and through, Mike's bikes are from another time and place.

This was the cycling world that Michael knew and loved. He'd grown up around bikes and most of his friends and his father's friends were cyclists. It was a world about as far away from my independent pure racing stock as could be imagined. I became fascinated with the idea of a cycling club run along those lines.

That growing fascination led me to ask why we couldn't recreate that club ethos ourselves – I now wanted to be part of it, and if it didn't exist then why not create it? That was how Velo Club Roca-corba, our own social cycling club, was born. Rocacorba is the nearest mountain to Girona and is a climb often used by pros for training and testing, so it seemed appropriate we should call our club after it.

Michael and I became passionate about the idea. We would meet in a Girona café to brainstorm with a sketchpad and notebook. Over time, we created the look and a basic manifesto for the club. I was to be president of Velo Club Rocacorba, Michael vice-president, and we invited carefully selected like-minded individuals to join us. Cycling was no longer just my job – it was my passion again. I was in a place in my life that I had never envisaged.

We held our inaugural Velo Club Rocacorba dinner a few nights after I had received the traumatic letter from the tax office. It made me appreciate even more how lucky I was to be able to do such

frivolous nonsensical things. Our first meeting, celebrated with a brilliant dinner at the renowned Can Roca restaurant, was a great success. The next day everybody from the club climbed Rocacorba.

I started my 2010 racing season with the fearless attitude of a neo-pro. I wanted to enjoy being a professional cyclist while my body could still carry me through the biggest, toughest races – I didn't care about goals or expectations any more, I was just determined to race my heart out.

In fact, I'd started every race since my comeback with that mindset, but without really understanding why. Now I knew. Now I lived in the moment when I raced, not caring or worrying about anything beyond, or before, the start and finish lines. It was the final lesson for me to take from all of my trials and tribulations.

After racing in Paris–Nice and a brief trip back to Malta for the first time since my birth, I went to the Classics, winning the Three Days of De Panne, considered to be one of the hardest and most dangerous races on the calendar. De Panne has special resonance for me: it was the scene of one of my very first professional wins, thirteen years earlier, and it was at De Panne that I'd asked Matt White to join Slipstream as a *directeur*. Appropriately, Whitey was directing as I clinched overall victory.

Then, fuelled by my new attitude, I raced in the Tour of Flanders, deemed one of the most brutal one-day races and the domain of specialists and Classics veterans. When Stuey saw me on the start line in Bruges he was genuinely shocked.

'What the fuck are you doing here, Dave?' he said in amazement.

'Fancied a change.' I shrugged. 'Something new, you know – thought I'd come and have a play with you boys.'

I was a *naif* in these cobbled Classics so there was no way I could be taken seriously. I decided just to have a laugh about it. Although I'd just won De Panne, I decided the best way to play it was that I wasn't serious, more inquisitive.

'After fourteen years …?!' Stuey exclaimed. '*Fuckin' 'ell, Dave!* I worry about you … !'

Starting Flanders turned out to be a good idea, because 250 kilometres later, I was off the front with Belgian champion Philippe Gilbert chasing Fabian Cancellera and Tom Boonen, all three Classics specialists. I don't think Stuey had expected that, but then neither had I.

Flanders is a wild event, deeply embedded in the Belgian sporting psyche and generating crowds similar to a Tour de France mountain stage. The main difference is that everybody is there to watch the race and to cheer their favourites on, unlike the Tour when people often wander out from a nearby campsite, simply to have a picnic and to catch random crap tossed from the publicity caravan.

I was a little out of my depth and my inexperience cost me dearly, because Flanders is like no other race we tackle. Not only do you have to be the strongest rider, but you also have to be the best bike handler, to know the roads like the back of your hand, and to be fearless when it comes to positioning yourself in the frenzied peloton.

I was in my element, but I had been too far back in the peloton when the attacks came, at one point finding myself walking up one of the many cobbled climbs. By the time I'd got back to the front, Cancellara and Boonen were long gone. Yet I was so euphoric just to have fought my way back up there that I attacked. Gilbert bridged up to me and then we were off, flogging ourselves in pursuit of the two leaders.

I wasn't in the habit of racing close to 270 kilometres, especially in one of the most difficult races that exists, so when we reached the bottom of the penultimate and legendary cobbled climb, the Muur de Grammont, my lights dimmed, flickered and then finally, as they say, went out.

I crawled up the Grammont 'wall'. But I was still one of the first on the road and on my own, an experience very few pros ever have on that hill. I can't really remember it, as I was having an out-of-body experience at the time, but I know it happened because I've seen a photo.

I was caught with 2 kilometres remaining, but recovered enough to lead out Tyler Farrar for the group sprint. I was empty when I crossed the line, rolling to a stop and sitting down against the barriers, just beyond the finish, trying to figure out what had just happened. Euphoric at winning the bunch sprint, Ty came and found me.

'Holy shit, Dave, *WE ROCK!* The Dave and Ty Show save the day!' he said exuberantly. 'That lead-out was *perfect*, man. Thank God you were there.'

Finally, taking in the state I was in, he paused. 'Er, you okay . . .?' he asked.

'I'm so fucked, Ty,' I said. 'Really, I don't think I've ever been this fucked. I was off the front with Gilbert, then, like a junior, I blew. They only caught me with 2 kilometres to go.' I put my head back in my hands.

Tyler stared at me. '*NO WAY!*'

Now I knew he was impressed.

13 JULY 2010, STAGE NINE OF THE TOUR DE FRANCE

Injured in a series of crashes on the opening days of the 2010 Tour, David Millar is fighting for survival as the race enters the Alps . . .

Despite the damage to my ribs – and the pain everywhere else – I decided not to take painkillers before the stage from Morzine-Avoriaz to St-Jean-de-Maurienne, confident that I was feeling better after spending the previous day, a rest day, in bed. This turned out to be a mistake.

From the moment the flag dropped, I felt weak. I knew straight away that I was in big trouble. After only 10 kilometres, the pace was frenzied and, as we descended a hill, the peloton was stretched taut, lined out, with me dangling precariously at the back of the train.

I was pedalling at my maximum, but couldn't hold the wheel and was losing ground on the guy in front of me. The rider behind came around me to fill the gap I'd allowed to open, a very bad sign so early in the day.

I crawled over the first small obstacle, the Chatillon, a short 2-kilometre climb that normally I'd barely notice. Only 100 metres further on that hill and I would have been left behind, sliding backwards through the peloton, beyond the riders and through the team cars. As we came over the top, I was suddenly horrifically aware that I had made a major error in thinking that I was better.

Next came the first major mountain pass, the Col de la Colombière. I prayed that the racing would settle down, that the bastards at the front would ease up and let me find a tempo, that we'd climb it at a controlled, steady, slower speed. This did not happen. Instead, things got worse.

From the lowest slopes of the Colombière, I was adrift, unable to stop my rapid slide out of the back of the bunch and into the convoy of following cars. Worse, every time I lifted myself out of the saddle to try to pedal a bit harder, my back began to spasm and there were stabbing pains from my ribs.

I had even less power standing on the pedals than I did planted in the saddle. I was dropped on my own – the first rider to go. There were just under 180 kilometres remaining in the stage and four mountains to climb. I was unequivocally, irredeemably, fucked.

Experience of racing has taught me not to panic. I did my best to remain calm, thinking that if I kept a steady pace I would be able to catch up with the *gruppetto*. But even if this panned out, I knew I'd be alone for a long time. Moments later, I passed my teammate Ryder Hesjedal, stopping for a piss at the side of the road. A few hundred metres later, he caught up, looked across and in his Canadian West Coast drawl, said: '*All right!* Let's go Millar Time!'

I stared back, open-mouthed.

'Ryder,' I spat, 'I'm fucked. I'm not going anywhere.'

With a stunned look on his face, Ryder rode on.

Soon he was out of sight, making his way back up through the cars in the convoy. I kept pedalling, and caught snatches of information from the race radios on the motorbikes overtaking me. The attacks were coming in waves at the front, leaving me even further behind.

For the last few kilometres of the Colombière, I was 90 seconds behind the other dropped riders, now forming little groups of chasers behind the ever-smaller front peloton. The descent, too fast and not technical enough to allow a lone rider to close a gap, didn't help me. By the time I got to the foot of the 2nd category Col des Aravis, I was minutes behind the group ahead of me.

And so, little by little, as the empty road stretched ahead of me, I began to think the unthinkable. The thought wormed its way into my head as I rode alone, almost unnoticed, past the spectators packing up their picnics and camping cars, suddenly looking up as I appeared, surprised to see me so far behind.

I realised that I could give up. I could quit.

I could abandon the Tour – after all, lots of great riders have found it all too much in the past. I'd hardly be the first. I was hurting all over and my ribs were more painful than they'd been at any point since the crash in Spa.

In front of me was empty, dead road. Behind me, as last rider on the road, was a convoy of vehicles crawling in my wake, one of them being the *voiture balai*. It hovered a few metres off my shoulder, reminding me that quitting was an option.

But I couldn't face it. There was no way I could climb off, stare at the floor while my race number was peeled off and then get in the broom wagon, enduring the humiliating public ritual that symbolises throwing in the towel like nothing else in sport.

Maybe I could have got into the team car; there was room as there were no guests, only Lionel and Kris from the team. But they seemed convinced that I was going to keep going – maybe they know me better than I know myself. Sometimes they sped ahead to take care of Tyler Farrar, in trouble in a group further ahead on the road. Most of the time they were with me, or nearby.

I'd round a corner and there they were, waiting for me, parked up at the side of the road. Each time they drove ahead, I decided that the next time they parked up, I would simply end it. I'd just pull over and get in the car. Game over. But I never did.

Once when they pulled alongside, Lionel leaned out of the car window and said: '*C'est bon, David, tu es seulement a une minute derrière le gruppetto.*'

'*It's good, David, you're only a minute behind the* gruppetto.'

Only a minute behind? I knew this couldn't be true, but I asked him, begged him, pleaded with him.

'*Oui?!*' I replied in astonishment. '*Véritablement?*'

He didn't respond – we both knew the truth. I could see far enough up the mountain to know that there were no riders, no team cars within reach.

But I'd forgotten one thing. I'd forgotten about the people at the roadside. Now they knew about my struggle and there they were, waiting for me, rooting for me.

They waited, and even now, writing this, I'm almost overwhelmed at the thought of it. Because when you're suffering that badly, I can't tell you how much it means. And there were thousands of them.

*

'COURAGE! COURAGE! COURAGE!'
   'Daveed, n'abandonne pas!'
   'Come on, Dave, don't give up!'
   'C'est Millar!? Oui, c'est lui! ALLEZ, DAVEED!'
   'Go, Dave! GO!'

At first, I felt bad that I was holding them up. Surely they just wanted to get in their cars and campervans and get off the mountain, after being there all day to watch the front of the race . . .?

But they cheered me with as much enthusiasm as if I was the first rider they'd seen. And then I started to hear my name, more and more, and I knew I had to keep going. This was the Tour de France – I couldn't give up, not here, not in front of them all.

Long after every other team helper had packed up and left, I rode into the feed zone at Le Mont Rond. Joachim from the team was standing there with my feedbag, waiting for me. He could have left long ago – Lionel in the team car was able to give me everything I needed. But he stood there, as usual, with my feedbag, expecting me to take it and to continue, as usual. So I did.

That was another option gone. I could have stopped there and then at the feed zone and been driven to the finish. But then what? Sit shamefully on the team bus as my teammates all came in after finishing the stage, the DNF (Did Not Finish) of the day. That wasn't me.

So I decided, no matter how unfeasible it was and no matter how late I was, that I would ride on to the finish. I had little chance of finishing inside the time limit, but at least finishing, albeit *hors delai* – outside the time limit – would carry some dignity.

The Col de Saisies was the third of four passes and as I began the climb, I started doing the maths. It was 15 kilometres to the summit so I'd cross the top of the pass with 97 kilometres ridden. The stage was 204 kilometres long, and the summit of the final mountain – the Col de la Madeleine – was 32 kilometres from the finish.

I shuddered. It was a long way from the top of the Saisies to the finish. Riding on my own along the valley to the next climb meant that I was going to lose even more time and further reduce my chances of making it inside the delay. It was demoralising.

334

As I began the climb of the Madeleine, I asked one of the drivers, in the convoy following me, how far behind the race I now was.

'*Je suis a combien des premiers?*' He looked at me with a pained expression.

'*Trente-cinq minutes*,' he said. Thirty-five minutes.

It was impossible.

I don't like the Madeleine. It holds very bad memories for me, of a different life, of a summer's day in 2001 when I got into a Cofidis team car and gave up my dreams, a time I've tried to forget. It's such a long climb that no matter how good you're feeling, you know that you're going to be spending a long time working your way up its slopes.

I couldn't cope with the thought of 25 kilometres of climbing, so I broke it up into 5-kilometre sections, working through them one by one. I found a rhythm of sorts and could feel myself strengthening, physically and spiritually. Even though it was a long shot, I started believing I could do it.

And, because I am a good descender, I knew I could descend the Madeleine faster than the front of the race, and on the flat roads to the finish there was no reason for my injuries to slow me as I didn't need to get out of the saddle.

The last few kilometres of the climb came quickly. I looked up towards the summit, at the thousands of people dwarfed by the monumental landscape, at the flags and banners outlining the ribbon of road all the way to the wonderful peak. I was slow but I wasn't weakening. I rode over the top, and zipped up my jersey, knowing that if I was to stay in the Tour, I had to throw myself down the mountainside.

The descent of the Madeleine is steep and technical, which makes it ideal for a lone rider. During the whole long day, my constant companion had been a gendarme motorbike outrider, opening the road ahead of me.

It must have been dull for him. We'd had only one moment of human contact, when he'd dropped back and offered me some water, but that was it. Other than that, he had simply ridden at my pace, doing his job, making sure the road ahead was safe for me.

But now, something unspoken between us surfaced. He understood me, understood my desperation. He read my intentions and for that wild, crazed descent off the Madeleine, we had the most exciting ride. From the first corners he knew what I needed, lifting his pace to match mine and carving a line through the bends, ahead of me. I put myself in his hands and followed his line. It was exhilarating.

But it was hairy too. The road was closed but crowds of fans, some on bikes and some walking, were already starting to head down the mountain. He dodged through them, siren wailing. Sparks flew off the pegs from his motorbike as he barrelled through the bends, with me tucked over the handlebars in his wake. I've rarely felt so alive.

Now, it felt as if everybody was with me. Lionel and Kris were behind me, careering through the bends in the team car, doing their best to keep up. The ambulance behind them was deliberately going slowly, delaying the race *commissaire* who had been with me all day. Even the French TV motorbike that had been assigned to me, moved in front of me, letting me ride briefly in his slipstream.

I felt proud that I hadn't given up, that I'd shut out the demons. On the flat road to the finish, I put my head down and rode like I was racing for the win.

When I crossed the line, I just kept going. I didn't want to stop – I couldn't face it, because I knew I'd lose it. I slalomed my way through the finish line crowds milling around the team bus, nerves jangling, on the edge of completely melting down.

I climbed off the bike, walked up the steps and into the sanctuary of the bus, making my way straight to my seat. Whitey just said: 'Nice one, Muzza.' Nobody else spoke to me, but then they knew not to.

I collapsed into my seat and left my glasses and helmet on. Then, inevitably, the tears came. I didn't want anybody to see that, so I just said quietly: 'Well, that wasn't so bad.'

Back at the hotel, Paul Kimmage was the first to greet me. It was typical of our up and down relationship that he should do that. He just shook my hand and said, 'Respect.'

There were others waiting too and I got pats on the back from almost all of them, along with words of kindness and admiration. I began to realise how important it was to have finished, and to understand that in no other race would simply finishing be considered such an achievement.

I went upstairs to my room, desperate for a few minutes alone, but I was shaking so much, I couldn't get the key in the door. Matt Rabin, our team chiropractor appeared, opened the door and ushered me into my room.

He looked at me. 'So how was it?'

The tears came again and I couldn't answer. I sat on the edge of the bed and started to quietly cry. Matt waited.

After a while I spoke.

'It was fucking horrible, Rabin. I should have taken my painkillers, because I lost my left side after a few kilometres, then my back started spasming when I tried to go any harder. I was sure I was out of the race. I don't know how I did it.'

'Fuck, mate,' he said. 'You did a great ride getting through.'

There was a pause before I spoke again.

'I can't figure out if I left a bit of myself out on the road or found a bit of myself.'

Rabin listened.

'You know what's weird? Nine years ago I pulled out of the Tour on almost this exact stage, on the descent of the Madeleine. Today I kept thinking, *I'm not that person any more*. I think I had to prove it to myself.'

He stood up. I wanted him to give me a hug, and I think he wanted to give me hug, but he didn't. Instead he just patted me on the back and sat back down.

I didn't tell him about what had happened on the Madeleine nine years earlier, when I quit on the same mountain, got into a team car and that night took my first steps into the world of doping.

A little later, my sister turned up, given leave from the SKY hotel to come and visit her brother. I knew France understood. She'd sat on the steps with me, by the beach in Biarritz. She knew about my demons, she knew, just like I did, that nine years before I was a different person, and that I wouldn't have made it through.

I both lost and found something on the road to St Jean-de-Maurienne. I'd finished when there was no reason to, when carrying on made no sense. It gave me great strength and resolve for the twelve stages still to come.

The 2010 Tour became my personal journey through suffering. It was something I didn't know I could endure, or perhaps more importantly, that I needed to endure. But I did. I kept going when it would have been easier to give up.

26

DAVE THE BRAVE

I've always loved the World Championships. The atmosphere is different from every other race on the calendar. It's festive and a little fresher than the occasionally battle-worn professional ambience we inhabit for the rest of the year.

When I rolled up at San Sebastian for my first Worlds in 1997 as a 20-year-old neo-pro, I was excited to be among English-speakers in a safe environment, having spent a horrible year learning about the harsh and hidden realities of the sport I loved.

Six years later, those realities had taken their toll. In 2003, I arrived in Hamilton a cold and calculating ruthless big hitter – unrecognisable in relation to the 20-year-old kid of 1997 – winning being the only reason I was there.

At the 2010 Worlds in Australia, I was neither of these younger versions, yet both of them remained part of me. At 33, I'd reawakened much of the neo-pro idealist, despite the 26-year-old having destroyed much of himself.

I was representing Team GB in the individual time trial, which would be run over two laps. I'd kept my strategy simple; give it everything in the first lap and then hang on with a wing and a prayer through the second.

Before the race, I sat chatting with Dave Brailsford and Luke Rowe, one of the younger guys in the British team. Luke reminded me of myself at the same age. He was charming and chatty, the big talent, the kid who stood out from the rest. I jokingly asked if he was going to be out on the road cheering me on, as the time trial route went straight past the Team GB hotel.

'Dave – of course I will,' he said. He seemed genuinely taken aback at the thought of not doing so.

'In that case, Luke, you're in charge of getting me a big crowd – in fact, why don't you make me a banner . . .?!' I was joshing with him, seeing how far I could push him.

'A banner . . .? Yeah, I can do that,' he said nonchalantly. 'Anything particular you want it to say?' I looked at Dave and saw that he was following our banter with amusement.

'I like you, Luke.' I laughed. 'It can say anything. What do you reckon, Dave?'

Brailsford put on his poker face.

'Luke, if you get a banner made and a crowd out there I'll do everything I can to make sure it's on TV or Graham Watson takes a photo of it. You've only got a couple of hours though, so you'd better start working on it.'

Luke, offered an opportunity to impress both Dave and I, was on his feet and out of the room almost instantly. Dave looked across at me and smiled.

Not many people knew what we'd been through together, or how far I'd really fallen, nor just how far Dave had gone to support me and pick me back up. Sitting there, the two of us jesting with one of the next generation, a couple of hours before I wore the British colours, squared the circle.

Just over three hours later, I came flying past the hotel. I had set the best time at all the time checks and was now leader on the road, desperately holding off the incoming express that was Fabian Cancellara. I knew that the British team would be watching me on TV in the hotel, and I felt so proud to be giving them something to cheer for, flying the flag at the very front of the race.

As I came careening onto the coastal road that passed our hotel I made sure that I lifted my head, taking a few seconds out from my race against the clock. I could see Team GB tracksuits lining the barriers and a big group, led by Luke, holding up a white sheet, presumably borrowed from the hotel.

Painted across it, in massive letters, were the words: 'DAVE THE BRAVE.'

If I hadn't been so wrapped up in my efforts to fend off Cancellara, I'd have had a lump in my throat. I didn't care that perhaps it was probably the only thing Luke could think of that rhymed – it was just nice to imagine that maybe he believed it.

Ten days later, after I'd been pushed into the silver medal position at the Worlds by the untouchable Cancellara, I arrived in Delhi to represent Scotland at the Commonwealth Games. This was another opportunity to say 'thank you', as it was among Scots that I'd found refuge when times had been at their worst.

Scotland had always welcomed me. When I'd been told I could compete for the nation in the Commonwealth Games and that the life-time ban enforced upon me by the British Olympic Association did not apply, I leapt at the opportunity.

When I'd been younger and consumed by the European racing scene, I had been dismissive of the Commonwealth Games. It was ignorant of me – I didn't see any benefits taking time out from my pro racing schedule to race for Scotland. I regretted that, and was thankful to have the opportunity to rectify it.

Mark Cavendish felt the same way about the Commie Games. It had never crossed our minds not to go – we'd both been with Team GB at the Worlds and we couldn't wait to get to India. We'd spent close to two weeks living in each other's pockets in Australia and had grown closer than we'd ever been.

I began to see a side of Cav that I'd never known. Behind the emotionally armed, verbal Gatling gun was a very focused and mature young man. I've met a few people in my time who like to think they suffer from OCD, but Mark was the real deal.

Within minutes of arrival at the team hotel, he'd emptied his expensive matching luggage ensemble and made his room his home. He was clearly intending to keep the room in a near perfect state of order and hygiene while he was staying there.

If I popped to see him in his hotel room in the morning, it already looked as if the housekeeping staff had done the rounds. But they hadn't – immediately after he woke up, Mark would make his bed and then keep everywhere else spotlessly clean and organised.

His behaviour behind closed doors was about as far from his public persona as was possible. As a result, he became much more interesting. I put aside the loyalties I had from being so close with Tyler Farrar, often the only competitor Mark had in the sprints, and opened my mind up to Planet Cav.

It was never boring hanging out with Mark. He's a charismatic little bastard, with an eccentric streak which makes him all the more appealing. I was amazed that he held the same desire to represent his country in the Commonwealth Games as I did. I'd assumed his rock star life in Tuscany had changed him, made him grander. I hadn't expected that representing his home, the Isle of Man, would mean as much to him as representing Scotland did to me.

His frivolity, generosity and occasionally manic behaviour reminded me of when I was his age. But Mark's vices were slightly less destructive than mine, probably due to the much healthier environment that surrounded him. He had come from the very nurturing Team GB set-up overseen by Brailsford, and then joined HTC, one of the new wave of clean professional teams.

At Team GB, Rod Ellingworth was his coach and confidant and had worked with him since he had been a teenager on the national team. Rod's a moral and ethical rock, immune to celebrity or wealth, and I have no doubt in my mind that he is one of the main reasons for Mark's incredible success. All of this had protected Mark from cycling's dark side.

I blended in as quietly as I could, and hung out a bit with the boys on the Scottish team, but I'm always a bit edgy when I find myself surrounded by other sports people. I'm always afraid that all they see me as is 'different', an unwelcome outsider. This probably isn't helped by the fact that I've only ever spent time with other non-cycling sportspeople at the Sydney Olympics, so the precedent didn't bode well.

Of the other riders out there, Mark and I had the most in common but we were also enjoying being in a completely alien environment. Being with athletes who had full-time jobs outside of sport, and for whom the Commonwealth Games was possibly the highlight of their sporting careers, was a refreshing and inspiring atmosphere. Mark and I loved being part of it all. In fact, Mark seemed more at ease and happier than I'd ever seen him.

We competed in the Commonwealth road race before the time trial. I'd never raced with any of my Scottish teammates before and yet we rode as if we'd spent the whole year racing together on the same professional team. We were all so proud to be wearing our white and blue, thistle-adorned jerseys, and we made sure everybody in the race knew it. But Scotland had never won a medal in any of the road events before and I wasn't expecting to be the person to change that record in the road race.

It was a pan-flat sprinter's course, raced around the central, deserted streets of Delhi. I had nothing to lose and raced like it, but the team was brilliant, doing everything I'd asked of them and setting me up perfectly to blow apart the second half of the race. I did as much as I could to rip the field to pieces, planning to tire out the sprinters in what I imagined would be a fairly impossible attempt to claim the elusive and unprecedented Scottish road cycling medal.

Yet the tactic worked and I finished in an exhausted but elated third place. It was a great feeling to be on the podium and watch the saltire being raised, even if it was for bronze and not for gold. The team was ecstatic and we all shared the joy of success, although I didn't join the festivities that evening as my main event, the individual time trial, was yet to come.

As an experienced time triallist, it was taken for granted that I'd win the gold medal in Delhi. I've been pre-race favourite many times in the past and it's never something I enjoy. It was made even more daunting by the time trial course, which, like the road race course, was completely flat. It was also dead straight; we raced 20 kilometres up the road, made a U-turn and then raced 20 kilometres back.

The weather was dry and dusty, with the temperature sitting in the low 40s. There was a howling tailwind on the outwards section, which ensured a horrendous headwind on the way back. None of this suggested a nice day out. I knew it was going to hurt like hell, as the flat and straight route meant that once I'd got up to speed, I'd only be shifting from my aerodynamic time-trialling position for the few seconds of braking, turning and accelerating at the 20 kilometre turnaround. This would put my body under a lot of stress, painful stress. That didn't bother me too much – it was more the psychological stress that worried me.

There would be no time checks, no supporters on the road – just me, the heat, the wind, the breathing and the pedalling. In other words, not much for me to concentrate on – just a painful, rasping meditation through time, racing against the clock.

Yet the amount of infrastructure the Games organisation had put into it compared to a Tour de France stage. Much of this was because they'd catered for a visit from a head of state, Scotland's First Minister Alex Salmond. He'd been told that he could count on a Scottish gold medal in the individual time trial. No pressure then.

I didn't feel good for most of the time trial, which wouldn't have been so bad if the course had been technical and fun. At least then I could have distracted myself with the technical intricacies of the race.

All I could think about was keeping my hands in the most aerodynamic position I could manage, focusing on my fingers being perfectly aligned and keeping my head down and out of the wind. I used my peripheral vision to guide me while balancing my maximal sustainable aerobic workload, against the delicate near overload of lactate.

I had no idea what the time gaps were to the riders I had to beat. The longer it went on for, the more insecure I became about my performance. Just when I thought it couldn't get any worse, I began to seriously overheat, which made the final kilometres excruciating, although it still looked effortless on TV.

Finally, with about 2 kilometres to go, I saw the Australian Luke Durbridge, who'd started a minute ahead of me. For the first time since I'd rolled down the start ramp, I knew I was going to win.

I crossed the finish line and wheeled to a halt, throat rasping. I craved water and downed bottle after bottle, finally cooling my badly over-heated body. Then I was able to enjoy it.

Everybody connected to the Scottish contingent was overjoyed. Although they'd expected me to win, that didn't detract from the joy that we were all sharing. This definitely wasn't business as usual – all the Scottish team had brought their kilts and put them on while I'd been out on the course. Alex Salmond was clearly ecstatic and appeared in the throng, giving me a big hug, live on BBC. I was a very, very proud Scot.

Mark was there to congratulate me too. He was in no rush to return to Europe and had spent the day helping out the Manx riders, working for the team, checking the kit, putting bikes on the roof rack and driving one of the following cars – the highest paid, most famous *directeur sportif* in the world.

By that evening, Mark had become an adopted Scot. There was a reception at 'Scotland House', a hotel that had been taken over by the Scottish federation for the duration of the Games.

Later, Mark and I commandeered the bar upstairs and invited everybody to join us. By the end of the night, we were in my room drinking Dom Perignon – Mark, not a big drinker, feels that when he does drink he must quaff only the finest champagne – celebrating the end of another season.

When I woke up a few hours later, there were two unfinished bottles by my bed. I got up and wandered over to the window, carefully avoiding the debris scattered across the floor, bleary-eyed but looking forward to the new day.

My planned cinematic sweeping opening of the curtains, to reveal a widescreen view of Delhi, stalled when I realised there was a technical glitch, preventing such a grandiose moment.

Finally, after some fiddling, I found the right cord and the curtains swept aside. I'd forgotten that I was on the top floor of the hotel and was taken aback by my eagle's view of this amazing city. Everything below looked so calm and peaceful, a long way from the reality.

I stood there for a while, my forehead pressed against the window and just stared. Below me, India was in its usual bustling frenzy, but up in my room, high above Delhi, it was so quiet. I don't know how long I stood there, but it was long enough for me to understand where I was, what I'd done and where I'd come from.

I had always been scared to push the fast-forward button France and I had wished we'd had six years earlier, sitting at the top of the steps down to the beach in Biarritz. Now finally, I did.

Everything that had come before ran through my mind: playing with my *Star Wars* toys, running through the RAF aircraft hangar with Dad watching over me, discovering cycling, my parents' separating in the dead of night, leaving Mum and France for Hong Kong and all its wonders, my dreams of turning pro, the success at Cofidis, Biarritz and loneliness, racing – always racing – the Tour de France, its beauty and pain, doping and lies, losing it all when I had it all, working with WADA, meeting Nicole, and then back to France and I, and the steps at my feet, leading down to the warm sand of the beach in Biarritz.

I stood, hungover, barefoot, a gold medal on the bedside table, forehead pressed against the window in a Delhi hotel room, quietly crying, a last wave washing over me, feeling something I thought I'd never know.

Redemption.

LIST OF ILLUSTRATIONS

PLATE SECTION PHOTOS:

Section 1
Graham Watson, Dauphine Libere 1999
Graham Watson, Etoile de Besseges 1997
Graham Watson, Tour de France 2000
Bruno Bade, Tour de France 2000
Graham Watson, Vuelta Espana 2001
Rodolphe Escher, Tour de France 2002
Tim De Waele, Tour de France 2003
Tim De Waele, Worlds 2003
Tim De Waele, Worlds 2003

Section 2
Bryn Lennon (Getty Images), Tour de France 2007
Pete Goding, Tour de France 2007
Damien Meyer (Getty Images), Giro d'Italia 2008
Tim De Waele, Tour de France 2008
Tim De Waele, Dauphine Libere 2009
Tim De Waele, Tour of Flanders 2010
Bruno Bade, Chrono des Nations 2010

Section 3
Timm Koelln, Girona, March 2011

INDEX